RIGHTS-BASED APPROACHES TO DEVELOPMENT

EXPLORING THE POTENTIAL AND PITFALLS

Edited by

Sam Hickey and Diana Mitlin

Kumarian Press
An Imprint of Stylus Publishing

Rights-based approaches to development
Published in 2009 in the United States of America by Kumarian Press
22883 Quicksilver Drive, Sterling, VA 20166-2012 USA

The text of this book is set in 10/12.5 New Baskerville

Proofread by Publication Services, Inc.
Index by Publication Services, Inc.

Production and design by Publication Services, Inc.

Printed in the United States of America by Thomson-Shore, Inc.
Text printed with vegetable oil-based ink.

∞ The paper used in this publication meets the minimum requirements of the American National Standard for Information Sciences-Permanence of Paper for printed Library Materials, ANSI Z39.48-1984

Library of Congress Cataloging-in-Publication Data
Rights-based approaches to development : exploring the potential and pitfalls/Sam Hickey and Diana Mitlin, [editors].
     p. cm.

  Includes bibliographical references and index.
  ISBN 978-1-56549-272-1 (pbk. : alk. paper)
  ISBN 978-1-56549-283-7 (cloth : alk. paper)
  1. Social planning. 2. Economic development—Social aspects.
3. Community development. 4. Social justice. 5. Human rights.
I. Hickey, Samuel, 1972- II. Mitlin, Diana
  HN28.R54 2009
  323.3'2942091724–dc22   2008053738

For Seth

Contents

Illustrations

Figures

Tables

Acknowledgments

This book is based on papers presented at a conference held in Manchester in late February 2005, entitled "The Winners and Losers from Rights-Based Approaches to Development." The funding for this conference came from the ESRC-funded Global Poverty Research Group, and we are very grateful for this generous support. As has been the case since the early 1990s, our conference administrator Debra Whitehead provided her usual excellent support to ensure that all ran smoothly. Regarding the book, the expert editorial assistance offered by Leonith Hinojosa, a researcher at IDPM, has been greatly appreciated and is largely responsible for keeping this project (more or less!) to time in the final stages. Thanks also to our publishers for their support and encouragement throughout, particularly our commissioning editor Jim Lance. Our collective intellectual debts for this book are too varied and numerous to list here. Inspiration has come from often close and long-standing ties with particular NGOs and NGO networks as well as more academic sources. Our thinking here benefited immensely from the contributions of and discussions with conference participants, including David Hulme, Giles Mohan, and Sheela Patel, who offered very insightful comments as discussants.

PART ONE

The Rise of Rights-Based
Approaches to Development

CHAPTER 1

Introduction

Diana Mitlin and Sam Hickey

The rights-based approach to development has grown in popularity during the last decade. In 1995, rights remained the preserve of lawyers, specialist nongovernmental organizations (NGOs), and United Nations (UN) treaties. By 2005, rights had entered the language, commitments and promotional material of development agencies (see, e.g., Moser and Norton 2001, 5; Eyben and Ferguson 2004, 163). This volume explores experiences of the rights-based approach, both from inside—through agencies that have adopted this approach—and from outside—through agencies and professionals working alongside development institutions and otherwise supporting rights. The volume therefore contributes to a stocktaking of what the rights-based approach means for progressive development and social transformation. This introduction first locates the debate within broader historical and contextual processes, and then introduces the chapters that follow by presenting five critical themes that have emerged from both the experiential learning of agency professionals and the observations of interested academics.

Rights, Rights-Based Approaches and Development in the 21st Century

The decade of the 1980s was marked by two contradictory and some-times contentious ideological trends, both of which came to be reflected within the policies of development institutions. First, development agencies and national governments replicated, and sometimes initiated, the neoliberalism embedded within the policy shifts of the international financial institutions in the 1980s, and supported the growth of market-oriented economic and social policies. These policy shifts had been catalyzed by the financial crises associated with balance-of-payments and public financing deficits, and in some cases with rising inflation, in the context of attendant conflicts over the scale of redistribution within the nation-state (Harvey 2006). The stabilization and restructuring packages of the ubiquitous structural adjustment programs were expected by the international financial institutions to lay the ground for economic growth and prosperity in the medium-to-long term. Whatever the anticipated benefits, however, in the short term many low- and middle-income groups suffered from the deflationary measures, which resulted in low and negative growth, state retrenchment, and the withdrawal of state-financed benefits such as health and education services and food subsidies (Cornia, Jolly and Stewart 1987).

The "old poor" (unskilled workers, those unable to work, and informal-sector workers) were joined by the "new poor" (newly unemployed middle-income households) (Minujin 1995). Households that had expected to receive adequate state assistance found themselves made vulnerable as the state–citizen relationship was redefined. Middle-class citizens who had previously received services were told they were no longer entitled to these benefits, or were entitled only if they could afford to pay for those provided on a cost-recovery basis; lower-income groups, many of whom had never received such benefits, continued to be ignored except for a few programs seeking to strengthen relations of dependency in a reference back to more populist policies. The state's position shifted from provider to enabler, with the private sector being identified as the key sector responsible for the efficient delivery of public services.

The widespread rise in poverty indicators was associated with active citizen protests as popular expectations of state programs and provision clashed with the roll-backs of the austerity era (Mayo 2005). The scale of protests prompted by the ideological trend toward neoliberalism appeared to threaten the stability of political regimes, and hence the economic reform programs being promoted by the international financial institutions. Social investment funds and other amelioration programs were introduced by donor agencies to address some of the worst social effects of neoliberalism and/or to demonstrate that at least some of the problems were being addressed (Robb 2004, 28).

In a context in which states were still held to be problematic and inefficient providers of public services and state expenditures were considered to be a major cause of economic crises, donors funding social programs sought nonstate mechanisms (Lewis 2007). However, the private sector, struggling even to respond to restructured economies and supposed new opportunities for growth, was generally not a credible alternative for social services. Hence civil society organizations, and more specifically their professional and formalized manifestation in the form of NGOs, were preferred suppliers of social programs (Hulme and Edwards 1997). In addition to donor programs, governments also started poverty-alleviation programs. These were often very limited and designed to bolster the governments' own political position with minimal financial commitment.

(See for illustration the discussions in Escobar Latapí and González de la Rocha 1995.)

For NGOs, the nature of the emerging opportunities was hard to assess. Many feared being co-opted through being drawn into donor-financed social provision outside the state line ministries (Hulme and Edwards 1997). But equally they were conscious that their legitimacy and indeed credibility was under threat: how could they refuse to participate when they had been vocal critics of both the lack of state programs and the inadequacy of what remained? Many became involved in amelioration-related activities in connection with social investment funds and structural adjustment programs. In this way, NGOs had ample opportunities to reflect on the inadequacies of these programs, including their partial nature (e.g., school buildings without adequate teachers), their limited range (e.g., serving one neighborhood but not another), and the short-term nature of their financial support. Some NGOs continued to develop the scale of their social service provision, but these and others went through an internal reflection on what they were providing in the context of their wider organizational mission, values, and principles. At the same time, there was increasing criticism and questioning of NGOs' integrity and legitimacy (Wallace 1997; Manji and O'Coill 2002). Challenged from both within and without, at least some NGOs sought an alternative position that was more consistent with their beliefs (Bebbington, Hickey, and Mitlin 2007).

Shortly after neoliberal economic policies extended their influence across governments North and South in the early 1980s, a second, very different global political and ideological trend became evident: authoritarian governments in a number of countries were challenged by organized citizen protests, and there was a significant shift to democracy (UNDP 2005, 20). These protests did not arise in a vacuum, but developed in many countries from previous ongoing citizen protest. Individuals and groups had long faced considerable risks as they campaigned against the state and its extensive repressive activities, often in relatively low-key ways granted little attention from the international media.

As noted by Gledhill (Chapter 3), these activities of civil society in some countries both sought to address specific political issues and, with rising momentum, demanded that respect for human rights be extended to those expressing dissenting political views. Once democratic openings were achieved, there were substantial and growing numbers of organized citizens and groups committed to ambitious programs for political change. In some cases such groups formed political parties contesting elections within the new democratic state. But in many cases these individuals and agencies chose instead to be involved in more specific campaigning work. Wherever they located themselves, their experiences of being social protesters in an authoritarian state were not easily forgotten, and they remained concerned citizens determined to secure and safeguard a better life for themselves and their compatriots.

Democratization, once underway, proved to be a complex process. The high expectations of citizens for the new democratic states met, perhaps inevitably, with some level of disappointment, as radical promises were frustrated by the realities of both the neoliberal hegemony of the international financial institutions and the need for pragmatic compromises with political elites. Concern about particular programs and policies of the state, impatience with the slow process of redistribution, and an awareness of the need to effect systemic change rather than simply swapping the seats at the top resulted in a raising of the political bar, and in at least some contexts led to a focus on constitutional reforms.

These experiences increased awareness of emerging international structures and processes in relation to human rights. As elaborated by Archer and Munro (Chapters 2 and 11), international human rights laws had been emerging since the end of World War II (Uvin 2004, 9–13; Gready and Ensor 2005). This increasingly complex framework of internationally proposed and partly accepted human rights provided a background for rights-based work at the local and national levels. A number of specialist NGOs had been pressing for the recognition and extension of this framework through bodies such as the United Nations Commission on Social and Economic Rights; see, for example, the work of the Habitat International Coalition, the Centre for Housing Rights and Evictions, and the local Southern civil society organizations involved in anti-eviction struggles (COHRE 1994; Environment and Urbanization 1994). The growing interest in rights included a 1986 UN Declaration that affirmed the right to development (Gaventa 2002). However, for several decades, the associations between human rights and the work of development activists had not been widespread, nor had there been that much attention to human rights from many international development agencies. In the mid to late 1990s this changed, as signaled most notably by the UN social development conference in Copenhagen in 1995; in the following years, rights became an observable framework and set of objectives of official agencies (Molyneux and Lazar 2003; Uvin 2004; Cornwall and Nyamu-Musembi 2005; Tomas 2005). As the hegemony of market-based economics strengthened following both the increased influence of the international financial institutions and the collapse of the Soviet Union, legal principles and instruments emerged as promising tools for those seeking to counter market-oriented economic imperatives.

The rise in popularity of the idea of "rights" in international development can therefore be understood as a product of the need to address tensions within and between experiences of neoliberalism and political transformation. Like many global ideas, rights rose to prominence because the Zeitgeist responded with all its multidimensionality to a particular moment. Accordingly, the growing enthusiasm for rights cannot be attributed to any single catalyst or cause.

For the democracy campaigners who feared that elected governments would start to backtrack on the promises of campaigns and betray the sacrifices of resistance movements, rights appeared to embed progressive commitments, making them difficult to overturn. With established legal rights, the courts could protect political transformation even if particular governments failed. Moreover, rights, and particularly the enactment of human rights legislation, guaranteed future resistance leaders a level of protection from the hypothetical risk of campaigning against future authoritarian states.

For the NGOs that had become service providers, maintaining a political status quo and implementing neoliberal economic policies, rights offered a complementary campaigning position that alleviated internal challenges and external questions about the legitimacy of their other work. As explained by Chapman and colleagues (Chapter 10), rights-oriented work spoke directly to NGO objectives to support participation and people-centered development.

For the middle class, rights offered a way back to a state-position that had previously protected their interests by virtue of their class status, but that was now denied to them. For bilateral development agencies pressured by criticism of their neoliberal policies from their own populaces, rights offered a way of extending their model of a liberal democratic state while not significantly changing economic policies (Edwards 2001; Mayo 2005, 23, 37–40; Tomas 2005). For some personnel in these agencies seeking to support economic growth through entrepreneurship, rights were seen as supporting stronger market economies, as these required a capacity to reinforce contracts and recognize the legal ownership of assets.

Rights, as the work of De Soto (2000) on land titling suggests, appear to be a way of addressing the perspective of neoliberalism with an explicit orientation to the needs of low-income groups. For agencies such as the UK Department for International Development (DFID), for example, "rights" resonated with Labour's historic concern for charitable endeavor and its longstanding commitment to pro-poor programming, while also allowing the agency to continue with pro-market strategies. The adoption of an idea therefore says little about the extent to which it is used to reconsider strategies and objectives rather than simply to rerepresent existing orientations. As summarized by Uvin (2004), some have argued that the embrace of "rights" yielded little substantive change in the case of major bilateral agencies. However, for at least some agencies, the adoption of a human rights framework involved major reconsiderations about organizational form and/or objectives.

As illustrated by the opening paragraph of Chapman and colleagues (Chapter 10), integrating rights into development work became associated with a set of measures packaged as the "rights-based approach" and adopted by a number of agencies, often without much consideration of what components were involved or of what was lost by this process of packaging. As is generally the case with such packages, there are a variety of interpretations of what should be included within the rights-based approach (see Moser and Norton 2001, 11–14; Molyneux and Lazar 2003; Uvin 2004; Mandar 2005; Piron 2005; Munro, Chapter 11 of this volume). Notable components include the following:

- (Pressure for) formal rights as laid down within some legal system, stipulation, rules, or regulations

- The implementation of such rights through legal campaigns and stronger links with the legal profession

- A more complete system of interconnected rights, rather than single rights

- Adherence to international rights and a hierarchy of rights at local, national, and international scales

- A perception of rights as a development goal to be achieved independent of other goals

- The explicit acknowledgement that engaging with rights requires an overtly political approach

There are also a number of nonlegal political processes that may be associated with the rights-based approach, with an emphasis on understanding individuals as participatory citizens rather than passive recipients, on the promotion of greater political transparency and accountability, and on consideration of those with the lowest incomes and those most excluded (Hinton and Groves 2004; Lewis 2007, 79–81). Particular emphasis is placed by some on the right of citizens to participation and on the need for rights-based approaches to be participatory in character (Cornwall 2002, 50; Gaventa 2002, 2; Uvin 2004). The adoption of a rights-based approach has been associated with offering a more coherent and consistent approach to development thinking and practice across North and South, and within and between agencies; among NGOs, the approach is associated with the more general shift away from service provision and toward advocacy (Molyneux and Lazar 2003, 6–7; Uvin 2004).

In some cases, the rights-based approach became a catchall for the complexity of the development issues and challenges facing institutions such as NGOs. If development is essentially about power, and rights are a way of securing structural change, addressing power inequalities, and protecting the poor, then rights became a way of addressing each and every development challenge. Molyneux and Lazar (2003) and Uvin (2004), for example, both draw a considerable diversity of development objectives, strategies, and approaches within their definition of the rights-based approach. Their definitions reflect an ambition among rights activists to reclaim the development imperative and reorient development policies and activities toward addressing the needs of those facing exploitation, exclusion, and dispossession.

Why This Conference, Why This Volume, Why These Themes?

The brief historical overview above outlines the background to our decision to hold a conference on the rights-based approach. The present volume is an outcome of this conference, held in Manchester, UK, in 2005.

Our interest (as conference conveners and editors) arose from an awareness that rights programming consistent with the rights-based approach had been operational for some years, and that diverse experiences were emerging. Some development professionals remained committed to the approach, while others were frustrated at the lack of progress in realizing its apparent potential. Some academics and activists expressed continuing skepticism and argued that the rights-based approach was one more example of Northern hegemony. Still others felt that the approach has shifted from being something of potential value to being a requirement of funding agencies regardless of its appropriateness in particular contexts. A further position was that the fulfillment of human rights was being conflated with the rights-based approaches to development regardless of whether or not the latter were effective in achieving their intended aims. It was hoped that appraising the rights-based approaches would throw light on these perspectives and aid efforts to achieve rights.

Those attending the conference and those contributing papers consisted of academics and NGO professionals in almost equal numbers. There were no contributions that were totally hostile to rights-based approaches, and so this position is not represented in this volume. Rather there was a series of measured contributions drawing on varied engagements with the rights-based approach, and on more general considerations about and experiences of rights. All of our authors believe that development should include a concern for rights, and that development professionals should support the effective acquisition of rights, particularly the rights of the lowest-income, most vulnerable, and otherwise most disadvantaged global citizens. But they express themselves with considerable diversity around this broad orientation, and there is no uniform support for a single or distinctive rights-based approach to development.

The purpose of this volume is to use experience to deepen our understanding of what it means to seek and realize rights and social justice in the context of development. Exploring a number of operational programs and research studies enables the emergence of the contours of a debate on the rights-based approach. Revealing the implications of the rights-based approach requires a close look at relationships between citizen and state in this evolving period of democratization. The following chapters enable us to use the rights-based approach as a lens through which to examine the issue of "governmentality" (see Gledhill, Chapter 3), and more broadly to review the relationship between citizen and state, the ways in which the state is extending its arena, and the implications for poverty reduction and empowerment. Equally, they enable us to understand how civil society is attempting to redefine social processes and its own strategies to be more effective in conceptualizing and realizing systemic alternatives.

This volume does not attempt a comprehensive analysis of the rights-based approach by drawing on a systematic analysis of concerns raised in the literature and responding to each with a measured assessment. Rather, the aim here is to present the debates that engaged the group that gathered in Manchester. These debates are encapsulated and developed by five sets of thematically paired chapters. The discussions within the chapters take positions that offer complementary, tangential, and alternative perspectives on the themes. This is not a simple "he said, she said"; rather the chapters and their pairing are better viewed as dual perspectives, with each perspective being contextualized within a particular locality and its associated events, activities, and relationships. The analyses offered by the authors are further enriched by their consideration of overlapping issues; none of the authors restricted themselves to the themes highlighted within the schema of this volume. The emerging analysis offers readers the possibility of multiple conclusions on the legitimacy and success of rights-based approaches. We offer our own conclusions in the final chapter.

Rights in Context

The first pair of chapters considers the evolution of rights and the rights-based approach, and hence their relationship to present ideological perspectives, development goals, and, in the case of Gledhill, emerging outcomes. The pairing takes up and develops the themes outlined at the start of this introduction: how rights have emerged as a campaign focus, and what this means for their realization within a project of progressive development.

Robert Archer's contribution (Chapter 2) discusses the growing engagement between development specialists and promoters of the human rights framework. Archer argues that the two traditions began at a similar time but then diverged in their development, coming together only in the last few years. He highlights a number of points at which the two agendas tend to challenge each other. A first theme is the systemic nature of the human rights framework, which, he suggests, makes it "more transparent and orderly. . . . more consistent and more logical" than other frameworks. Archer argues that the pragmatism of development practices may be a weakness as well as a strength, and that one contribution of rights is the rigor that it offers. He goes on to note also the value of compromise and negotiation, observing that increasing numbers of human rights organizations are "associating with government institutions in reform processes . . . because they see that shaming and blaming are not enough." A second, related theme is the inability (or limited ability) of rights approaches to make trade-offs between options in a context of scarce resources. Archer concludes by arguing that the development and human rights standards used to measure progress are neither explicit nor shared, and that it is difficult for the traditions to assess each other and identify complementarities. He suggests that if this process is more rigorously undertaken, the potential contribution of the human rights framework will be better recognized by development specialists.

John Gledhill (Chapter 3) outlines the emergence of the rights-based approach in Latin America and examines the relationship of rights with the strengthening of neoliberalism. He suggests that, while rights may be associated with neoliberal regimes and the promotion of capitalist economic systems, in Latin America debates on rights and related campaigns have also been catalyzed by socially excluded groups. Gledhill challenges several assumptions of supporters of rights-based approaches, and argues that rights may not lead to inclusion as rich and poor see a need to protect themselves from particular groups, particularly in contexts of rising crime and violence. The discussion highlights the significance of state and civil society capacity if amended and improved laws are to be realized and, more fundamentally, if shared values are to evolve. Such shared values, Gledhill argues, underpin concepts of fairness and redistribution, which in turn set a framework for rights.

Generally speaking, Gledhill argues, there is little interest within the state in taking on bigger agendas of income or asset redistribution. Neoliberalism is associated with individualism, with positive values being given to market participation. However, this trend is somewhat softened by growing concerns for the strength of civic virtue. To be effective rights need to be about more than just participation. The "poor citizens" need to develop a capacity for self-representation in the public sphere, identifying alternative economic possibilities and catalyzing their realization.

In understanding the contribution of rights, Gledhill emphasizes the need for detailed analysis of the particular context in which the rights lobby is emerging. He finds reasons to be positive but remains somewhat ambivalent about the contribution of rights to progressive policies in Latin America.

Rights, Governmentality, and Citizenship

The second pair of chapters deals with issues of identity and inclusion, considering how distinct underprivileged groups subject to discrimination can be assisted by a rights-based approach. Central to ideas of rights is equality of resources, assets, and opportunities. This pairing explores two particular development interventions that have sought to address the needs of and discrimination against distinct groups broadly identified by their ethnicity, one in Nepal and one in Cameroon. The two chapters both emphasize (albeit sometimes indirectly) the issue of self-determination for minority groups seeking to secure rights. Taken together they raise questions about what such self-determination might mean for a group that may be ambiguously defined, and that is, inevitably, an amalgam of different interests with intragroup differentials in access to power and associated benefits. The discussion also raises questions about the benefits and limitations of gaining inclusion within dominant political formations.

Katsuhiko Masaki (Chapter 5) draws on research in Majuwa, a village in Nepal, to analyze the potential offered by the adoption in 2006 of the UN Declaration of the Rights of Indigenous Peoples. In particular, he considers the principle of free, prior, and informed consent (FPIC) and the related principle of self-determination. Masaki notes that rights-based approaches have catalyzed a stronger recognition that development projects cannot be imposed on indigenous groups, and raised awareness of the need to protect minority cultures from mainstream domination. However, he argues that the subsequent processes are complex, due to the multiple identities held by individuals who belong to "hybrid" indigenous groups. His argument is illustrated by the case of a group called the Tharus, who have been disadvantaged since the region they inhabit was colonized by the state of Nepal, and who are also divided by class, party politics, and gender. The struggles of indigenous groups are difficult for numerous reasons, including the fact that, in their struggle for recognition, such groups are often forced to "assimilate themselves to societal norms that have placed them at a disadvantage." Rights, Masaki concludes, cannot easily be introduced from outside through development interventions or well-intentioned strategies for inclusion, and instead need to emerge from the groups themselves in a process of self-determination that engages with the inequalities within such groups.

Duni and colleagues (Chapter 4) explore a positive experience with the rights-based approach in the Cameroon in which an ethnic minority, the Mbororo'en, has been able to consolidate its livelihood strategies after securing more favorable legal processes. Relatively wealthy in cattle but with limited and usually only informal access to grazing land, the Mbororo had tended to settle disputes outside the courts, even when exploited by others. A paralegal program sought to challenge these arrangements and, as a result, the group is now more likely to use the law and to reduce their involvement in excessive exploitation and use of bribes. Moreover, the authors suggest that legal officials show an increasing concern to be accountable to local citizens. While the group may not have realized full rights, it has improved its position—albeit within a system that remains clientelist.

Despite finding that the program has been successful in catalyzing processes of citizenship formation and good governance, Duni et al. raise critical questions about this rights-based approach. First, there are indications that vertical relationships linking the Mbororo with the state have become less exploitative, but horizontal relations between the Mbororo and their farming peers may have worsened. This perhaps indicates that improved individualized rights have come with the cost of reduced commonality and collectivity. Second, the authors are concerned that gender relations are not a priority for the program, as issues important for Mbororo women have not been taken up by the paralegal staff. In some ways, the program has concentrated more on areas that matter for economic productivity than on those associated with the development priorities of the more vulnerable.

Rights and Poverty Reduction: Between Collectivism and Individualism

The third pair of chapters considers the interface between rights and collective and/or individual strategies for poverty reduction. Does the use of a rights-based approach strengthen individual property rights and help to address poverty through ensuring greater income-earning opportunities? Or is the collective essential to poverty reduction, in providing a basis for political action that addresses basic needs and secures redistribution? This pairing juxtaposes the experiences of households in rural Peru, needing individual legal rights over property to improve their livelihood options, with the efforts of pavement dwellers (and other squatters) to secure tenure in Mumbai, India. The two contributions explore the extent to which the rights-based approach may help to protect the interests of the poor by offering rights, or may undermine their longer-term political interests by placing an increasing emphasis on individualism within social norms and values. Additionally, this debate contrasts rights strategies that strengthen the collective power of the poor, enabling them to renegotiate and bargain for a greater distribution of resources, with strategies that place greater reliance on individual entitlements, protected by law and the legal system, for personal livelihood development.

Leonith Hinojosa-Valencia (Chapter 6) analyzes the livelihoods of peasant groups in the South Peruvian Andes, and argues for the value of property rights. Drawing from research on the livelihoods of 400 households, she finds that investments in land make an important contribution to the livelihood strategies of agricultural producers. Yet the regime of land tenure is problematic for some families as individual land-use allocations are made but not officially recognized; the state and NGOs have preferred to strengthen communal land management despite the partial breakdown of these systems. This situation puts Andean highland peasants at a disadvantage compared to agricultural producers elsewhere in the country. The failure to translate rights over land use into legal ownership reduces the value of the land, as users may be reluctant to make major capital investments and there are no title deeds to be used as loan collateral. Moreover, the present system of collective land ownership and the use of informal negotiations to advance individual access does not work in favor of either women or the lowest-income groups. Hinojosa-Valencia concludes that a greater allocation of property rights is required, and that such property rights may help individuals to diversify their livelihoods, increasing their development opportunities through improving their ability to participate in new agricultural markets.

Sheela Patel and Diana Mitlin (Chapter 7) examine strategies used to acquire shelter by landless and homeless federations in Southern towns and cities, and particularly by the women-led savings schemes active in several countries and the work of the National Slum Dwellers Federation in Mumbai (India). The women, who make up the majority of members in the local federations (which are themselves aggregations of local savings schemes), do not believe that an openly aggressive and critical rights campaign against the state is likely to be successful, given the present imbalance in power and vulnerabilities that disadvantages low-income groups, women, and other targets of discrimination. Therefore, while savings scheme members may be critical of the state, in general they seek to negotiate with local and national government to advance their rights in matters of shelter, services, and livelihood. The women also believe that there is no simple answer to their needs for tenure, basic services, and housing, and that, in this context, it does not make sense to simply press the state to deliver established (but inadequate) entitlements. For these women, realizing rights requires an active engagement in finding solutions to problems, and savings schemes therefore aim to develop new alternatives in collaboration with the relevant ministries and departments.

Once the women have identified such solutions, they also seek to build in an active role for local community groups in the realization of shelter improvements. Savings scheme and federation leaders believe that organized, active local groups will build a constituency able to negotiate successfully for redistribution and social justice.

The Rights-Based Approach and the Agency of the Poor

The fourth pair of chapters examines the contribution of rights to strengthening the agency of the poor. Michael Drinkwater (Chapter 9) uses an examination of efforts to address gender inequality to argue that rights approaches are crucial because they encourage greater human agency. Frances Cleaver (Chapter 8), offering a second perspective, argues that the creation of agency is complex and multidimensional, and that while factors such as rights may help to strengthen a sense of agency (and the attainment of further rights), they do not necessarily do so.

Drinkwater argues that the rise of rights-based approaches in development organizations has brought a different perspective to their work—how to deal more effectively with the endemic social problems of poverty, marginalization, and discrimination. He argues that "a rights-based approach to development can further the ability of initiatives seeking to address the more pervasive factors that perpetuate gender inequality" by advancing the simple but powerful proposition that all humans are equal. Examples illustrate that a rights-based understanding of development has achieved success in securing gender inclusion partly because the perspective has encouraged work on strategic as well as practical gender needs. Drinkwater argues that previous attempts to pursue women's empowerment have foundered if and when they have come to question systematic inequities and inequalities. By contrast, a rights-based approach to women's empowerment requires the challenge to the natural order to be posed at the outset: "we are also human and require treatment as such." This, he suggests, is far more effective in catalyzing a reflective process that results in a transformative change in power relations at a local level. Drinkwater argues that the effectiveness of rights-based approaches in catalyzing relational change lies in the deep analysis of existing power inequities, in the educational use of information about rights within projects, and in the way in which men are encouraged to reflect on their relationship to women and on the benefits of women's empowerment.

Cleaver explores the realization of rights from the perspective of human agency and the variety of forces that constrain and promote such agency. She seeks to move beyond a review of claims for greater rights by problematizing the processes that are central to the identification, claiming, and realization of such rights through local decision-making institutions and collective action. "Taken-for-granted" institutions are, she suggests, far more complex than assumed, and only through a detailed analysis of both processes and outcomes in the promotion of rights can their positive contribution be identified and understood. Cleaver questions assumptions about community participation in the common management of natural resources, particularly water resources. Participation is associated with good governance, and both, she suggests, are seen as a good thing. However, she finds that little attention has been given to the actual dynamics of involvement in local governance institutions. Cleaver argues that there is a need to understand who controls access to resources and how the poor gain access. She goes on to explore constraints on agency, notably with respect to the limited ability of some participants to make choices. She considers how moral "worldviews" act to reinforce some behaviors, and how the multiple identities that people hold may influence access to natural resources; she then examines a number of other constraining factors that affect how people may understand and claim rights.

The Rights-Based Approach and Operational Effectiveness

The final pairing considers issues related to the policies and programming of international development agencies. Does an emphasis on rights and the implementation of the rights-based approach assist agencies to become more effective in reaching low-income groups and addressing poverty? Or does it lead to ineffective decision making and a confused set of activities? Has an emphasis on rights led to more sensitive and people-oriented programs, or has it resulted in poor targeting and a lack of direction? These two chapters draw on the experiences of two organizations, the United Nations Children's Fund (UNICEF) and ActionAid, to explore the implications of the rights-based approach for development agencies.

Lauchlan Munro (Chapter 11) argues that the complications of rights-based programming for UNICEF have proved to be considerable. The agency embraced a rights-based approach to planning and programming, believing that human rights principles such as universality and indivisibility must inform and be embedded within every stage of the planning and programming process. However, the author suggests that this led to an absolutist stance that, while consistent with a legal interpretation of the rights-based approach, led to organizational paralysis through the inability to select intervention points. If "to plan is to choose" (Julius Nyerere), can the universalist requirement of rights-based approaches be consistent with good programming and planning, which must necessarily be selective? The proponents of a rights-based approach to development insist that the existence of international human rights conventions means that development policy is a matter of law, not of charity, morality, social preference, or economic or social benefit. However, Munro suggests that UNICEF struggled to manage the consequences of rights-based programming, producing a reduction in activity, a lack of clarity in language, overly complex goals, an inability to act due to failures of prioritization, and increasing dissent between staff members. Munro concludes that, to be effective in realizing rights, a rights-based perspective needs to be implemented in conjunction with other frameworks assisting in a range of management dimensions.

Jennifer Chapman and colleagues (Chapter 10) discuss the experience of ActionAid with the rights-based approach, and draw more positive conclusions. The authors argue that rights-based approaches hold considerable potential for repoliticizing development work and encouraging development workers to be more reflective about their actions, and hence to understand some inherent contradictions belonging to an international development agency. In many cases, they suggest, the rights-based approach has inspired staff members to make more connections between their work and the social processes within which the activities take place. This deepening of analysis and, they suggest, strengthening of people's power, can help to ensure that agencies have greater long-term impact and make a difference in the lives of poor and excluded communities. However, the authors emphasize that the rights-based approach will result in more effective development only if it is grounded within a careful analysis of power in all its forms, and if the resultant strategies incorporate a sufficiently complex understanding of how change happens and how it is sustained. In particular, existing lessons about grassroots development work on issues of participation, empowerment, conscientization, organizing and leadership development need to be built on and integrated into rights-based approaches. Transforming unequal power relationships requires a simultaneous engagement with unjust legal processes, reform of such processes, changing of widely held societal attitudes and behaviors that support inequity and discrimination, and empowerment of the poor and marginalized with greater self-organization. Chapman and colleagues conclude by emphasizing the importance of contextualized analysis, and of avoiding a narrow simplistic strategy that equates "rights-based approaches primarily with policy and advocacy work" and sees "rights as the sole solution to poverty."

References

Bebbington, A., S. Hickey, and D. Mitlin (eds.). *Can NGOs make a difference? The challenge of development alternatives.* London: Zed Books.

COHRE. 1994. Centre for Housing Rights and Evictions (COHRE). *Environment and Urbanization* 6, no. 1:147–157.

Cornia, G., R. Jolly and F. Stewart, eds. 1987. *Adjustment with a human face: Protecting the vulnerable and promoting growth.* New York: Oxford University Press.

Cornwall, A. 2002. Locating citizen participation. *IDS Bulletin* 33, no. 2:49–58.

Cornwall, A. and C. Nyamu-Musembi. 2005. Why rights, why now? Reflections on the rise of rights in international development discourse. *IDS Bulletin* 36, no. 1:9–18.

De Soto, H. 2000. *The mystery of capital: Why capitalism triumphs in the West and fails everywhere else.* New York: Basic Books.

Edwards, M. 2001. Introduction. In *Global citizen action,* edited by M. Edwards and J. Gaventa, 1–16. Boulder: Lynne Rienner Publishers.

Environment and Urbanization. 1994. *Environment and Urbanization* 6, no. 1:3–216 (special issue on evictions).

Escobar Latapí, A. and M. González de la Rocha. 1995. Crisis, restructuring and urban poverty in Mexico. *Environment and Urbanization* 7, no. 1:57–76.

Eyben, R. and C. Ferguson. 2004. How can donors become more accountable to poor people? In *Inclusive aid: Changing power and relationships in international development,* edited by L. Groves and R. Hinton, 57–75. London: Earthscan Publications.

Gaventa, J. 2002. Introduction: Exploring citizenship, participation and accountability. *IDS Bulletin* 33, no. 2:1–11.

Gready, P. and J. Ensor. 2005. Introduction. In *Reinventing development? Translating rights-based approaches from theory into practice,* edited by P. Gready and J. Ensor, 1–46. London and New York: Zed Books.

Harvey, D. 2006. *Spaces of global capitalism: Towards a theory of uneven geographical development.* London and New York: Verso.

Hinton, R. and L. Groves. 2004. The complexity of inclusive aid. In *Inclusive aid: Changing power and relationships in international development,* edited by L. Groves and R. Hinton, 3–20. London: Earthscan Publications.

Hulme, D. and M. Edwards, eds. 1997. *NGOs, states and donors: Too close for comfort?* Basingstoke: Macmillan Press.

Lewis, D. 2007. *Management of non-governmental development organizations.* 2nd ed. Abingdon: Routledge.

Mandar, H. 2005. Right as struggle—Towards a more just and humane world. In *Reinventing development? Translating rights-based approaches from theory into practice,* edited by P. Gready and J. Ensor, 233–253. London and New York: Zed Books.

Manji, F. and C. O'Coill. 2002. The missionary position: NGOs and development in Africa, *International Affairs* 78, no. 2:567–583.

Mayo, Marjorie. 2005. *Global citizens: Social movements and the challenge of globalization.* London and New York: Zed Books.

Minujin, A. 1995. Squeezed: The middle class in Latin America. *Environment and Urbanization* 7, no. 2:153–165.

Molyneux, M. and S. Lazar. 2003. *Doing the rights thing: Rights-based development and Latin American NGOs.* London: ITDG Publications.

Moser, C. and A. Norton with T. Conway, C. Ferguson and P. Vizard. 2001. *To claim our rights: Livelihood security, human rights and sustainable development.* London: Overseas Development Institute.

Piron, L-H. 2005. Rights-based approaches and bilateral aid agencies: More than a metaphor? *IDS Bulletin* 36, no. 1:19–30.

Robb, C. 2004. Changing power relations in the history of aid. In *Inclusive aid: Changing power and relationships in international development,* edited by L. Groves and R. Hinton, 21–41. London: Earthscan Publications.

Tomas, A. 2005. Reforms that benefit poor people—Practical solutions and dilemmas of rights-based approaches to legal and justice reform. In *Reinventing development? Translating rights-based approaches from theory into practice,* edited by P. Gready and J. Ensor, 171–184. London and New York: Zed Books.

UNDP [United Nations Development Programme]. 2005. *Human development report.* New York: UNDP.

Uvin, P. 2004. *Human rights and development.* Bloomfield, Conn.: Kumarian Press.

Wallace, T. 1997. New development agendas: Changes in UK NGO policies and procedures. *Review of African Political Economy* 24, no. 71:35–55.

CHAPTER 2

Linking Rights and Development: Some Critical Challenges

Robert Archer[1]

Introduction

The emergence and growing influence of rights-based approaches to development has caused policymakers, practitioners, organizations, and academics involved with "rights" on one hand and "development" on the other to reengage with one another. Although both communities date from the period after World War II, they took different institutional paths for much of the rest of the century.[2] The new dialogue between rights proponents and development practitioners is just a few years old—mainstreaming at the UN level only started at the end of the last century—and we are at the start rather than the end of an institutional exchange that will determine how much rights and development can offer one another.

This chapter will focus on the characteristics of each tradition that are relevant to this exchange. The range of issues involved cannot be fully covered here, and some shorthand will be necessary. I start by identifying characteristics of the human rights tradition that distinguish it from development. I am perhaps particularly conscious of these because, though I now work for an organization that focuses on human rights policy questions, I am not a lawyer and my background is in development, broadly defined. In my view, these differences help explain why attempts to mainstream human rights—whether in development, governance, economics, or environmental matters, and whether at the UN, government, or NGO level—continue to experience difficulties and require time to sort out. I then go on to discuss challenges that both communities face before making the case for taking rights seriously in development circles. In particular I will argue that the human rights framework, contrary to the concerns of development economists, can provide the development approach with some significant political and social benchmarks, both for testing decisions within development and for evaluating them (see

Munro, Chapter 11). However, it is important that this useful borrowing is not perceived as "capture": in general, at least for the foreseeable future, development professionals will not be willing to jettison their tradition in favor of a formally constructed rights-based model.

Rights and Development: Understanding the Differences

An immediate difference between the two methods concerns the systematic character of the human rights approach and the more pragmatic traditions that underpin development. Unlike political and economic theorists or development and governance practitioners, whose traditions are pragmatic (and, for that matter, unlike the Anglo-Saxon legal tradition) the human rights approach is systemic. It is built around a body of principles and derives policy from them. Many things follow from this basic structure, including many of the approach's real and claimed weaknesses.

The systematic approach means that the human rights framework is more transparent and orderly than other frameworks. It is more consistent and more logical. Not for nothing do human rights proponents emphasize the value of universality and interdependence. They believe that the system they advance is powerful because it has very wide application and because rights are consistent with one another (in most cases) and mutually supportive. For example, freedom of expression is inconsistent with the continued practice of torture; it underpins not just political participation but access to economic and social rights. It follows, however, that human rights supporters cannot change course easily. They are not flexible and do not easily engage in policymaking in one area (provision of water, for example) without regard for other areas (education, political participation). They find it difficult to negotiate and trade (see Munro, Chapter 11, and also Chapman, Chapter 10). In these respects the human rights approach differs from other traditions, whose practitioners can change their methodologies quickly if it makes sense to do so. From the opposite perspective, of course, the pragmatism that is part of much development practice is a weakness: it can generate inconsistent and discriminatory effects. As such, it is conceivable that the systematic and disciplinary character of rights-based discourse and instruments might bring a certain rigor to development thinking and practice, and strengthen the meaning of ideas that are widely used and often abused.[3]

It does not help communication that many human rights activists are unfamiliar with the history and traditions of other disciplines. They do not necessarily know that development professionals worked for many years to arrive at their notions of participation and inclusion. Many advocates of the human rights approach believe that human rights invented such ideas and brought them to development. This makes it difficult for them to engage with a concern expressed by some development practitioners: that advocates of a human rights approach are simply repackaging existing development values and ideas in new language. The lack of knowledge is mutual, of course: most development practitioners are not familiar with the history or content of human rights, and therefore find it difficult to understand the form of human rights arguments or the reasons why proponents of human rights are preoccupied by certain ideas.

It is unfortunate but not surprising that, partly as a result of ignorance, human rights proponents have earned a reputation for moral grandstanding and for judging the performances of others without dirtying their own hands in the mucky business of development. Relations between human rights professionals and professionals rooted in other disciplines—economists, development experts, governance advisers—are often hedged with private criticisms that underpin the unwillingness of many institutions (NGO, government, and international) to engage fully with a rights approach.

What are these criticisms, and are they justified? Although space prevents a detailed discussion, these observations need to be brought to light in order to understand where the human rights framework can be helpful and where it needs help. I will briefly outline the main points, to put them on the table.

The first criticism concerns the "political" character of human rights. Some claim that human rights advocates are inherently critical of government, interested in blaming institutions rather than changing them. This is one face of the "won't dirty their hands" critique mentioned above. Personally, I don't think the claim stands up. The role of watchdog is a vital one even if it is inconvenient. Moreover, many more human rights organizations are associating with government institutions in reform processes. Interestingly, they are doing so precisely because they see that shaming and blaming are not enough: if institutions are too weak, or are dysfunctional, shouting at them won't help. Mainly, however, the political criticism is weak because the fault of being political can be (and frequently is) leveled as tellingly against development agencies. They are said to intervene in other countries in the agency's own national interest or to suit their own convictions, and to do so without accountability because of the power their aid budgets bestow.

Another criticism is that human rights methods focus on individuals and individual rights rather than on duties or larger public benefits. Leaving aside the right to development and other attempts to promote collective rights, this judgment has a degree of truth. It is a strength of development and economics approaches that they address macro-objectives and long-term investments. They can envision large processes of change and plan through short-term disruption and loss while working toward long-term gain, even though (as we see below) such trade-offs are also controversial in the development tradition.

This observation can be linked with two other criticisms leveled against human rights advocates: that they think only in the present tense and that they allow only unidirectional progress. This approach, it is argued, is deeply at odds with the experience of development. Development advocates consider themselves to be modernists and progressives, but many accept that some or many people who are caught up in development processes will suffer as a result: people living now will suffer some loss for the benefit of the next generation or their children. It is understood that development is a long and mucky process. A realist of this kind thinks human rights advocates are not able to balance benefits for the many against losses for a minority or to weigh great benefits in the future against manageable losses now. It is clear, they would say, that a major new road system or water delivery system can bring long-term and immediate benefits to large populations, but such systems cannot be constructed in most societies without displacing and disrupting and harming the interests of some people. As a result (it is claimed), obsessed by detail, human rights proponents cannot see the big picture: they condemn progress that takes one step back in order to go two steps forward. They are only concerned about violations *now,* here, in this place.

There is some truth in this. Human rights advocates do find it difficult to contextualize loss and violations, either in space or time, or to relativize the loss of one group of people against the gains of a larger group. However, this weakness is also a strength. It is clearly one of the cardinal failures of development, and certainly economic planning, that those responsible often concentrate on long-term benefits or benefits to the majority while ignoring losses suffered by more invisible communities or minorities. This too is a matter of controversy within development, of course. Whereas most economists and planners are willing to put up with short-term losses in return for long-term gain, those operating from either an environmental or social development focus tend to challenge this thinking.[4] They are often unwilling to accept that any losses are justified. In this area, the very particular interest that human rights has for individuals, and in those who suffer discrimination or loss, provides some sharp and helpful tools and techniques that will not remove arguments about justice but could assist planners in making transparent—and responding to—the human costs of large-scale development and economic programs.

In addition, there is the "refusal to choose" criticism. Human rights advocates are said to duck hard decisions, for example, between two goods (education or health, roads or sanitation), and to reject the discipline of working with limited resources and scarcity that economists take for granted (see Munro, Chapter 11).

This is a real challenge. For the reasons already mentioned, human rights advocates do find it difficult to trade, to prefer one right at the expense of another. They don't like to allow that a schoolteacher should be employed *instead* of a nurse whose services are equally essential. However justified theoretically, this attitude can encourage a soft or aspirational approach to decision making.

That said, I will make two comments. First, work is now being done—for example, on budget analysis—that may enable decision makers to apply human rights principles and methods to decision making in rather focused ways.[5] Second, it is a strength of the human rights approach that it perceives progress in an interconnected way. It is widely accepted in development circles, too, that sustainable economic and social progress requires a multidimensional approach. Education cannot be improved successfully without improving health, health cannot be improved without improving access to food, and so forth. This parallel discipline, complementary to the discipline of scarcity, usefully discourages the "quick fix" or "single cause" approaches that have plagued many development models in the past.

Shared Values, Shared Problems

We could continue. What emerges from such a list, I think, is that success and failure depend on the standard of judgment used. The standards against which development approaches and human rights approaches are judged (and judge one another) are often neither explicit nor shared and may not be the best or most appropriate ones to use.

For example, neither development nor human rights has a good record when it comes to influencing or profoundly changing worst cases. The very poorest countries, the least strategic and least resourced, have not made the fastest progress toward ending poverty, in spite of (or, some would say, because of) the large amounts of aid they have received. Currently, the big success stories are countries such as China; in the past countries such as South Korea saw the biggest advances. Human rights reform works best in states that have the capacity to be rule-based, where there is an active civil society and a sound judicial system (see Gledhill, Chapter 3). It is an odd idea to suppose that economic and social development would work best in the poorest and weakest societies, or that human rights reform would advance easily in societies that are most resistant to its values. Yet both movements are most often judged against the worst cases.

It might also be said that the human rights and development movements are both progressive: they seek to change, to modernize, to bring into being new worlds that are more prosperous, more humanly fulfilling, and more just. In so doing, they also seek to expunge forms of behavior and relationships that impede what they perceive to be progress. In some respects both are therefore revolutionary movements; at least their proponents think they are. From other points of view, they may be conservative, entrenching already out-of-date ideas such as the notion that Western ethical and legal principles are universal, that aid promotes rather than obstructs independent economic development, or that rich countries will disinterestedly help the poor. Many who are outside both movements see them as ultimately oppressive, representing the values of a powerful establishment that desires to entrench its legal and economic institutions across the world.

A crucial goal, therefore, is to understand which criticisms are sound and which ones are "straw men." To what extent do the two sides have different or comparable strengths? To what extent are they complementary? Or antagonistic? To what extent do they share the same weaknesses?

The truth is that no system works in theory: it works in practice, because people make it work and fit it together. A human rights framework that is applied to the letter, without judgment, will produce absurd results. And development plans—especially large ones—introduced without judgment produce white elephants and catastrophes.

We are at the point where we must try things out, working together to see whether we are using the same terminology to mean the same things and making careful observations to see what works. My own bet is that the human rights framework will not always be useful but that it will provide some very useful political, economic, and social tests for identifying and monitoring risks and for taking decisions and evaluating them.

Toward Convergence: Reasons for Development to Take Rights Seriously

In this final section I want to suggest that the human rights framework can bring at least two core strengths to the development tradition. Both are linked to a characteristic that both traditions share: an inclusiveness that is central to their political and moral credibility.

The first strength is the opposite face of another criticism: that human rights is an abstract and legalistic concept. I have said already that the framework is systematic and that this is a source both of strength and weakness. The human rights approach is legal as well—in my view, inescapably—and this means that it is relatively complex to use. The complexity results from the fact that human rights is both a popular language with which almost everyone can identify (the language of human dignity resonates powerfully in founding documents such as the Universal Declaration of Human Rights) and at the same time a set of rather precise understandings that governments have reached by negotiation. The latter texts are not romantic: they represent what governments believe to be the realistic limits of their moral, political, and economic obligations in relation to their citizens and other people under their jurisdiction. Certainly a lot of politics and rhetoric are there, but a great deal of realism as well. Without question, this is one of the human rights movement's great strengths. Their language is grounded, relatively precise, and can be used by governments to negotiate with one another. The collateral of this is that the simple and noble assumption of human rights is girded with legal conditions that limit their application in practice. This is what makes them realistic and potentially (if not actually) effective—and it is another reason why their application is complicated and often counterintuitive.

No other public or official language is available that provides the same range, power, and precision as the human rights framework. This makes it very important. In comparison, development can be morally appealing, but it does not have the force of law. The same can be said about good government. Law may not be applied and governments may behave illegally, but the human rights framework offers levers of influence that other discourses do not.

This quality serves as a fundamental source of human rights' legitimacy. Human rights law may be described as legitimate because it has been signed by governments—yet it is independent of the interests of a single government. It therefore has legal authority. In addition to the useful forms of practical leverage that human rights techniques can provide, this is another reason why those working on economic and development policy should look carefully at where they can adopt the language of rights. Very often their own policies do not have the same legitimate roots and are often accused of being illegitimate in important ways.

A second underlying strength has particular relevance to the issue of poverty. Let's be hopeful and imagine ourselves a few years from now. The major Organisation for Economic Co-operation and Development (OECD) governments have signed up to 0.7. The G8 has agreed to cancel the poorest countries' debt and has approved new financial mechanisms that have freed for development an amount of new money equal to the aid budget. The IMF has revalued its gold reserves. The world has united around "MDGs+." What core obstacles would still stand in the way of progress in the fight to end poverty?

Well, quite a number of things, of course. But the most important might be capacity: the ability of poorer countries to absorb and manage, to invest and reinvest, much larger flows of resources effectively. This of course is a political problem as much as an economic concern. Absorption capacity has been a source of political risk since the OECD refocused aid on the poorest nations rather than on a wider range of developing countries. The same risk occurs when large donors, impressed by the quality of work of some small NGOs, overgive and destroy them.

There is no simple way to grow effective financial and governance institutions quickly.[6] They need to be rooted in societies and to have earned their legitimacy. That said, human rights can make a distinctive and vital contribution in this area. Here I will refer to yet another criticism, which is particularly misplaced. Human rights advocates are still sometimes blamed for undermining sovereignty and imposing foreign values on countries. This is a variant of the "human rights are political" argument. It is misplaced because the human rights framework is in fact highly focused on national obligations. It puts the responsibility and authority of national governments at the center of its arrangements, and it does so precisely for the reasons indicated earlier: the framework was negotiated and agreed by governments in all their realism. (This strength also carries a weakness because it is so difficult for states to agree on when it acceptable for international actors to intervene—peacefully, or even forcefully—in the affairs of other countries to protect certain rights, for example, life. But that is another story.)

A fundamental merit of the human rights framework is that it puts in place a range of mechanisms and tests that oblige governments to be more transparent and accountable than they would normally wish to be. The big practical tests that the human rights framework requires—inclusiveness (nondiscrimination), communication of information, political participation in decisions, and accountability—all have the effect of sharpening the performance of public (and eventually private) institutions. But they also make them legitimate. If a rights regime is in place, those whom institutions affect have access to information about the institutions' policies, are able to make their views known, and can see that the institutions concerned are obliged to report upon and justify their conduct. In addition, the system has a legal foundation, with the additional precision and legitimacy that this implies.

Once again, no short cuts are available. There is no magic wand. Human rights activists are as dismayed as everyone else by the glacial pace of most institutional improvement, and they are as depressed as developmentalists by the ineffectiveness of their advocacy. In the longer term, nevertheless, the human rights framework offers a route toward achieving better institutions. And it is a sounder route than most because it creates mechanisms that generate local, national, and international legitimacy—as well as better performance. The system does not impose foreign values (development does that far more often, and more arbitrarily). It puts the onus firmly on national governments to be publicly accountable. And it does so legitimately, because national governments have signed the standards in question.

For me, this is another fundamental reason why governance and development professionals should look for ways of drawing on the human rights framework wherever they can when they seek to strengthen capacity and institutional performance. It is not always easy to do so, neither is the human rights framework quick or always effective. But it builds in political and democratic legitimacy, and this is a priceless commodity if one is seeking sustainable change.

Conclusion

Let me end with a final comment about poverty and inclusiveness. I have tried to argue that one of the strengths of human rights is that it focuses on those who are excluded. It requires policymakers to ask, Who has not benefited? Who has been forgotten? Who has been excluded? It offers valuable corrective tools to development planners, who are predisposed to add up overall progress and overlook the often invisible minorities who do not benefit.

For very good reasons, development organizations have refocused on poverty in recent years. The political test of development policies now is whether they reduce extreme poverty. I have suggested this creates a political risk—that the wider public could become disillusioned with the whole project (at national level and in donor countries) if quick progress is not made (although quick progress may be impossible).

There is another political risk, however, that both movements ought to avoid. Neither are minority movements. The objective of development is, or ought to be, that the whole of society benefits from it. Of course that must include the very poor, the marginalized and excluded, the least resourced, the most oppressed. They are the acid test of commitment. But *all* should benefit from development and progress, and those who are poor cannot in fact be made better off unless society as a whole prospers. This is a crucial political message, if we want pro-poor policies to win the support of the middle class in middle-income countries, or of the broader public in industrialized countries. Development is about everyone, not just the prosperous—but not just the poor either.

The same is true of human rights. Every person is entitled to claim his or her rights. They empower everyone. This is a much broader message than one which focuses only on the very poor, only on political prisoners, only those who suffer systemic discrimination. In this respect, the universality of human rights is central to its credibility. If a human rights approach is to work politically, it must appeal to the prosperous as well as the poor—and it must remain relevant to both. In fact this is where the true power lies: we all benefit if everyone is treated justly, if we all feel safe, if people are protected against extreme poverty, if all are healthy and educated. The obligation to include the excluded is clearly there: it is the acid test of justice. But the legitimacy and authority of human rights—and the legitimacy and authority of the development movement too—lie in their universal interest and appeal. If we do not communicate this, we will fail in the end to achieve either.

References

Grindle, M. 2004. Good enough governance: Poverty reduction and reform in developing countries. *Governance* 17, no. 4:525–548.

Holland, J., M. A. Brocklesby and C. Aburgre. 2004. Beyond the technical fix? Participation in donor approaches to rights-based development. In *Participation: From tyranny to transformation? Exploring new approaches to participation in development*, edited by S. Hickey and G. Mohan, 252–268. London: Zed Books.

Kanbur, R. 2001. Economic policy, distribution and poverty: The nature of disagreements. *World Development* 29, no. 6:1083–1094.

Norton, A., and D. Elson. 2002. *What's behind the budget?: Politics, entitlements and accountability in the budget process.* London: ODI.

Slim, H. 2000. Dissolving the difference between humanitarianism and development: The mixing of a rights-based solution. *Development in Practice* 10, no. 3–4:287–291.

Notes

1. This chapter derives from the author's keynote address to conference. The footnotes have been added by the editors as a means of linking up certain points to wider debates that the reader may be interested in. This should not be taken to imply that the author takes a particular position vis-à-vis these debates.

2. See Slim (2000) for an elaboration of this divergence and of why the two should reconverge.

3. For example, Holland et al. (2004) and others argue that participatory approaches to development, which have been particularly prone to co-option and dilution, can be given added rigor and "bite" when linked up with rights-based approaches.

4. See Kanbur (2001) for a fuller exploration of this central divide within the development community.

5. On the potential of rights-based approaches to inform budgeting, see Norton and Elson (2002).

6. On the difficulties facing efforts to impose "good governance" and for moves toward a more realistic agenda, see Grindle (2004).

CHAPTER 3

The Rights of the Rich versus the Rights of the Poor

John Gledhill[1]

In this chapter I produce a "balance sheet" of the possibilities and contradictions of the rights-based approach to development from the
perspective of poor people and popular organizations, illustrated principally with examples from Latin America, a region that has a strong
historical affinity with the politics of rights. But I begin by scrutinizing the
rights-based approach's claims to universalism and its relationship to
neoliberal techniques of government. The rights-based approach clearly
resonates with the global discourses of "participation," "empowerment,"
and "social inclusion" that pervaded the field of "development" from the
late 1990s onwards. Is it simply another "Third Way" strategy of "drawing
potential adversaries into managed dialogues and partnerships" (Craig
and Porter 2005, 257), in order to minimize disruption to the trajectories
of capitalist development favored by global elites and the multilateral
institutions that serve them? I argue that the rights-based approach
amounts to more than that, because it is in part driven "from below," but
that it is important to be realistic about what can be achieved in very
unequal societies if the rights of the rich are treated as sacrosanct.

Exploring the Tensions of the Rights-Based Approach

Rights as a "Popular" Demand

The gains from a rights-based approach are especially apparent when
linked to past histories of authoritarianism (Molyneux and Lazar 2003, 31).
In Latin America, the struggle for democracy was impelled by social
movement activism that embraced the global human rights agenda and
brought its different dimensions together. Gender issues, for example,
became articulated to human rights through the public protests of mothers against the "disappearances" of their children. Although the mothers
generally began by appealing to patriarchal ideologies in efforts to shame

the military, the brutal reactions that these tactics provoked drew many women not only toward more radical perspectives on women's rights but also into broader campaigns for civil rights, justice, and an end to impunity (Stephen 1997). As global trends and regional democratization combined to create an environment that favored movements for indigenous rights and autonomy in the 1990s, established networks of women's organizations and NGOs ensured that the indigenous activists could not ignore the demands of women within indigenous communities (Hernández Castillo 2005). These intersections between rights agendas are productive and important.

However, the impulse behind the rights-based approach in Latin America is not simply grassroots struggles and the support such movements receive from organizations inside the region, such as churches, and outside it, such as transnational NGOs and voluntary support networks. Another side of the coin is the transition to the new modes of "governmentality" of neoliberal regimes. A "rights-based approach" is not necessarily invalidated by its affinities, explored in more detail below, with neoliberal "government at a distance" and "active citizenship" (Rose 1999, 49–50, 164–165). Yet in Latin America—where even the IMF now concedes "trends in poverty and income inequality have not improved substantially over the past decade" (Singh et al. 2005), while other commentators paint darker pictures of pervasive insecurity and violence (Kruijt, Sojo and Grynspan 2002)—these neoliberal affinities are one of several complicating factors for those who see the rights-based approach as a way of achieving a more inclusionary society.

People who have gained the right to live in an electoral democracy are still routine losers in terms of economic and physical security. Under conditions of increasing stress, sociability deteriorates between people whom members of other social classes might see as equally poor, but who make important distinctions among themselves—between, for example, people who dwell in slums and those who live in different kinds of "neighborhoods," or between hardworking, respectable, "original" colonizers of an informal urban settlement and more recently arrived "invaders" seen by established families as having greater dispositions to criminality. These tensions affect popular ideas about who should enjoy "human rights." People may be increasingly eager to demand respect for *their own* rights, but poor Brazilians seldom think that people they themselves see as "marginals" or "bandits" should enjoy such "privileges" (Scheper-Hughes 1992, 227–228), and often applaud police who engage in extrajudicial executions (Caldeira 2002, 251–252)—without regard to the fact that all are victimized by the combined class and racial prejudices embedded in the police and justice systems. As the rich and the middle classes guarantee their own security by living more segregated lives protected by gates and walls, the way in which lower-class people react to their own everyday situations of poverty and insecurity also reinforces the deployment of violent force as a means of addressing social problems.

Civil Society and the State

The development of neoliberal "government at a distance" has a direct impact on the organizations that promote rights-based development. Social movements and NGOs face increasing dilemmas as governments invite them to enter into "partnerships," which often undermine their capacity to press for structural changes that might have greater long-term impacts on social inequality. When NGOs become providers of services previously supplied by the state, they risk becoming parastatal organizations, compromised in their ability to represent grassroots demands and obliged to work with official agendas inconsistent with their original aims in order to maintain their funding (Molyneux and Lazar 2003, 84–85).

Social movements too may find their radical edge blunted through institutionalization, even if they avoid being disarticulated by clientelistic relations with NGOs administering poverty alleviation programs (Auyero 2000, 110). Such institutionalization of movements occurs particularly when their urban-middle-class professional advisors gravitate toward more compliant positions under neoliberal democratic regimes. As Assies argues in discussing the urban social movements of Recife, radical demands for "participation" and "empowerment" began to "blend into a strategy of neoliberal reform" in democratic Brazil as they acquired "connotations of self-advancement and self-reliance to participate as economic subjects" (Assies 1999, 222–223). Foweraker has argued that democratization weakened grassroots mobilization in Brazil and Chile as "organization" grew at the expense of autonomy, producing "tensions between leaders and base, elite and mass, professionals and volunteers." The response to these tensions was yet more institutionalization, condemning the represented to political silence and renewed clientelization (Foweraker 2001, 864–865). Despite shifts of government to the Left in some countries, Foweraker's diagnosis remains relevant to understanding the frequently divisive and demobilizing consequences of engagement by radical social movements with "progressive" governments such as that of Néstor Kirchner in Argentina (Zibechi 2004).

Practicing rights-based politics is difficult in societies in which laws are routinely disregarded in the case of the poor. Rights-based struggle clearly seeks to overcome this challenge, but it is often difficult even to access national judicial and administrative institutions in more remote rural areas (Molyneux and Lazar 2003, 83). State capacity is therefore central to the practical value of a model whereby "citizens claim and the state delivers." The concern with state capacity invites contrasts between regions, but we need to be careful about how we draw them.

Comparative Perspectives on Civic Cultures and the State

It is tempting to contrast state capacity in, say, East Asia and Africa in terms of the ability of central government to intervene in civil society to implement desired policies and affect the allocation of resources. Even within Latin America, central governments' "capacity" in this abstract sense is a variable. Yet we must unpack a greater range of variables to do anything analytically useful with "state capacity" and related abstractions such as "strong" and "weak" states.

In comparison with their Latin American peers, the "illiberal" developmental states in East Asian countries enjoyed strong powers to control the actions of social and economic elites (Wade 1990). Singapore offers an extreme example of a "nanny state" that preempted social and ethnic tensions by addressing social rights such as public housing (Castells 2000, 261). Most of these "hard" East Asian states nonetheless faced some resistance from below, as exemplified by the trade union movement in South Korea, and their impressive achievements in reducing social inequalities have led to more middle-class engagement with liberal politics and to the social movements' mobilization around gender relations and the environment (Castells 2000, 377). There are, however, still cultural differences between East Asia and Euro-America that affect the meaning of citizenship, notions of rights, and citizens' concepts of their relationships with the state and the state's duties toward them.

Totalizing characterizations of these cultural differences obscure the way in which the meanings of "shared values" are internally contested and renegotiated in the course of historical change. For example, Yang has argued that the range of practices labeled *guanxi* in China have no historically unchanging meaning: they disappear from some social, political, and business contexts only to reappear in different contexts in which they take on new significance (Yang 2002). Nevertheless, it remains clear that the process of "citizens claiming and the state delivering" will continue to reflect significant differences in the way rights are grounded and in the moral discourses of entitlement that are constructed in different cultural contexts. Even if ideas derived from "advanced liberal" societies in the West actively permeate the public spheres of non-Western countries, they will be resignified by governments and citizens in ways that adapt them to differing institutional arrangements and local understandings.

The same is true of Africa, the region that suffers most from blanket generalizations about cultural differences and state incapacity in debates about development. There may be grounds for agreeing with Chabal and Daloz (1999) that Africa will not replicate Western models of economic and political development, but there are few justifications for ignoring differences within the region or neglecting to examine the substance of the civic cultures that have evolved in it. Botswana is clearly not Congo (Werbner 2004).

Monga contends that "groups, organizations, and personalities that pursue freedom, justice and the rights of citizenship against authoritarian states" have emerged in many postcolonial African countries, constituting a civil society that represents "new spaces for communication and discussion over which the state has no control" (Monga 1996, 4). His study documents how an alternative kind of civic culture can propagate through informal rural–urban networks, in addition to being forged by dissident artists and intellectuals in cities. Yet the frequent co-optation of dissidents recorded in this same study suggests that Monga's restriction of "civil society" to groups that stand up against patrimonial state power begs too many questions. It replicates a particular model—as much ideological as historical—of the "civil society" of the Western European bourgeoisie confronting the "Old Corruption" of the Absolutist Monarchies. The bourgeoisie's notion of "freedom" did lay the basis, in Western Europe and North America, for subsequent struggles by other social classes and women not only to be included in the "right to have rights" but also to extend the substance of those rights. But the universal association of this model with a "strong civil society" is misleading.

First, it may lead us to assume that societies not dominated by a "strong" bourgeoisie in the European sense, such as those of Latin America in the nineteenth century, were incapable of producing rights-based movements. Second, the idea of civil society being in "natural" opposition to the state becomes incoherent when generalized beyond the original European case. In other contexts, "civil society" would have to include a wide variety of groups distinct from the state but with privileged access to and influence upon it (including both mafias and respectable business associations). This is important today given that neoliberal governmentality projects offer "participation" to organizations of the poor on the debatable premise that their voices will "count" equally to those of other components of civil society with greater social power, such as property developers.

Important concerns can therefore be raised about projecting "rights-based development" as an abstract and universal model that transcends cultural differences and historically specific institutional configurations of state–society relations. By focusing in the remainder of this chapter on

Latin America, I am looking at what may be in some respects a particularly favorable context for the rights-based approach.

The Rights-Based Approach in Latin America: Possibilities and Constraints

Historical Antecedents

At first sight it seems obvious why Latin America has proved fertile ground for rights-based approaches. Liberal constitutions were adopted throughout the region in the postcolonial era, with the result that "the values of liberalism and democracy, while insecurely implanted and politically contested by left and right, were nevertheless the dominant cultural referents for much of the continent's modern history" (Molyneux and Lazar 2003, 33). Yet constitutions could not guarantee that citizens' rights would actually be respected, and the classical liberal tradition qualified entitlement to rights with ideas that only citizens with the right class and educational background were truly fit to enjoy them (Gledhill 1997, 82–84).

National elites in Latin America were not slow to think up further grounds for disqualifying some of their new citizens. Women were deprived of the promise of equal rights through the sanctifying ideology of *marianismo*, which honored their spiritual superiority while justifying inequalities on grounds of this "natural" difference (Arrom 1985). Nineteenth-century elites also redefined "the Indian problem" in ways that reflected new European ideas about race and about state- and nation-building (Larson 1999). A strong body of elite opinion argued that worthy citizens for a modern nation could be created only by "whitening out" the indigenous population through miscegenation or displacing it through European immigration. In 1910 Cândido Rondon, a soldier, telegraph engineer, and leading member of the Positivist Church, founded the Brazilian government's Indian Protection Service, with the paternalistic goal of "nationalizing" Brazil's tiny minority of surviving indigenous people through the creation of a "great wall of state authority between indigenes and local society" (Diacon 2004, 120). State tutelage infantilized Brazil's indigenous people juridically as well as metaphorically, hardly enhancing their capacity to exercise rights as the equals of other citizens in defense of their lands and way of life (Ramos 1998).

Nonindigenous people also suffered from racialized understandings of what was required to "catch up" with North Atlantic exemplars of a "modernity" that seemed to be leaving Latin America behind. The government of Brazil, which did not abolish slavery until 1888, dispatched its "civilizing" forces to conduct wars of annihilation against the "fanaticism" of regional religious movements of ethnically mixed people; the most famous of these was the Canudos massacre in the Bahian backlands in 1897. The nationalist ideologies propagated by the dictatorial "New State" of Getúlio Vargas in the 1930s incorporated more positive views on race mixing and African heritage, fostered by the work of intellectuals such as the anthropologist Gilberto Freyre. Yet such changes had little effect on everyday practices of racial discrimination against people seen as "black," and perceptions of class difference in Brazil remain strongly racialized, with lower-class people being "blackened" in the eyes of others, and the upwardly mobile "whitened" (Sheriff 2001).

Throughout Latin America, these ideas about the innate incapacities of indigenous and black people affected elite models of the lower classes in general. Although the Brazilian state's "rationally planned" development projects of the 1950s and 1960s aimed to promote greater social equality, government did not see the poor rural migrants whose labor underpinned these projects as possessing the capacity to exercise the full rights of "citizenship" (Caldeira and Holston 2004, 401). The irony is that Latin American history abounds with struggles by powerless people to make constitutional promises of fuller rights of "citizenship" real in terms that were meaningful for them. As Molyneux and Lazar point out, "poor peasants, indigenous people and even slaves" had been taking their ethnic and social superiors to court in the name of rights throughout the colonial period (Molyneux and Lazar 2003, 34).

The violence of Latin American history in the nineteenth century could be read as an index of the liveliness of civil society rather than of its debility, though its vitality lay among different sectors of society to those envisaged by the European model. Movements against the arbitrary rule of racist local oligarchies sprang up in marginal regions such as Chachapoyas in Peru (Nugent 1997). Indigenous militias in Mexico fought for national independence alongside mestizos, and Indians sometimes fought with liberals against conservatives in the civil wars of the later nineteenth century. Long-term alliances with liberals tended to collapse because the latter were generally determined to privatize communal lands and forests, which most indigenous communities wished to defend as the basis for their economic well-being and their ability to manage their own affairs. Yet Indians were willing to invest in the liberal concept of a society of "free and equal citizens" as an improvement over the tributary relations and racial caste hierarchies of the colonial order. When they talked the language of rights—and they frequently did (Mallon 1995)—they did not work with the conception of rights that motivated liberal models of "possessive individualism" (Gledhill 1997, 76), but they did engage energetically with changing state law.

In Alta Verapaz, Guatemala, for example, indigenous plantation workers sought to exploit the conflict of interest that developed between local landlords and the centralizing political project of the dictator Jorge Ubico, who was finally overthrown by the 1944 revolution (Sieder 2000). Men demanded payment of the wages specified by the law, while women demanded the right to leave husbands who abused them and compensation for violence. The fact that the plaintiffs were Indians meant that racial as well as class bias affected the administration of justice. Such biases continue today, prompting NGO capacity building efforts to train indigenous people to defend members of their own communities within the official justice system, rather than rely on the generally poor advocacy of public defenders or paid nonindigenous lawyers. But there is nothing historically novel in disadvantaged people trying to use the law to have their rights respected and a desired citizenship made real in Latin America.

Back to the Future? "Communitarianism" and the Limits of Neoliberal Inclusion

Past rights struggles in Latin America had an ambiguous character. "Modernization" threatened some kinds of rights, such as the right to possess communal territories, while simultaneously promising emancipation from past forms of domination. This ambiguity continues today.

Contemporary indigenous demands for special rights within a multicultural nation seem to reassert the collective rights abolished by nineteenth century liberal "reformers." Neoliberal states and multilateral institutions now seem relatively comfortable with making concessions in this area, at least where no strong conflict with capitalist interests in land or subsoil resources is involved—despite other tendencies toward growing privatization of state functions and public space, increasing individualization, and emphasis on the reproduction and configuration of the "person" through participation in the market and consumption. At the same time, indigenous people themselves are caught up in these latter movements: it is proving increasingly difficult to persuade young people to commit themselves to the construction of rural utopias rather than migrate to less marginal places. Moreover, despite a long history of popular struggle over rights, negotiation of bureaucratic "favors" or resorting to the levers of personal patronage remain more certain means of getting one's rights as a citizen attended to in Latin America.

It is true that past traditions of deference to social and ethnic superiors are in decline in many contexts. The culture of the Bahian backlands, once viewed by the government as "fanatic," is now seen as a rich "folkloric" patrimony worthy of state promotion for religious tourists (Pessar 2004), and due to the decline of traditional agro-export economies, migrants from rural hinterlands move in increasing numbers toward the "divided cities" of Brazil, where they encounter a new political emphasis on the need to include the poor as "citizens" (Caldeira and Holston 2004, 402). This new emphasis on poor "citizenship," however, remains in continuing contradiction with the priority of market mechanisms in determining the future of urban space (Fix 2001). For example, in 2007 center-left political parties enjoyed power in the metropolitan city of Salvador, the state of Bahia, and Brazil as a whole. Yet when confronted with criticisms of local government approval of urban development plans authorizing additional horizontal condominiums for upper-income families in areas where poor people had also established settlements, one official responded that public funds were scarce, that the land was already in private hands, and that the only way to conserve more Atlantic forest in the area was to rely on the environmental self-interest of the rich to take care of the problem, since the overcrowded and unplanned settlements of the poor were inevitably environmentally catastrophic.

This posture seemed unresponsive not only to the demands for green spaces and environmental improvements made by organizations representing the poorer residents, but also to their offers to collaborate in developing systems of regulation. It revealed how the "rights to the city" of the poor can still be disqualified by finding new ways of characterizing them as "different" from better-off citizens. The social implications of the property rights and lifestyle choices of the rich no longer incite the passions of the Left, which manifests a strong commitment to the use of public resources for "poverty alleviation" but shows little stomach for a fight over income or asset redistribution. The poor residents of Salvador's urban periphery are more conscious than ever of their potential "rights"—civil, human, gender, sexual, and social as well as political—and have not abandoned longstanding traditions of organization and militancy. Although the interventions of a wide range of NGOs, churches and political parties have promoted a certain fragmentation of popular forms of association, there is grassroots interest in putting the pieces back together. The question is, however, whether the neoliberalization evident in governments of the Left in Brazil constitutes an insuperable impediment to the delivery of the rights that subaltern actors seek.

The new tendency in neoliberalism is perhaps best defined as the extension of the concept of "market society" to embrace the production of personhood, identity, and social life itself. This can lend neoliberal governmentality a strongly authoritarian, disciplinary, and normalizing thrust, present even in its "softer" Third Way versions (Gledhill 2004, 340); refusal to accept what capitalist labor markets have to offer (however poorly remunerated and socially degrading), or lack of prudence in providing for one's own future security, is taken as both individual moral failure and failure to exercise social responsibility. An older liberal language of "obligation and social citizenship" has been displaced in neoliberalism by a focus on "the political forms that are adequate to the existence of persons as essentially, naturally, creatures striving to actualize themselves in their everyday, secular lives" (Rose 1999, 166). Yet contemporary elite opinion seldom favors a purely individualistic social model in which the unfettered pursuit of self-interest guarantees the greatest good. US neoconservatives and Blairite Third Wayers alike worried about the apparent decline in "civic virtues" that accompanied the transformations of the 1970s and 1980s, and such concerns produced agreement across a wide political spectrum that it was essential to rebuild "community" (Rose 1999, 186).

Contemporary neoliberal attitudes place responsibility for this restoration of civic virtues that the individual has lost in the hands of nonstate entities, including not simply churches and NGOs but "communities" with historically shared ties of culture. As Hale (2002) notes in a discussion of indigenous rights politics in Guatemala, the logic of the new relationship between community, identity, and political subjectivity thus favored the rise of multiculturalism. Yet the problem that neoliberal multiculturalism poses for popular aspirations is that "the state does not merely 'recognize' community, civil society, indigenous culture and the like, but actively reconstitutes them in its own image, *sheering them of radical excesses,* inciting them to do the work of subject-formation that would otherwise fall to the state itself" (Hale 2002, 496; emphasis added). In this case, the professionalized NGO becomes the neoliberal substitute for Bentham's panopticon (Hale 2002).

In highlighting the manner in which some grassroots demands are accommodated and others classified as "too radical," Hale observes that indigenous communities lose the capacity to define themselves and are constrained by "neoliberal multiculturalism's investment in neatly bounded categories of cultural difference" (Hale 2002, 324). The scope of concessions made to indigenous groups, and the political options of leaders who enter mainstream public life, are also constrained by the "backlash effects" that greater participation can create. Hale illustrates the latter among non-Indian members of the provincial middle-class *ladinos.* I found similar effects in my own research in Mexico when I interviewed a local notable living in a settlement where the original indigenous inhabitants had been dispossessed by invading mestizo ranchers through manipulation of the liberal land privatization laws.[1] His wife was one of the few remaining inhabitants of Nahua stock. When I asked how he felt about the fact that indigenous people had won control of the municipal government, he responded with a candid: "Well, we used to screw them, so now it's their turn to screw us!" Yet he then turned to a litany of complaint about how the children of indigenous families got scholarships to study outside the community, whereas mestizos had to scrimp and save to get their children educated; he ended with a disquisition on his belief that while there was nothing wrong with indigenous people winning elections, the "radicalism" of some of their leaders was bound to increase ethnic conflict.

In fact, interethnic conflicts over land already had a long history, and the present situation differed from these simply in the extent to which the mestizos could now remain confident that state agents would be as partial toward their interests as they had proved in the past. Yet there was a further problem. While my interviewee was relatively affluent by local standards, owning a share in a hotel as well as irrigated land and cattle, the region also contained many mestizos who were as poor as their indigenous neighbors. As a result of ruthless efforts by the regional nonindigenous elite to displace the indigenous population from the land before the 1910 revolution, and subsequent political manipulation of the poor mestizos by richer ranchers in the period of agrarian reform that was cynically intended to carry forward this older project by new means, the indigenous people of the zone had not only become deeply antagonistic to *all* mestizos, but had also internalized the racist ideologies imported by their erstwhile upper class enemies—even to the point of presenting conflicts between different indigenous communities as the result of differences of "origin" understood as "racial." This points us toward further problems in neoliberal multicultural politics.

First, it fixes identities that are historical products of processes of class and state formation. Hale suggests that the incongruity of poor indigenous people being unable to solidarize with poor mestizos (and vice versa) can only be addressed by a cultural politics that deconstructs these bounded categories from below. This is, in fact, precisely what the Zapatista rebels in the Mexican state of Chiapas have tried to do. Yet histories of interethnic violence and duplicity are not easily erased from collective memory. Furthermore, if working with "difference" proves the best strategy for winning marginal increases in resources from government in an environment of fiscal austerity, the danger is that indigenous rights politics will broaden the wedge between the indigenous and nonindigenous poor, while indigenous representatives themselves become socially distanced from the people whom they represent as they move into the urban worlds of NGO funding, government agencies, and party politics.

Second, when indigenous people adopt strongly bounded notions of local "community" in their struggles for recognition and resources, this can generate problems for the protection of individual rights. In Mexico, the state generally allows indigenous communities a degree of autonomy to solve their own problems in their own way and in terms of their own concepts of justice, turning a blind eye to irregular practices and organizational idiosyncrasies unless they pose a threat to wider political interests or regional stability. The downside of this system has been that indigenous leaderships can acquire a good deal of impunity by displaying loyalty to the political forces dominating nonindigenous society, favoring local boss rule and a style of politics in which dissenters are accused of threatening the integrity of the "community" itself by challenging established patterns of authority (Collier 1997).

In communities whose ideologies of "harmony" mask deep divisions, defenses of "tradition" have often led to the expulsion and dispossession of dissident minorities, in particular non-Catholics who refuse to fulfill public duties associated with Catholicism and may also prove strong opponents of boss rule. As Hernández (2005) points out, neither these patterns of intolerance, nor issues such as the exclusion of women from an active role in community governance, represent unsolvable problems. A good deal of the internal politics of indigenous communities today revolves around addressing these challenges. Interventions by government agents in the name of "the defense of individual rights and guarantees" are often selective and politically motivated, while the official justice system has also been known to adopt a stance of "multiculturalist" relativism when doing so serves to defend male prerogatives against indigenous women's aspirations for change in community "uses and customs." Contemporary discourses about rights in the neoliberal political field always need to be situated within an analysis of the local and translocal power relations that underlie them.

Third, we should consider the irony that neoliberalism has finally given indigenous minorities a kind of advantage over the mestizo groups that most modern national states previously treated as better equipped to enjoy the rights of citizens in the modern nation than "backward" Indians. The older class-based politics offered mestizos substantial opportunities to demand benefits from the state, but the urban poor have now become socially anonymous in the neoliberal public sphere (Boltvinik and Hernández Laos 2000, 14). The only way to contest the discretionary and politically motivated use of "poverty alleviation" funding (a classic example of which was Carlos Salinas's "Solidarity" program in Mexico), and to transcend individualistic, clientelistic relations with NGO service providers and political intermediaries (Auyero 2000, 110), is to build collective "communities" of the kind the neoliberal state will recognize as interlocutors. The most prominent examples in urban contexts are place-based residents' or community associations, though cultural, religious, and gender-based organizations are increasingly common as a result of the proliferation of the rights-based approach. Yet it is difficult for these organizations to achieve substantial leverage on government in isolation, and this often requires the mediation of NGOs or political parties.

As I noted earlier, the 1990s brought a good deal of pessimism about the future of popular struggles in Latin America. Some of it reflected the effects of deepening impoverishment. González de la Rocha (2004, 194) argues, for example, that bonds of interhousehold reciprocity—once one of the "resources of poverty" on which people could draw to adapt to hard times—have become increasingly eroded by the absolute "poverty of resources" produced by a sustained decline in real incomes. Emphasis on the waning of social movements now seems exaggerated in light of the new opposition to neoliberal capitalism that has developed in some Latin American countries in recent years, and many rights-based NGOs should not be portrayed simply as Trojan Horses of neoliberal governmentality. Nevertheless, the contradictions discussed in this section remain real, and social movement participants are consciously reflecting upon them.

Conclusion

Although rights-based development is sometimes seen as contributing to an individualizing ethos, it can equally well be oriented toward the cultivation of a sense of social responsibility to and for others. Although sectors of the middle classes remain central to social and political activism, neoliberal capitalism has made the poor responsible for themselves. It has also fostered the detachment of other classes from any inclusive social project. In an analysis relevant to other "global cities," Caldeira (2000) shows how the São Paulo elite, sequestered in fortified condominiums, has withdrawn from its public responsibilities in a radical way. Defending a justice system in which their children enjoy impunity, and no longer capable of practicing sociability even with each other, such elites have driven a strong, though still contested, tendency toward social fragmentation (Caldeira 2000, 258–259).

Neoliberal notions of participation empower unequal actors equally, leaving the socially powerful in the dominant position. Even those "included" as interlocutors of government sometimes represent little more than themselves where they have become disarticulated from their base, or where that base is more virtual than real. Meanwhile, the current model of capitalist globalization is generating inequalities of a kind that should reawaken scrutiny of the rights currently accorded to better off citizens. It is not realistic to imagine that spontaneous "bottom up" action by poor citizens will be sufficient by itself to bring about changes, but there is everything to be said for measures that enhance their capacity to organize, not merely to make demands, but to take greater direct control in the production of their own identities and of public understanding of their lives and their problems. For those faced with the power of the media industries and political machines for which "truth" about social issues is whatever brings in the most votes, the problem of achieving a capacity for self-representation in the public sphere is as acute as that of overcoming the politics of the pork barrel or securing justice from a biased legal system. These are clearly all areas in which a rights-based approach has much to offer. What needs to be added is new thinking about alternative economic possibilities and the kinds of political coalitions that might be constructed to promote them. In the absence of such efforts, the rights-based approach may prove another depoliticizing delusion.

References

Arrom, S. M. 1985. *The women of Mexico City, 1790–1857.* Berkeley: University of California Press.

Assies, W. 1999. Theory, practice and "external actors" in the making of new urban social movements in Brazil. *Bulletin of Latin American Research* 18, no. 2:211–226.

Auyero, J. 2000. The hyper-shantytown: Neo-liberal violence(s) in the Argentine slum. *Ethnography* 1, no. 1:93–116.

Boltvinik, J. and E. Hernández Laos. 2000. *Pobreza y distribución del ingreso en México.* Mexico City: Siglo XXI Editores.

Caldeira, T. 2000. *City of walls: Crime, segregation, and citizenship in São Paulo.* Berkeley: University of California Press.

Caldeira, T. 2002. The paradox of police violence in democratic Brazil. *Ethnography* 3, no. 3:235–263.

Caldeira, T. and J. Holston. 2004. State and urban space in Brazil: From modernist planning to democratic intervention. In *Global assemblages: Technology, politics and ethics as anthropological problems,* edited by A. Ong and S. Collier, 393–416. Malden, MA: Blackwell Publishing.

Castells, M. 2000. *End of millennium.* Malden, MA: Blackwell Publishing.

Chabal, P. and J-P. Daloz. 1999. *Africa works: Disorder as a political instrument.* Oxford, Bloomington and Indianapolis: The International African Institute in association with James Currey and Indiana University Press.

Collier, G. 1997. Reaction and retrenchment in the highlands of Chiapas in the wake of the Zapatista rebellion. *Journal of Latin American Anthropology* 3, no. 1:14–31.

Craig, D. and D. Porter. 2005. The Third Way and the third world: Poverty reduction and social inclusion strategies in the rise of "inclusive" liberalism. *Review of International Political Economy* 12, no. 2:226–263.

Diacon, T. 2004. *Stringing together a nation: Cândido Mariano Da Silva Rondon and the construction of a modern Brazil, 1906–1930.* Durham and London: Duke University Press.

Fix, M. 2001. *Parceiros da exclusão: Duas histórias da construção de uma "nova cidade" em São Paulo.* São Paulo: Boitempo Editorial.

Foweraker, J. 2001. Grassroots movements and political activism in Latin America: A critical comparison of Chile and Brazil. *Journal of Latin American Studies* 33, no. 4:839–865.

Gledhill, J. 1997. Liberalism, socio-economic rights and the politics of identity: From moral economy to indigenous rights. In *Human rights, culture and context: Anthropological approaches,* edited by R. A. Wilson, 70–110. London: Pluto Press.

Gledhill, J. 2004. Neoliberalism. In *A companion to the anthropology of politics,* edited by D. Nugent and J. Vincent, 332–348. Malden, MA: Blackwell Publishing.

González de la Rocha, M. 2004. De los "recursos de la pobreza" a la "pobreza de los recursos" y a las "desventajas acumuladas." *Latin American Research Review* 39, no. 1:192–195.

Hale, C. 2002. Does multiculturalism menace? Governance, cultural rights and the politics of identity in Guatemala. *Journal of Latin American Studies* 34, no. 1:485–524.

Hernández Castillo, R. A. 2005. Gender and differentiated citizenship in Mexico: Indigenous women and men re-invent culture and redefine the nation. In *Citizenship, political culture and state transformation in Latin America,* edited by W. Assies, M. A. Calderon and T. Salman, 323–340. Amsterdam: Dutch University Press.

Kruijt, D., C. Sojo and R. Grynspan. 2002. *Informal citizens: Poverty, informality and social exclusion in Latin America.* Amsterdam: Rozenberg Publishers.

Larson, B. 1999. Andean highland peasants and the trials of nation-making during the nineteenth century. In *The Cambridge history of the native peoples of the Americas,* Vol. 1, Part 2, *South America,* edited by F. Salomon and S. B. Schwartz, 558–703. Cambridge: Cambridge University Press.

Mallon, F. 1995. *Peasant and nation: The making of postcolonial Mexico and Peru.* Berkeley: University of California Press.

Molyneux, M. and S. Lazar. 2003. *Doing the rights thing: Rights-based development and Latin American NGOs.* London: ITDG Publishing.

Monga, C. 1996. *The anthropology of anger: Civil society and democracy in Africa.* Boulder, CO: Lynne Rienner Publishers.

Nugent, D. 1997. *Modernity at the edge of empire: State, individual and nation in the Northern Peruvian Andes, 1885–1935.* Stanford: Stanford University Press.

Pessar, P. 2004. *From fanatics to folk: Brazilian millenarianism and popular culture.* Durham and London: Duke University Press.

Ramos, A. R. 1998. *Indigenism: Ethnic politics in Brazil.* Madison: University of Wisconsin Press.

Rose, N. 1999. *Powers of freedom: Reframing political thought.* Cambridge: Cambridge University Press.

Scheper-Hughes, N. 1992. *Death without weeping: The violence of everyday life in Brazil.* Berkeley: University of California Press.

Sheriff, R. 2001. *Dreaming equality: Color, race and racism in urban Brazil.* New Brunswick: Rutgers University Press.

Sieder, R. 2000. Paz, progreso, justicia y honradez: Law and citizenship in Alta Verapaz during the regime of Jorge Ubico. *Bulletin of Latin American Research* 19, no. 3:283–302.

Singh, A., A. Belaisch, C. Collins, P. de Masi, R. Krieger, G. Meredith and R. Rennhack. 2005. *Stabilization and reform in Latin America: A macroeconomic perspective on the experience since the early 1990s.* IMF Occasional Paper 238. Washington, DC: International Monetary Fund.

Stephen, L. 1997. *Women and social movements in Latin America: Power from below.* Austin: University of Texas Press.

Wade, R. 1990. *Governing the market: Economic theory and the role of government in East Asian industrialization.* Princeton, NJ: Princeton University Press.

Werbner, R. P. 2004. *Reasonable radicals and citizenship in Botswana: The public anthropology of Kalanga elites.* Bloomington: Indiana University Press.

Yang, M. 2002. The resilience of Guanxi and its new deployments: A critique of some Guanxi scholarship. *China Quarterly* 170:459–476.

Zibechi, R. 2004. Dangerous liaisons: Center-left governments and the grassroots. Americas Program, Interhemispheric Resource Center. http://www.americaspolicy.org/reports/2004/0412movements.html.

Notes

1. I gratefully acknowledge the support given by the Mexican National Council for Science and Technology (CONACYT) and the UK Economic and Social Research Council to this study.

PART TWO

Rights, Governmentality, and Citizenship

Exploring a Political Approach to Rights-Based Development in North West Cameroon: From Rights and Marginality to Citizenship and Justice

Jeidoh Duni, Robert Fon,
Sam Hickey and Nuhu Salihu

Introduction

Rights-based approaches to development promise to deliver many of the goals toward which development actors currently work, particularly in terms of creating a political environment conducive to development. Good governance will emerge, particularly in the form of increased levels of accountability, as states fulfill their obligations to citizens, not least because citizens become empowered through rights-based approaches to make increased demands on the state. This vision of a virtuous circle evinces a liberal democratic confidence in the power of civic actors to reshape the state, already weakened by neoliberal reforms in many developing countries. It is therefore not surprising that NGOs claim to have taken a leading role in promoting rights-based approaches for and on behalf of poor and excluded citizens (e.g., Molyneux and Lazar 2003; Nyamu-Musembi and Cornwall 2004).

This is an ambitious agenda. Although moving toward more effective and accountable states and empowered citizenship is certainly desirable (Green 2008), it is not clear that the promotion of rights-based approaches by NGOs is likely to achieve this. Process of state and citizenship formation are indeed critical for development (DFID 2004)—but the sequencing of such processes and their outcomes, and the patterns of causality between them, remain historically and contextually specific rather than in any sense universal (Gledhill, Chapter 3). For example, some states may be effective at delivering development without necessarily allowing citizens to take a central role in determining the direction or content of this development. And the promise being made for participatory rights-based approaches is not simply one of meeting a tough political challenge; it extends to catalyzing processes of long-term social change whereby previously excluded people develop sufficient agency to make demands on various duty bearers, either directly or through representatives in civil and political society. This places very high expectations on people whose exclusion is partially caused by a relative lack of agency (e.g., some women or disabled people; see Cleaver, Chapter 8), not only vis-à-vis the state but also in relation to other social groups whose claims to rights may in some instances conflict with theirs. It remains unclear whether the participatory approaches that NGOs employ to overcome this challenge are capable of these types of transformation (VeneKlasen et al. 2004; Hickey and Mohan 2004).

We explore this challenge of transformation through a case study of a participatory rights-based program that seeks to assist a marginal pastoral group in North West Cameroon to be empowered citizens. The project involves providing paralegal support aimed at challenging the practices of state and social actors who regularly seek to exploit this marginal (and in some ways isolationist) group. It is run by a local social movement, and funded by an international NGO with a growing reputation for innovative work on empowerment issues (Mohan 2002; Hickey 2002; Waddington and Mohan 2004). This effort to counter exclusion and support minority rights is inherently political, and it reveals both the potential and the problems that arise when certain rights-based approaches engage with the politics of promoting progressive social change.[1] We argue that the program has been relatively successful in catalyzing underlying processes of sociopolitical change—particularly shifts from clientelism to citizenship among the program's participants—and that it has also improved the quality of local governance. However, the program's explicit, often confrontational engagement with the power relations underpinning exclusion and exploitation—between state and citizens and between social groups in a context of ethnic and gendered inequality and difference—has been both a strength and a liability in advancing progressive social change. This raises critical challenges for the strategic, theoretical, and philosophical dimensions of rights-based approaches.

Rights and Citizenship in Cameroon: The Politics of Belonging

Cameroon offers a challenging context for the pursuit of rights-based approaches. The process of "democratization" that begun in the early 1990s has stalled, as evidenced most graphically by a series of discredited presidential elections and the prevalence of human rights abuses (Amnesty

International 2003; Krieger and Takougang 1998). President Paul Biya's government, in power since 1982, has skillfully manipulated the process of political liberalization, while opposition parties have failed to unite and consolidate the wave of popular unrest, and international actors have offered little support for democratization (Takougang 2003). Political liberalization has tended to intensify rather than undermine the neopatrimonial practices that dominate national and local political processes in Cameroon. This expresses itself in various ways, including the use of public resources for private gain and for the personalization of political rule, and the tendency of predatory state agents to co-opt ethnically constituted power bases at local levels (Gabriel 1999; Nyamnjoh 1999). This neopatrimonial politics is closely linked to the politics of belonging in Cameroon, whereby the importance of belonging to a particular "native" community in a particular place is stressed. Such discourse is often employed by political entrepreneurs at election time, and in efforts to secure "natives" privileged access ahead of "strangers" to reproductive resources and political power.

In this context, human right abuses remain rife, despite the fact that the 1996 amended Constitution commits the government to protect the inalienable and sacred rights of all human persons, and affirms Cameroon's attachment to the various UN declarations on human rights. The national institutions required to guarantee these rights have yet to be established, leaving arbitrary arrest and detention, extrajudiciary execution of civilians, imprisonment of journalists, torture, and corruption commonplace (Amnesty International 2003). Further obstacles arise because Cameroon's colonial legacy left it with a bifurcated legal system, such that eight of its ten provinces are French-speaking and operate the civil law system, while the two English-speaking provinces operate the common law system. The 1996 Constitution in fact "classifies Cameroonians into natives and foreigners (allogenes, indigenes) and makes large groups foreigners in their own country" (Nkwi and Socpa 1997, 139); its apparent commitment to protecting minority rights seems to reflect the state's desire to play the politics of belonging for political gain, rather than a genuine dedication to challenging exclusion.

The Mbororo Fulani in North West Province: Citizens at the Margins

These political tendencies play out in particular ways in the North West province of Cameroon, where the paralegal program is set. The Anglophone North West is home to Cameroon's main opposition party and to a fairly vibrant civic arena, including human rights groups, hometown development associations, credit and savings groups, and farmers' cooperatives. Education rates are relatively high compared to other provinces, and North Westerners pride themselves on this and on their respect for democracy. "Citizenship" in the North West also relates closely to membership of subnational political communities, which coalesce around traditional ethno-territorial groupings that were reified as political units through the colonial policy of co-opting them as the basis of native administration. Traditional structures have been somewhat resurgent in recent years in terms of local political influence and control over land; access to land is particularly significant here given the heavy reliance on small-holder agriculture and the cultural significance with which land is invested by most groups.

Within this context, the pastoral Mbororo Fulani have historically constituted something of an anomaly.[2] Arriving into the Grassfields from 1916 as a seminomadic pastoralist group, they were markedly distinguished from the "native" farming populations by their livelihood, attachment to Islam, dispersed and fragmented sociopolitical structures, and apparent disinclination toward community development. They have typically been viewed as strangers by both their neighbors and successive state regimes. Their tendency to settle toward the spatial peripheries of the Province entailed reduced access to government services, while their relatively dispersed settlement patterns further excluded them from the territorial definitions of "community" on which development efforts are generally based. Often lacking formal education, the Mbororo'en have historically been underrepresented in all branches of local government and administration, while their traditional leaders are viewed as subordinate to native chiefs. However, a tendency toward self-isolation is also characteristic among the Mbororo people, most notably through a code of conduct known as *pulaaku* that emphasizes a general sense of reserve, otherness, and ethnic exclusivity (Burnham 1996).

This experience of citizenship formation—of how the Mbororo have engaged with the broader political community and on what terms—is differentiated among the Mbororo by gender, intergenerational, and urban–rural disparities. Both within Mbororo communities and more broadly, particular injustices are experienced by women, including domestic violence and asset stripping in the event of widowhood. Mbororo women tend to have lower literacy levels and experience greatly reduced social mobility compared to men, on whom they are largely economically dependent. The shift to a sedentary lifestyle, and the increased Islamicization that has accompanied it, have also further restricted women's role in broader social life.

However, the marginality experienced and often reinforced by the Mbororo'en is entwined with a high degree of incorporation within more patronage-based forms of politics at both local and national levels. With both colonial and postcolonial administrations viewing the Mbororo

Fulani as temporary residents rather than full citizens, the pastoralists relied on paying tribute to local landowners for grazing rights, and this tradition involved developing close patron–client links with local chiefs and administrators. While this informal mode of political incorporation has benefited the Mbororo'en in several respects, it has also left them vulnerable to the more predatory elements of the system. The outstanding example of this involves a campaign by a wealthy industrialist and erstwhile member of the ruling party's central committee—Baba Ahmadou Danpullo—to co-opt the Mbororo'en as his client group. This campaign has been characterized by land evictions and cattle confiscation, human rights abuses and repression, and the co-optation and imprisonment of Mbororo leaders (for details see Davis 1995; Hickey 2004).

Similar (if less dramatic) forms of exploitation occur on a more everyday basis in the North West, most notably in relation to farmer–grazier disputes over land that are often framed as being between "native farmers" and "stranger pastoralists." The conflict resolution process is widely considered to be ineffectual and corrupt, and the many points of engagement between officials and plaintiffs are open to bribery. The chief beneficiary here tends to be the local Divisional Officer as head of the Farmer–Grazier Commission, and with corruption institutionalized in the legal system the graziers' relative wealth in cattle makes them a valuable focus for extortion. Their ability and inclination to pay bribes is resented by women farmers in particular, and has led to major public protests. For their part, Mbororo graziers argue that their low status in terms of land rights leaves them with little choice over how they pursue access to land. They cite their lack of representation in the administration, and claim that the Commission is staffed by the cultural "relatives" of the farmers and is thus biased against them. When matters reach the courts, the balance of power is reversed, as farmers generally have a superior knowledge of the law and legal system compared to the pastoralists. Similar types of adverse power relations persist beyond the land tenure system. Corrupt members of the security forces frequently target Mbororo men on trumped-up charges in the hope of securing bribes. To compound this, the preference of the Mbororo to allow third parties to represent them encourages other social groups (notably the Hausa or Fulbe) to take on this role and to then connive with state officials to exploit them.

Challenging Exclusion and Promoting Citizenship through a Rights-Based Approach

In the early 1990s, some Mbororo started to build alliances with lawyers, NGOs, political parties, and human rights activists in order to challenge these processes of exclusion, adverse incorporation, and self-isolation.

This emerging elite—largely urban, often educated and comprising key female as well as male actors—formed the Mbororo Social and Cultural Development Association (MBOSCUDA) in 1992 with the explicit objectives of protecting the rights and promoting the culture of all Mbororo people in Cameroon. Immediate conflicts with Baba Ahmadou Danpullo (the political patron introduced above) offered an early introduction to the perils of promoting rights in this political context. By the late 1990s, rights and exclusion issues were gaining currency among international NGOs, and in 1998 MBOSCUDA and three other local NGOs formed a partnership with a UK-based development NGO, Village AiD (Hickey 2002). This effort was in several ways more politically engaged than many NGO interventions, particularly through the partnership with MBOSCUDA and the adoption of the REFLECT approach to literacy (Regenerated Freirean Literacy through Empowering Community Techniques), which incorporates an explicitly political challenge toward "structures of oppression." In 1999, a second project was started, focusing explicitly on challenging social exclusion and heralding a shift toward a rights-based approach. A key element of this project was a paralegal extension scheme, which started in 2001 as a pilot in one division before being extended across the Province in 2003. Given the relative newness of the paralegal component, any evaluation of its impact so far is necessarily provisional and cautionary.

The Paralegal Program

The paralegal program has employed two key approaches to improve the citizenship status and rights of the Mbororo Fulani in the North West Province, namely *legal literacy* and *paralegal extension* (Orvis 2003). Legal literacy is a process of acquiring critical awareness about rights and the law, the ability to assert rights, and the capacity to mobilize for change. Paralegal extension uses community-based volunteers to extend legal advice and services to members of the public. Community-based paralegal officers work closely with community members, and engage in community education, legal advice, counseling, and court representation. These activities are monitored and supervised on a monthly basis by a chief paralegal from the regional office. Where matters are beyond the capacities of the paralegal officers, the case is referred to the legal consultant of the project, who offers professional support to the paralegals and takes cases of human rights abuses to court if required. The process of developing legal and political literacy among clients has been achieved through the REFLECT method of literacy development (Archer and Cottingham 1997). The radical edge to this method is gained through a Freiran approach that explores the structures of oppression facing marginal groups; this struck a chord with members of MBOSCUDA and key program staff, as it resonated with the social movement's broader objective of challenging exclusion. This suggests that the focus in integrating participatory and rights-based approaches needs to move beyond questions of methodological innovation (e.g., Holland et al. 2004; VeneKlasen et al. 2004), by also considering the extent to which shared understandings of social change underpin each approach.

The program is based around seven regional paralegal offices, each of which is managed by a trained paralegal. Each office handles an average of forty cases annually, while the lawyer handles an average of 30 matters of human rights abuses in court each year, the most frequent perpetrators being state officials. Land disputes are also a key focus, as elsewhere in rural-based paralegal programs (Orvis 2003). In practice, a mixture of direct and fairly confrontational approaches (for example written complaints, workshops and court cases) and more discursive strategies have been used to good effect, with the latter involving framing the program in terms of broader discourses and institutions associated with wider drives within Cameroon toward good governance. A largely unplanned benefit has derived from the success of the cases, whereby the program has taken on significant dispersion and demonstration effects.

The most common strategy has involved paralegal officers writing to the relevant authorities, setting out the precise legal grounds on which an injustice is being challenged and also the action that will be taken if the authorities fail to act lawfully regarding the particular problem. The use of phrases such as "the matter will be pursued to a logical end," including hints at court action, have often been enough for cases to be addressed in their primary stages—as noted by one claimant, "as soon as the letter was delivered to the Divisional Officer the matter died a natural death." Where no action is forthcoming, the complaint is forwarded to the next official in the state hierarchy, with a note that the lower official has failed to resolve the issue and with copies of the earlier letter attached. This form of exposure has proved strikingly effective, and has turned on using Cameroon's often disempowering norms of bureaucratic practice—a heavily centralized, top-down, and patronage-based system—to the advantage of citizens.

These strategies have been employed within the context of a growing discourse around issues of good governance in Cameroon, which are often promoted by international agencies. The paralegal program has made linkages to some of the institutions associated with this discourse, such as the National Anti-Corruption Unit. This reflects the fact that "recourse to political discourses and practices of naming [is] extremely important in most political struggles, and . . . marginalised groups may take advantage of such discourses as one of their few assets"

(Engberg-Pedersen and Webster 2002, 267), and that the good governance discourse, although much criticized by development academics, has a genuine resonance with citizens in poorly governed countries (Corbridge et al. 2005).

Tracing the Impacts So Far

The outcomes of the program so far appear to be promising. Members of the Mororo community and state officials in Donga Mantung Division believe that Mororo–state relations have improved significantly over the period of MBOSCUDA activity and, more specifically, the lifetime of the paralegal project. A key judicial official stated that "there has been a remarkable change in the relationship between the Mororo and the administration . . . over the past two years," a view with which the Divisional Delegate for Livestock concurs, arguing that "the Mororo people now see themselves more as citizens." According to one North West government official, "Years back, this community [the Mororo] were serving as the milking cow of the administration[,] especially the forces of law and order. Nowadays this relationship has ceased from being unidirectional and has become mutual." A lawyer who practices in the region stated that, in the past, the Mororos were "very juicy" clients who paid any fee that was quoted to them, but that they now negotiate fees with lawyers based on the services rendered to them. Those Mororo associated with the program draw similar comparisons with the past, claiming that contrary to earlier experience, "Now we have a say in any matter we have." One Mororo woman whose son was wrongfully accused of cattle theft states:

> I am vigilant now and any thing that I see is not satisfactory for me I will go to the paralegal for advice and redress. Now we are no longer in the dark . . . we have "eyes" and as such these people now know that they can not treat us like in the past.

The following section analyzes the key impacts of the paralegal program so far, in terms of good governance and citizenship formation, before exploring the critical challenges that face the program, particularly in terms of power relations and exclusive forms of citizenship.

Toward Good Governance?

The paralegal program seems to have had a positive impact on governance practices toward the Mororo'en in the North West. The broad sense of success expressed in the assessments above can be evidenced according to a number of indicators, including the number of bribes the administration has been forced to pay back, the transfer of errant staff to posts elsewhere in the Province, and reduced levels of predation faced by the Mbororo'en.

The strategy of aiming for high-profile cases has been largely effective. Successfully prosecuted targets have included Brigadier Commanders, Divisional Delegates of Livestock, and prominent gendarmes. One of the latter used his Company Commander's car to move around the Division arresting Mbororo graziers and extorting large sums of money; program staff managed to secure an investigation by the Anti-Corruption Unit of the Prime Minister's Office, with the result that the Company Commander's imminent promotion was suspended and both he and the gendarme were transferred out of the province. In several cases, the mere presence of a lawyer committed to the Mbororo'en seems to have had an immediate impact, ensuring that due process is followed, and balancing the generally superior capacity of the farmers to represent themselves at this level. In other instances, farmer–grazier conflicts have been removed from the courts where they were being improperly tried. The threat of being taken to court has led several officials to contact local paralegal officers, pleading that if an issue arises concerning them, then all efforts should be made to resolve the problem informally.

One of the key elements of the program has involved enabling the state and the Mbororo'en to see each other in a different way (Corbridge et al. 2005). In particular, government officials have been removed from the pedestals upon which the Mbororo tended to place them: "Now we no longer have that extreme fear for the officers that we had in the past." This could in time constitute a key challenge to the vertical patron–client relations on which the Mbororo have relied, and which officials have exploited for personal gain. Therefore, although it is not yet possible to argue that the program has ensured higher levels of good governance, there does seem to be progress toward what Merilee Grindle (2004) terms "good enough" governance. Patron–client relations persist, but the terms of the relationship have become more "democratic," with greater negotiating power from below.

From Clientelism to Citizenship?

This apparently increased capacity among the Mbororo'en to negotiate patron–client relations is one of the key aspects of progress toward citizenship empowerment. Others include a stronger sense of self- and group-empowerment, increased levels of legal and political literacy, and the removal of exploitative middlemen in dealing with the administration. The capacity and willingness of many Mbororo graziers to pay their way out of conflict situations, and the propensity of state officials and middlemen to demand bribes, has been directly challenged. In numerous cases, claimants reveal that legal support has empowered them to either avoid or at least negotiate lower payments. Relating the details of one case, a Mbororo grazier proudly stated that he had shouted at the Divisional Officer, and paid only CFA 20,000—significantly less than the 100,000 plus that was being demanded. In many instances, this empowering confidence has been retained in subsequent cases without direct paralegal involvement. This newfound ability to stand up to local authorities is often reported by clients of paralegal programs (Orvis 2003, 261).

Increased levels of legal and political literacy among the Mbororo are becoming evident, with claimants now showing much clearer awareness concerning what they are entitled to and which processes are open to them. Much of this learning has been done experientially, through particular cases rather than training workshops. Successful claimants disseminate their increased understanding, both informally at markets and through helping others (usually family members) with cases. One judicial official noted that "More Mbororo seem to be aware of their rights and duties . . . they feel themselves as citizens to a greater extent now . . . they do not shy away from most of the things the other citizens do." Several claimants support this view, suggesting that whereas the Mbororo "used to be frightened by the name 'court,'" they "no longer fear the Gendarmes like in the past," and claiming that "If someone is arrested I question the arrest even in the presence of the Commander." Such statements indicate that these rural subjects are not longer intimidated by the institutions of civil society (Mamdani 1996), and are indeed seeing the state in a different light. According to a Divisional Officer, "Cases have now come up where Mbororo people quote the Constitution—they say, 'We have stayed here for over 30 years so why are we not citizens? The so-called natives have also moved [here] from another place.'" This altered attitude to the state appears to extend to the uptake of the obligations as well as the rights of citizenship. One judicial official praised MBOSUDA's sensitization efforts, which ensured that the Mbororo made the best response regarding a campaign for registration of children with birth certificates.

This more legalistic culture appears to have led to a reduction rather than an increase in the number of incidents requiring legal intervention, probably because improper use of the legal system itself was a large part of the previous problem. However, there are more mixed reports concerning the impact on local relations between the Mbororo'en and their farming neighbors. One grazier who won a case against his farming neighbor reported that: "We were enemies before we went to the court but not as bad as we are now. Before, we used to meet and discuss other things." Gains in vertical citizenship relations may therefore come with the cost of damage to horizontal forms of citizenship (Kabeer 2005, 23–4).

A significant impact of the paralegal program has been the reduced reliance of some Mbororo'en on the exploitative middlemen who previously acted as interlocutors between themselves and the state. These middlemen have been replaced by a mixture of paralegal staff and empowered Mbororo individuals acting for themselves and each other. As one Divisional Delegate for Livestock relates, "You see many Mbororo people now going to the [government] offices without a Hausa man leading them to help talk with the administrators; it means that they too are citizens and can take their worries to the appropriate places."

Advocates of rights-based approaches generally welcome challenges to exploitative patron–client relationships as an indication of empowerment. However, shifting from clientelism to citizenship raises at least two potential dangers. First, it may deny people the benefits of patron–client relationships (such as security), and may even leave them at risk of a backlash from erstwhile patrons. For example, Kabeer (2003, 37) notes that rights-based approaches often "require poor people to break with past relationships of dependency on patrons and to stand up for themselves, often at some personal and economic cost," and thus have some contradictory implications. As yet, few graziers have reported worsening relations with the state or reduced ability to secure grazing permits and other crucial state-controlled resources. Moreover, the association of previous patron–client relationships with high economic costs suggests that a more progressive outcome is possible here. However, it would be naive to imagine that the decades-long experience of certain patterns of political engagement can be overturned so easily without negative implications.

The second danger is that one form of patron–client relationship might be simply replaced by another, potentially even more unaccountable form of dependence. The relationship between program trustees and clients remains highly skewed, with little evidence that rights-based approaches have prompted development agencies to become more accountable to their clients despite this being central to the claims of such approaches (Nyamu-Musembi and Cornwall 2004). However, paralegals have sought to minimize the risk of creating new forms of dependence by trying to ensure that claimants (rather than paralegals) take the cases forward wherever possible. In one case, a paralegal simply excused himself from the government office just before the case was to be taken to the officer concerned, effectively forcing the client to stand for himself.

Power Relations and Progressive Politics

Given the particular problems women face in exercising their citizenship (Molyneux and Lazar 2003; Cornwall and Wellbourn 2002), it is concerning that so few have made use of the services offered by the paralegal program. Although the Village AiD–MBOSCUDA partnership began with an almost exclusive focus on women's groups, the onset of paralegal work has shifted the focus distinctly toward men, largely because cases of exploitation tend to center on male-dominated livelihood issues involving land and cattle ownership. The public–private division between male and female spheres of responsibility that characterizes exclusive models of citizenship in many polities (Lister 2004) ensures that matters requiring legal redress disproportionately involve men, and obscures the forms of exploitation experienced by women in the private sphere. So although Mbororo women may gain from the benefits of the program (e.g., since less household income is spent on illicit payments), there are a series of gendered patterns of injustice that the program could address, notably with regard to cases of divorce, child custody, property rights, and inheritance. Indeed, women form the majority of clients in other paralegal programs (Orvis 2003, 257), particularly in cases of marital and domestic violence. Significantly, women from local farming communities have taken up the services offered by the program, particularly with regard to the common problem of asset stripping in the event of widowhood. This has achieved some notable successes; as one successful claimant noted, "the whole community knows that a [woman] has stood up against a group of men and [has] successfully challenged them . . . just the fact that I am currently living in the compound is satisfactory testimony of success." However, whereas most paralegal work involves demanding the enforcement of existing laws, some of the problems faced by women require changes to present rules in state and traditional practice, and potentially also new legislation (Nott 2003)—a challenge yet to be addressed by the program.

This gendered reading of the program's relevance and impact highlights the challenge for rights-based approaches in addressing the relational field within which rights emerge and are realized (see Cleaver, Chapter 8). In everyday life, rights are neither universal nor inalienable, but rather need to be continually negotiated and fought for through a series of encounters with social others, public discourse, and the wider political system. A particular challenge here concerns the historically informed but continually evolving sets of interethnic relations with which Mbororo households are involved. As already noted, the program seems to have gone some way toward reshaping certain power relations, particularly between the Mbororo'en and the state, and between the Mbororo'en and other ethnic groups. This has involved granting Mbororo graziers the freedom to exercise their rights in quite powerful ways, but with little advance thought given to how such freedom might create new forms of inequality in local social relations. This reflects an individualized and legalistic tendency within rights-based approaches that essentializes individuals and groups, and casts rights as their private property in a way that disregards the social context in which those rights will be exercised (Englund, 2004, 12). At the individual level, some graziers report worsening relations with neighbors as a result of their defeat via legal redress, and there is a wider fear that Mbororo empowerment may be occurring at the expense of other groups. Successful Mbororo claimants frequently boast of their "victories" over their farming neighbors and of the Mbororo'en becoming a stronger group, raising the specter of rights-based approaches converging with local discourses in ways that deepen problems of citizenship (Hickey 2002). Such claimant responses need to be understood in the context of decades of subordination, and they may also be accentuated by the adversarial nature of the legal process. However, there remains a genuine concern that understandings of citizenship in Cameroon tend toward narrow rather than universal readings, whereby the gain of one group is seen as occurring at the expense of others. In a context where ethnicity is highly politicized, and in a country united only by ethnic difference (Nyamnjoh 1999), to consolidate this dimension of politics would hardly constitute a progressive move—particularly considering the extent to which the Mbororo are economically wealthier than their farming neighbors, despite their status as second-class citizens.

In practical terms, the paralegal program has started to recognize this problem, with paralegal offices now seeking to act as citizens' advice bureaus for all. In strategic terms, however, it has been apparent that a rights-based perspective in itself offers little guidance for achieving an equitable balance in advancing the rights of some at the expense of others. This is complicated by the fact that the marginal group in question are denied civic and political rights, yet at the same time envied for economic power (cattle rearing being more productive than agriculture). Therefore, while their historic marginalization needs to be addressed, the prospect of the Mbororo gaining comparatively increased citizenship status across all three forms of Marshallian citizenship rights (civil, political, and social) is hardly an equitable or just one, not least because women farmers would have very strong claims to being a still more subordinated set of second-class citizens in North West Cameroon. As noted by Munro (Chapter 11), the emphasis placed in rights-based discourse on achieving all rights fully leaves issues of sequencing and prioritizing unaddressed.

However, the challenge is also both theoretical and philosophical. Simplistic celebrations of minority rights within multiethnic communities and polities are of growing concern, and we would concur with Englund's advice that

> If the current aesthetic of recognition allows little more than
> discrete individuals, groups and communities pursuing their

own agendas, an alternative aesthetic must attempt to do more justice to the relational field in which the politics of recognition emerges (2004, 12–13).

For Englund and for us, such an alternative aesthetic involves engaging with particular understandings and forms of citizenship rather than of rights per se. Molyneux and Lazar (2003, 74) likewise argue that the key challenge for Latin American NGOs keen to promote rights-based approaches is to absorb the issue of citizenship into that project. Clearly, rights constitute a significant element of citizenship and might be seen as providing the overarching framework within which notions of citizenship are located. However, whereas rights-based discourses often appear to emerge out of a cosmopolitan ether, citizenship—or membership of political communities—exists and emerges in specific times and places, and is inextricably linked to actual political practice. Thinking in terms of citizenship helps to ground delocalized discussions of rights, placing them in relation to the specific histories of how political communities emerge and how people become incorporated into and make claims on these communities. This requires that we recognize citizenship as a substantive rather than legalistic phenomenon, as taking both an ethnic and national form, and also as a form of practice often undertaken by marginal groups through informal and private means (Mohan and Hickey 2004). A focus on citizenship thus offers a way of grounding rights-based approaches within local political realities. These realities can be operationalized within program research, monitoring, and evaluation in a more tangible and contextualized form than more abstract notions of "global" human rights.

The philosophical challenge here is to detach the promotion of rights from a wider project of securing *freedom* and to link it more directly to struggles for *justice.* Associating rights with freedom fails to offer a benchmark for assessing when the rights of some are being asserted to the detriment of others. Moreover, to curtail the progress of one group in such cases would be contrary to the wider project of freedom, under which they would be free to assert their rights fully. However, the word "right" is derived from the Latin word *rectus,* which means "that to which a person has a just and valid claim." Notions of social justice offer clearer guidance concerning which claims have the most validity in particular contexts at particular times. Our preference in pursuing this avenue would be to relocate rights-based approaches within a wider philosophical and political project of "relational justice" whereby injustice is understood to be located in unequal and "unjustifiable" relations within and between states or groups, rather than in abstract notions of a "good society" (Forst 2001). Under such an approach,

> A judgement of injustice differs from moral judgements about human need and suffering or about inequalities in that it not only identifies asymmetrical social relations as unjustified, it also locates the responsibilities for that situation (Forst 2001, 167).

It is arguably in promoting inclusive forms of citizenship as part of a wider project of social justice that rights-based approaches can make their most significant contribution.

Conclusion

The move from marginality and exploitative patron–client relations toward a "negotiated clientelism" facilitated by the paralegal program calls into question the feasibility of any easy shifts toward ideal forms of participatory citizenship. Nonetheless the changes that have occurred in the Mbororo community are significant, and suggest that a broader and largely progressive process of social change has been catalyzed, alongside moves toward a "good enough" form of governance (Grindle 2004). Our findings with respect to paralegal approaches to development indicate that such initiatives can have relatively high levels of impact on citizenship formation within fairly short periods of time, and this conclusion is supported elsewhere (e.g., Orvis 2003). Although these results are promising, the success of paralegal approaches will rely heavily on the character, expertise, and dedication of the facilitators and legal representatives involved. Program staff need to confront a series of tensions that emerge when adopting a rights-based approach to work with marginalized groups in contexts where the discourse on rights and ethnic citizenship is associated with exploitation, patronage, and privilege. A commitment to political activism as well as development professionalism seems to be important (see also Orvis 2003, 261).

As with several social movements and NGOs in Latin America (Molyneux and Lazar 2003, 44), MBOSCUDA and Village AiD have shown creativity in designing development work that connects rights to participation and empowerment. The case reinforces the extent to which global discourses around human rights can be mobilized as a strategically important ideological resource in local struggles for citizenship. This mobilization of rights discourse has rested on an engagement with changing power relations in the context of pursuing a broader project of social change (VeneKlasen et al. 2004, 10). The national and politicized character of MBOSCUDA as a social movement has often been critical here, revealing once again the benefits of NGOs working directly with such movements. However, it would not be entirely accurate to say that rights-based approaches have offered MBOSCUDA a needed means of "legitimising a more progressive, even radical, approach to development" (Nyamu-Musembi and Cornwall 2004, 4). MBOSCUDA was arguably already pursuing a fairly radical agenda before Village AiD became a partner, and the political challenge of confronting the state held little fear for a cadre of leaders who had experienced the threat, and in some cases the reality, of imprisonment for their activities. Moreover, the more radical challenge remains, and will involve the MBOSCUDA–Village AiD partnership moving beyond issues of minority rights and into broader struggles for social justice.

References

Amnesty International. 2003. *Cameroon Annual Report 2003*. http://www.amnesty.org

Archer, D. and S. Cottingham. 1997. REFLECT: A new approach to literacy and social change. *Development in Practice* 7, no. 2:199–202.

Burnham, P. 1996. *The politics of cultural difference in Northern Cameroon*. Edinburgh: Edinburgh University Press.

Corbridge, S., G. Williams, M. Srivastava and R. Véron. 2005. *Seeing the state: Governance and governmentality in India*. Cambridge: Cambridge University Press.

Cornwall, A. and A. Wellbourn, eds. 2002. *Realizing rights: Transforming approaches to sexual and reproductive well-being*. London: Zed Books.

Davis, L. 1995. Opening political space in Cameroon: The ambiguous response of the Mbororo. *Review of African Political Economy* 22, no. 64:213–228.

DFID [UK Department for International Development]. 2004. Better government for poverty reduction: More effective partnerships for change. Paper produced for Drivers of Change Policy Division Team. London.

Dicklitch, S. 2002. Failed democratic transition in Cameroon: A human rights explanation. *Human Rights Quarterly* 24, no. 1:152–176.

Engberg-Pedersen, L. and N. Webster. 2002. Political agencies and spaces. In *In the name of the poor: Contesting political space for poverty reduction*, edited by N. Webster and L. Engberg-Pedersen 255–271. London: Zed Books.

Englund, H. 2004. Recognizing identities, imagining alternatives. In *Rights and the politics of recognition in Africa*, edited by H. Englund and F. B. Nyamnjoh, 1–29. London: Zed Books.

Forst, R. 2001. Towards a critical theory of transnational justice. *Metaphilosophy* 321, no. 2:160–179.

Gabriel, J.M. 1999. Cameroon's neopatrimonial dilemma. *Journal of Contemporary African Studies* 17, no. 2:173–196.

Green, D. 2008. *From poverty to power: How active citizens and effective states can change the world.* Oxford: OXFAM International.

Grindle, M. 2004. Good enough governance: Poverty reduction and reform in developing countries. *Governance* 17, no. 4:525–548.

Hickey, S. 2002. Transnational NGDOs and participatory forms of rights-based development: Converging with the local politics of citizenship in Cameroon. *Journal of International Development* 14, no. 6:841–857.

Hickey, S. 2004. "Hometown associations" as social movements for citizenship: A case study from Northwest Cameroon. Paper presented at the 47th Annual Meeting of the African Studies-US Association. New Orleans, LA, November.

Hickey, S. 2007. Caught at the crossroads: Citizenship, marginality and the Mbororo Fulani in Northwest Cameroon. In *Citizenship in Africa,* edited by D. Hammet, P. Nugent and S. Rich-Dorman, 83–104. Leiden: Brill Publishers.

Hickey, S. and G. Mohan. 2004. Relocating participation within a radical politics of development: Insights from political action and practice. In *Participation: From tyranny to transformation? New approaches to participation in development,* edited by S. Hickey and G. Mohan, 159–174. London: Zed Books.

Holland, J., M. A. Brocklesby and C. Abugre. 2004. Beyond the technical fix? Participation in donor approaches to rights-based development. In *Participation: From tyranny to transformation? New approaches to participation in development,* edited by S. Hickey and G. Mohan, 252–268. London: Zed Books.

Kabeer, N. 2003. Making rights work for the poor: Nijera Kori and the construction of "collective capabilities" in rural Bangladesh. IDS Working Paper no. 200. Brighton: Institute of Development Studies.

Kabeer, N., ed. 2005. *Inclusive citizenship: Meanings and expressions.* London: Zed Books.

Krieger, M. and J. Takougang. 1998. *State and society in Africa: Cameroon at the crossroads.* Boulder, Co: Westview Press.

Lister, R. 2004. *Citizenship: Feminist perspectives.* 2nd ed. Hampshire: Macmillan.

Mamdani, M. 1996. *Citizen and subject: Contemporary Africa and the legacy of late colonialism.* London: James Currey.

Mohan, G. 2002. The disappointments of civil society: NGOs, citizenship and institution building in Northern Ghana. *Political Geography* 21, no. 1:125–154.

Mohan, G. and S. Hickey. 2004. Relocating participation within a radical politics of development: Critical modernism and citizenship. In *Participation: From tyranny to transformation? New approaches to participation in development*, edited by S. Hickey and G. Mohan, 59–74. London: Zed Books.

Molyneux, M. and S. Lazar. 2003. *Doing the rights thing: Rights-based development and Latin American NGOs*. London: ITDG Publishing.

Nkwi, P. N. and A. Socpa. 1997. Ethnicity and party politics in Cameroon: The politics of divide and rule. In *Regional balance and national integration in Cameroon: Lessons learned and the uncertain future*, edited by P. N. Nkwi and F. B. Nyamnjoh, 138–149. Leiden: ASC/Yaounde, ICASSRT.

Nott, S. 2003. Gender mainstreaming as an instrument for combating poverty. In *Law and poverty: The legal system and poverty reduction*, edited by L. Williams, A. Kjønstad and P. Robson, 205–222. London: Zed Books.

Nyamnjoh, F. B. 1999. Cameroon: A country united by ethnic ambition and difference. *African Affairs* 98, 390:101–118.

Nyamu-Musembi, C. and A. Cornwall. 2004. What is the "rights-based approach" all about? Perspectives from international development agencies. IDS Working Paper no. 234. Brighton: Institute of Development Studies.

Orvis, S. 2003. Kenyan civil society: Bridging the urban–rural divide? *Journal of Modern African Studies* 41, no. 2:247–268.

Takougang, J. 2003. The 2002 legislative election in Cameroon: A retrospective on Cameroon's stalled democracy movement. *Journal of Modern African Studies* 41, no. 3:421–435.

VeneKlasen, L., V. Miller, C. Clark and M. Reilly. 2004. Rights-based approaches and beyond: Challenges of linking rights and participation. IDS Working Paper no. 235. Brighton: Institute of Development Studies.

Waddington, M. and Mohan, G. 2004. Failing forward: Going beyond imposed forms of participation. In *Participation: From tyranny to transformation? New approaches to participation in development*, edited by S. Hickey and G. Mohan, 219–234. London: Zed Books.

Notes

1. The findings presented here are based on evaluative and qualitative research carried out during October and November 2004. The authors are all more or less implicated in the actual program, and

although seeking to be critically reflexive, cannot be said to constitute independent witnesses. Jeidoh Duni and Robert Fon are respectively the paralegal coordinator and the lawyer on the program discussed here; Nuhu Salihu is Africa Programme Coordinator for Village AiD, the funder-partner in the program, and Sam Hickey was a trustee of Village AiD at the time the research was carried out.

2. This section draws on Hickey (2007).

CHAPTER 5

Recognition or Misrecognition? Pitfalls of Indigenous Peoples' Free, Prior, and Informed Consent (FPIC)

Katsuhiko Masaki

Introduction

In 2006, indigenous peoples' protest and lobbying culminated in the UN Human Rights Council's adoption of the UN Declaration on the Rights of Indigenous Peoples. The full implementation of the declaration remains tenuous in the international community of nation-states, as attested by the subsequent adoption by a UN General Assembly subcommittee of a resolution to defer action on the declaration and to consider concerns raised by some member countries. Some governments have called for qualification regarding the principle of self-determination, while others are concerned that the promotion of ethnic minority rights and identities constitutes a threat to national integrity and political stability. Despite this setback, the declaration is "the most comprehensive statement of the rights of Indigenous Peoples to date, establishing collective rights to a greater extent than any other document in international human rights law," and is expected to "exercise a considerable amount of moral force" (University of Minnesota Human Rights Center 2003).

One key feature of the declaration is that it explicitly recognizes the principle of free, prior, and informed consent (FPIC). Underlying FPIC is the right of "all peoples" to self-determination and to sovereignty over their own land and natural resources, both of which have been stipulated in some existing international legal instruments. The declaration spells out indigenous peoples' right to FPIC in this context, in order to respect their decisions to give or withhold consent for development projects affecting their well-being. According to a paper that laid out a basic framework for the drafting of the declaration, it is therefore crucial that indigenous people are "not coerced, pressured or intimidated in their choices," that they are given "full information about the scope and impacts of the proposed development activities," and that they participate in decision making "prior to the authorization and start of development activities" (United Nations 2005, 15).

The history of planned development is replete with the imposition of projects resulting in the destruction or loss of indigenous peoples' lands and resources, as well as their political, economic, and sociocultural systems. Respect for indigenous cultures and modes of living should therefore be a constitutive part of rights-based approaches to development that lay emphasis on the processes through which rights are promoted, rather than only on the outcomes of development endeavors (Uvin 2004, 180). In line with the principle of FPIC, it is imperative that development agencies involve indigenous peoples in decision making in order to mitigate the negative consequences of their activities. At the same time, existing literature on participatory assessments points out that such "methodological revisionism," in meddling with the procedures and methodologies of popular participation, diverts attention away from an unjustified exercise of power embodied in the discourse of FPIC itself (e.g., Cooke and Kothari 2001; Hickey and Mohan 2004).

What "unjustified" elements are entailed in the discourse of FPIC? With this question in view, this chapter takes up the case of a lowland village in the Bardiya District of Western Nepal, drawing on research carried out from 2000 to 2001 (Masaki 2007).[1] The village, called Majuwa, had been inhabited by an indigenous people called the Tharus, until Bardiya and its surrounding areas were annexed to Nepal in the nineteenth century. As a result of colonization, Tharus became laborers or tenants for the new migrants called Pahadis. Moreover, Pahadis historically drew on their caste and kinship affiliations with political leaders and functionaries to dominate decision making concerning public works projects. Pahadis even exacted unpaid labor and services from Tharus for the construction of physical infrastructure such as irrigation canals and roads. There consequently existed a common feeling of grievance among Tharus regarding Pahadi dominance, which attests to the relevance of FPIC to Majuwa.

However, does the dichotomized view of the colonizer–colonized interface implied in the discourse of FPIC provide a complete picture of the circumstances surrounding members of an indigenous community? As observed by Bhabha (1996), who elucidates the "hybridity" and "liminality" entailed in colonial relations, one should avoid analyzing such relations in terms of two discrete, opposing forces. If the identity of an indigenous community is "hybrid," is it feasible to define a clear-cut benchmark of "full consent," drawing on a "centered" image of deliberation—underlying the principle of FPIC—that regards decision making as a set of goal-oriented activities with a definite beginning and end? According to Butler

(2005), recognition is given or obtained not unilaterally, but via reciprocal relations in which one's subjectivity is formed by virtue of recognizing
or being recognized by the other. Does such "fundamental dependency
on the other" compel an indigenous community to tailor its demands to
conform with social norms when seeking recognition as a rights holder
entitled to FIPC? The following section delineates theoretical frameworks
to address these questions, and is then followed by the case study of the
Tharus in the village of Majuwa.

Analytical Frameworks

Pitfalls in the Politics of Recognition

A group of indigenous people have certain social and cultural affinities,
and thereby hold similar interpretations of social reality. At the same
time, each of them is multiply positioned because their status as the
indigenous populace cuts across other attributes, such as class, gender,
and religion. To belong to an indigenous community should not merely
be equated with speaking or thinking as "aboriginals." Depending on
whom they interact with, and what issues they attend to, indigenous
people move around a variety of perspectives available to them. According to Young, it is therefore crucial to promote a "differentiated solidarity," balancing our commitment to combat oppression and discrimination
with the "differentiated relationship" among the indigenous populace,
who are "engaged in a process extending over space and time" beyond
their immediate surroundings (2000, 123).

The notion of "differentiated solidarity" also leads us to abstain from
the "centered" image of decision making lurking beneath the principle of
FPIC, which relegates the deliberative process to a step-by-step sequence
of arriving at a "rational" consensus. The UN Declaration on the Rights of
Indigenous Peoples envisages an idealized situation in which a group
of indigenous people are present in one place, and articulate their
demands in solidarity. However, seeking to identify the "shared will" of an
indigenous community entails arbitrarily fixating their "consensus," while
disregarding the multiple and fragmented nature of the members' subject
positions. Young therefore calls for a "decentered" view of decision making
as mediated through and dispersed over space and time (2000, 46), which
gives prominence to flows and exchanges among various social sectors,
while avoiding setting any final moment of decision. Accordingly, rather
than seeking to determine the "single will" of an indigenous group by
bringing their struggles under decision-making control, we should regard
FPIC as a goal that is to be pursued within the context of intricate wider
social processes.

Another basis for caution against positioning a group of indigenous people as a unified entity deprived of dignity is elucidated by Butler, who capitalizes on the Hegelian philosophy of recognition to emphasize one's "fundamental dependency on the other" (2005, 33). In keeping with her analysis, indigenous people are required in their struggles for recognition to assimilate themselves to societal norms that have placed them at a disadvantage. Butler also develops a further dimension to this reading of Hegel, pointing out that "a vacillation between loss and ecstasy is inevitable" (Butler 2005, 28) within the structural condition of reciprocal recognition. Thus, in the eyes of indigenous peoples, one's fundamental dependency on the other both poses restrictions on one's thoughts and actions and enables one's struggles for recognition.

The "Liminality" of Colonial Relations

To gain insight into indigenous peoples' experiences of suppression and resistance, it is also helpful to turn to Bhabha, who offers a warning against reducing a colonial situation to a simplistic dichotomy between the colonizer and the colonized. Even when a group of indigenous people have a sense of the shared history of oppression, their subject positions are not merely defined by their interactions with the colonial authority, but are forged at complex intersections of a range of social relations along lines of ethnicity, class, gender, and other sociocultural differences. Their collective identity is therefore constructed by eliminating plurality and difference, thus entailing agonistic confrontations as the fundamental condition of its existence. This is in line with Mouffe's assertion that a political community is composed of "adversaries," or "friendly enemies . . . who share a common symbolic space but . . . want to organize this common symbolic space in different ways" (2000, 13).

It is crucial to avoid dichotomizing a colonial relationship into two discrete, opposing forces, the interactions of which lead to the hybridity of their identities, and the borderlines of which exhibit the liminality of the colonizer–colonized divide. We should instead regard a colonial relationship not merely as the reflection of pre-given ethnic or cultural attributes, but as being founded "'in-between', or in excess of, the sum of the 'parts' of difference" (Bhabha 1996, 2). Both indigenous people as well as their "masters" hold multifaceted, incoherent identities in a composite society that cannot be solely determined by the colonizer–colonized line. What is at stake in the promotion of indigenous rights is the "performative nature of group identifications: the regulation and negotiation of those spaces that are continually, *contingently*, 'opening out,' remaking of [*sic*] the boundaries, exposing the limits of any claim to a singular or autonomous sign of difference" (Bhabha 1996, 219). A new mode of representation is therefore needed to replace the simplistic model dichotomizing indigenous peoples and external actors infringing their rights (such as dominant ethnic or "racial" groups, the governments, aid organizations, and private sector operators).

Setting the Context: The "Liminal" Pahadi–Tharu Divide

The village of Majuwa is situated in Bardiya, which is the third Tarai district from the western border with India. The Tarai, which is an extension of India's Gangetic plains, stretches along the southern frontier adjoining India. Bardiya had been thinly populated, mostly by Tharus, until it was annexed to the Nepalese state in 1861. The ruler then granted large tracts of land in Bardiya as rewards to his loyal courtiers and generals, who were Pahadis. The colonization by the state impacted the Tharus in Majuwa in several ways. First, they were relegated to being laborers or tenants of the Pahadi landlords, and became economically dependent on them. Second, the Pahadis started exacting unpaid labor from the Tharus for the construction and maintenance of village infrastructure, such as irrigation canals, bridges, and roads. Third, the Tharus came to be marginalized in the decision-making processes of public works, while the Pahadi migrants drew on their caste and kinship ties with political leaders and local functionaries to preempt negotiations with the government.

As of November 2000, there were a total of 138 households in Majuwa. Thirty-eight households were those of Pahadis,[2] while the remaining majority of the village populace were Tharus. The promotion of "free, prior and informed consent" (FPIC), upheld in the UN Declaration on the Rights of Indigenous Peoples, could potentially serve to ameliorate the inequitable access to engagement in decision making concerning village public works. The Tharus would surely benefit if offered equal opportunities, on a par with the Pahadis, to make informed choices and to express their wants and needs. At the same time, it is imperative to address the more fundamental question of whether we can view Pahadis and Tharus in dichotomized terms, given Bhabha's demonstration of the implausibility of a clear-cut divide between the colonizer and the colonized (see above).

In Majuwa, not all of the Tharus were landless or small farmers, but a fraction of them were well-off owner-cultivators, who had managed to obtain some land at the time of the land reform program in 1964. The latter group corresponds to the Tharu "elites" upon whom the Pahadi landlords had depended while managing village affairs. One of the Tharu "leaders" waiting on the Pahadi landlords was a Tharu who had been the elected representative of the village for more than 20 years, before the country's transition to the multiparty system in 1990. During his tenure this Tharu, together with his kin and some other landed families, both Tharu and Pahadi, had suppressed the poor majority who had failed to benefit from the land reform program. As a consequence, the Tharu peasants had long suffered from the double burden of high rents and corvée obligations.

In Majuwa, therefore, though ethnic tensions largely overlapped class conflicts, the two did not necessarily go hand in hand. On the contrary, class tensions existed that cut across the Pahadi–Tharu divide. Moreover, class struggles had been refracting with party politics that had already penetrated the village in the latter half of the 1980s. Some Pahadi activists of an underground communist party had been covertly organizing protests by capitalizing on the mounting discontent among Tharu peasants. Therefore, the polarized picture of Pahadi–Tharu rivalries indicated in the first paragraph of this section does not capture the entirety of village politics—which, in the 1990s, came to be played out at the increasingly complex intersections of struggles along lines of party identification, ethnicity, class, gender, and other differences (Masaki 2007, 77–94).

The "Hybridity" of the Tharu Community

Party Politics

With the advent of the multiparty system in 1990 in Nepal, this historical rivalry came out in the open in the form of party politics. Those who took part in the protests against the old Tharu representative and his followers generally supported the Communist Party of Nepal–Unified Marxist-Leninist (CPN-UML), while others usually turned to the Nepali Congress (NC) party. Although the CPN-UML occupied all the elected posts in Majuwa during the 1990s, the two parties polled nearly equal votes, and had an almost equal support base. In Nepal, the multiparty system degenerated into a "naked power struggle" (Hachhethu 2000, 91), which forced party leaders at the center to exert pressure on their local cadres to strengthen their support bases by fair means or foul.[3] In Majuwa, the intensification of party politics manifested itself in the growing "liminality" of the Pahadi–Tharu divide, as well as the increasing "in-between spaces" between the Pahadi and the Tharus, to use the terms coined by Bhabha.

First, party politics provided more space for the Tharus to ally with the Pahadis in their ongoing struggles against the historical Pahadi dominance. For example, aiming to stand in the way of the elected leaders from the CPN-UML responsible for executing village public works, Pahadis affiliated with the NC often called into question the use of corvée, which required Tharus to forgo wages for days on end despite their hand-to-mouth lives. The Tharus were able to capitalize on this NC protest, refusing at times to provide unpaid labor for village public works. Second, party politics bred intragroup tensions among the Tharus by penetrating into the *khel* system of indigenous communal labor, which the Pahadis had appropriated to exact unpaid Tharu work. This is attested to by the fact that the post of the *badghar* (leader), the occupant of which the Pahadis had historically entrusted to take the lead in organizing labor contributions for village public works, was divided into two in 1993 along the party line.

Gender Struggles

Another factor that rendered the Pahadi–Tharu dichotomy untenable in the 1990s was gender politics. In Majuwa, all the elected representative posts had been filled by males, except for one seat reserved for a female, and the village administration had largely failed to address issues of particular concern to women. In 1993 a group of women, both Pahadi and Tharu, started a mothers' group to tackle issues hitherto overlooked by male leaders, such as hygiene, sanitation, alcoholism, and domestic violence. Within two years' time, the membership swelled to encompass more than eighty women. Nearly thirty of these were Pahadis, while about fifty were Tharus. During the early 1990s, women's groups had sprung up throughout the country following the relaxation of political restrictions, such as those hindering freedom of speech and association, and encouraged by the constitutional guarantee of the promotion of gender equality. This provided a favorable ground for the emergence of the mothers' group in Majuwa. The founding members had also been inspired by the mushrooming of female savings groups in the surrounding localities.

The existence of female activism in Majuwa, which cut across the Pahadi–Tharu line, illustrates a potential pitfall of promoting FPIC without regard for the "hybrid" Tharu identity. The complex intersections of ethnic, gender, and party politics in Majuwa added to this hybridity (Masaki 2007, 77–94). For example, the river in Majuwa had been shifting its course to cause the riverbank to be washed away; several small-scale riverbank protection structures had been built, mostly using boulders and steel wire. In 1996 the mothers' group planted trees and shrubs by the river with the objective of promoting vegetation along the riverside, a crucial measure for flood mitigation that had been neglected in Majuwa. Yet this program was also partly instigated by activists from the NC, who had noticed that some Tharu peasants supportive of the CPN-UML were encroaching on and cultivating the government land. What made the matter even more complicated was that all the executive members of the mothers' group were Pahadis. This had caused suspicion among some Tharus that the program was yet another plot by the Pahadis to repress the Tharus.

Suppose that, in line with the notion of FPIC, we had sought the local Tharus' decision to give or withhold consent on the project: whose perspective should we have sided with? Would it have been plausible to decide straightforwardly whether to give priority to the rights of the Tharu peasants to subsist by the river, or to the importance of protecting the village from a potential flood? Could we have determined whether the mothers' group's commitment to addressing the issue, hitherto unaddressed by the male leadership, overrode the concern held by some Tharus that the mother's group was yet another forum for the Pahadi to extend their domination? It would have been infeasible to give preference to one particular standpoint, whether that of the CPN-UML-affiliated Tharu squatters, that of the Tharu women from the mothers' group, or that of Tharu males resenting the Pahadi-led mothers' group.

What would have been at stake is the "liminality" of the Pahadi–Tharu interface. Tharus' interactions with Pahadis were not always confrontational. Depending on who interacted with whom, and which issues were under consideration, these interactions were also instrumental for the Tharus to resist and challenge various forms of social domination. Such "emancipative" potential, inherent in the Pahadi–Tharu interface, is exemplified by the female activism described in this section, or by the party politics that often served to ease the Tharus' corvée burden (explained in the preceding section). It would have been inapt to box Tharus squarely into the underclass category in analyzing these interactions, and we could not have identified a "shared will" of the Tharu community.

Newcomers' Settlements

The above section corroborates Bhabha's assertion that "[w]hat does need to be questioned . . . is the *mode of representation*" (1996, 68), in that the identity of the Tharus was neither unitary nor coherent, contrary to the solidarity of indigenous groups assumed in the UN Declaration on the Rights of Indigenous Peoples. The Tharus in Majuwa did not simply subjugate themselves to the Pahadis, but were variably positioned in the composite society—which encompassed struggles not only between these two groups, but also along lines of gender, class, and party. The cohesiveness of the Tharu identity was further diminished by the mobility of landless Tharus in Baridiya, who migrated from one place to another in search of better livelihood.

For example, there existed a group of six "migrant" Tharu households that had been living on the fringe of a community forest since the late 1990s, with few neighbors to depend on and no kin in the vicinity. Another case in point was a settlement of fifteen Tharu households located at the southern end of the village. The residents had been squatting at this location after clearing some of the woodland in the early 1960s. The newcomers' area had not been allocated a fair share of the trail improvements that were annually undertaken with the villagers' unpaid labor contributions. This was because, according to a local informant, the "indigenous" Tharu residents had colluded with the Pahadis to preempt the decisions concerning resource distribution. Even when the maintenance of trails in the squatters' area was carried out, the other Tharus had not attended to their tasks as conscientiously as the new Tharus did for other areas.

To summarize the overall situation in Majuwa, village politics were played out at the intersections of differences not only in ethnicity, but also in class, gender, and party affiliation. This had brought about the hybridity of the Tharu identity, as well as the liminality of the Pahadi–Tharu divide. It therefore would have been neither feasible nor desirable to promote FPIC for the "Tharu community" across the board. Not all Tharus were equally downtrodden, and they were differently situated according to their economic status, their proximity to political influence, and/or their involvement in organized activities. Could we then have geared FPIC toward the more deprived segments of the Tharus, who lacked political, social, and economic clout? I examine this question in the next section, by drawing on an anecdote concerning the migrant Tharus who had settled at the southern fringe of Majuwa.

"Decision Making" Extending over Space and Time: An Anecdote

Majuwa is of quadrangular shape, with two sides bordered by a sinuous river that causes adjacent land to be washed away. The river control projects undertaken in 1993, 1994, and 1996 only protected the northern end of the village inhabited by the "native" Tharus, disregarding the settlement of the Tharu "newcomers" in the south. According to the "migrant" Tharus, the proposals of all the river control projects had been tabled as a foregone, unobjectionable conclusion in village meetings. Although these Tharus had expressed in the meetings their reservations about the plan protecting only the northern side, in their view their opinion had not been seriously attended to. The elected representatives insisted on focusing upon the northern end in a high-handed manner, and had even reprehended the "newcomer" Tharus for not forgoing their narrow interests and for failing to see flooding in perspective.

A proponent of FPIC would have suggested providing an opportunity for the "migrant" Tharus to make an informed choice, based on adequate briefing on how the engineer in charge had derived the project design. Moreover, public deliberations could have taken place in an environment conducive for the participants to be open and attentive to one another, in order to arrive at an optimal solution acceptable to all the villagers. However, supposing these conditions had been met, would they have made a difference?

Underlying such an FPIC strategy is a "centered" image of decision making that proceeds in a linear, purposive manner with a clear-cut beginning and end. However, as pointed out by Young (2000, 37–51), this type of deliberative model is flawed in that its tacit norm of "articulateness" privileges those accustomed to public speaking, and in that it is liable to conceal particularistic values of order lurking beneath a supposedly "common good." Accordingly, it can be surmised that even with a more orderly sequence of public deliberations, the proposals to protect the northern side of Majuwa would have been given the appearance of being an optimal course of action, using neutral, technical language. This, in turn, would have restrained the "migrant" Tharus from openly questioning the idea, since they would be pressured into keeping up the pretence of contributing to the "greater good" of society. The disadvantaged Tharus, even if they had decided to break their silence, would have been able only to make an "impaired inquiry," because they were not fully conversant with "scientific" terminology.

Whatever the case might have been, there occurred an "unexpected" course of events in 1997. The village's elected representatives proposed the construction of river control structures on the southern side. Their proposal to help the marginal area evolved out of ongoing societal dynamics, rather than a technocratic process of administering village-level public works. As described in the preceding section, with the advent of the multiparty system in 1990, village politics had come to be contested at intersections of party, ethnicity, gender, class, and other coordinates. This had provided fertile soil for the landless Tharus to seek to rectify various forms of injustice, especially through recourse to party politics. Accordingly, at the time of the 1997 proposal these Tharus had just won a lawsuit they had filed with the help of the NC, revoking a 1994 move by the CPN-UML to condemn part of the land the Tharus had been tilling.[4] The village elected representatives affiliated with the CPN-UML had thus felt compelled to make up for their party's blunder in the form of a hand-out, and the ostensibly unforeseen decision was taken. Contrary to assumptions lurking beneath the notion of FPIC, it was not imperative for an external agent to deliberately bring the deprived Tharus' voices to the attention of policymakers.

This episode corroborates the value of what Young calls a "decentered" model of decision making, in which it is seen as mediated and dispersed, in contrast to the "centered" view. "Society," Young contends, "... outruns political institutions, and thus democratic politics must be thought of as taking place within the context of large and complex social processes the whole of which cannot come into view, let alone under decision-making control" (2000, 46). Moreover, because a step-by-step sequence of decision making can potentially play into the hands of "loudmouths," it is crucial to conceive an alternative to the FPIC focus on singling out the "shared will" of an indigenous community through a series of goal-oriented deliberations. The concluding section, drawing on lessons learnt from Majuwa, considers how best to safeguard indigenous peoples against development programs infringing on their lands and ecosystems.

Conclusions: Avoiding the Pitfalls of FPIC

This article, drawing on the case of the Tharus in Majuwa village, illustrates that the identity of an indigenous community is neither homogeneous nor consistent, even when its members have a shared history of colonization and suppression.[5] Indigenous people are multiply positioned in a composite society, and move around a range of perspectives, depending on whom they interact with, and what issues they attend to. This is because their identity as the "colonized" cuts across other social coordinates, such as party affiliation, class, and gender, thus according them multiple and incoherent subjectivities. Therefore, in contrast with the dichotomized view upheld in the UN Declaration on the Rights on Indigenous Peoples, we should abstain from viewing the oppressor–oppressed interface solely in terms of two discrete, opposing forces. Moreover, given the hybridity of an indigenous community, it is not feasible to identify its "shared will" regarding whether to give or withhold consent to a particular development project.

This does not mean, however, that we should abort the promotion of free, prior and informed consent (FPIC). It is instead crucial that we seek to balance our commitment to combat oppression and discrimination against indigenous peoples with the liminality of the colonizer–colonized interface. The FPIC principle is of particular relevance to large-scale undertakings such as the construction of mega-hydraulic dams and highways, the commercial extraction of oil and minerals, or the designation of environmentally protected areas. To prevent these types of projects from causing adverse impacts—particularly ecosystem degradation and massive displacements—it is imperative to ensure the effective participation of indigenous peoples in decision making, while providing them with complete information regarding the objective nature of projects and their probable results, including their foreseeable benefits and risks of harm.

Should we then conclude that, while advancing FPIC, we should refrain from pushing through a step-by-step sequence of deliberations in order that we would not hastily fix the "single will" of an indigenous community? Would it suffice to suggest making special efforts to heed community members' differing experiences and views? It would be technically feasible to explore various research methods to grasp the fluid, contingent, overlapping nature of the boundaries of an indigenous group. For example, focus group interviews would help to elucidate the existence of varying perspectives held by different subsets of a particular group. Participatory observations, as employed in ethnographic studies, would also provide clues for comprehending the transient and multiple nature of individuals' identities. These methods could prevent us from uncritically setting up the rigid inside–outside distinction that fabricates the internal unity of an indigenous community. However, should we be content to eschew misconstruing a particular viewpoint as representative of a group, while uncritically continuing to seek that group's decision whether to give consent on a development project?

Such concern with the procedures of seeking FPIC diverts attention away from the larger workings of power, as explained at the beginning of this article. Which broader dynamics of power remain unaddressed when indigenous rights promotion is relegated to a procedural matter of getting an indigenous community to partake in decision making? In our endeavors to go beyond such "methodological revisionism," it is crucial to pay attention to an antinomy inherent in the principle of FPIC. As stated at the outset, underlying the notion of FPIC is the self-determination of indigenous communities as well as their sovereignty over their own land and natural resources. The ideal of indigenous peoples' self-determination, however, is in irreconcilable tension with the objective of FPIC to enlist them through their acceptance of an externally conceived project.

This point can be elucidated by considering the following hypothetical project in Majuwa. As stated already, the river running along the village is a sinuous stream, causing problems of bank erosion and flood discharge. In order to tame the river, continuous dikes as well as meander-loop cutoff channels are to be built along its entire stretch. Since Majuwa is located on the river bend, this project will dislocate a significant portion of the village populace to make way for cutoff work. The project may give the impression that it is indispensable in protecting locals from the unfavorable natural conditions. It is to be noted, however, that the project forecloses alternatives to flood mitigation, such as nonstructural measures including land use regulations, disaster insurance, and upper watershed conservation. More importantly, a natural event would not turn into a disaster unless people reside or undertake livelihood activities in flood-prone areas. One important aspect of disaster reduction, then, is to address such sociopolitical dynamics which put at risk the livelihoods of marginal groups (Masaki 2007, 48–50).

The notion of FPIC, given its objective to seek consent to a preconceived project, is liable to lapse into what Foucault terms a "political technology" (Dreyfus and Rabinow 1982, 196), reducing a complex political issue entailing conflicts of interests to a technical matter of identifying an optimal solution. It risks legitimizing the proliferation of state intervention, rather than allowing locals to shape and pursue their own strategies. This corroborates Butler's assertion, referred to above, about one's "fundamental dependency on the other" (2005, 33). An indigenous group is immersed in reciprocal relations by which it is required to assimilate itself to existing norms governing how people gain recognition. When acting as rights-holders entitled to FPIC, the group's members are likely to exercise their rights—realized by virtue of being conferred recognition—within parameters laid out by an external agent. This corresponds to what Bhabha terms the "uncanny double of democracy," by which one exercises autonomy over one's own territory under responsibility to others (1996, 96).

At the same time, as pointed out by Butler (2005), this "uncanny double" of recognition is not always prohibitive or dyadic, but can open up opportunities beyond our routine comprehension of what is possible. The productive and facilitative nature of one's "primary dependency on the other" is attested to by the Tharus in Majuwa drawing on Pahadi-dominated politics, which opened up room for them to challenge the status quo. Wider movements and organizing principles, such as party, class, and gender politics, were assimilated into the Tharu community, the members of which then contested their respective positions in society. With recourse to extralocal processes, moreover, the Tharus continually waged their struggles beyond the time frame of any specific public works project. The need to heed broader processes extending over space and time is exemplified by the anecdote about the project proposal to protect the hitherto neglected settlement of the deprived Tharus. As described in the preceding section, the idea that the project should extend help to the "newcomer" Tharus evolved out of ongoing local politics, rather than being an administrative process of according them opportunities to voice their concerns in public.

A clue to how to mitigate the risk that FPIC will lapse into a political technology—a liability emanating from one's fundamental dependency on the other—lies in our adopting a "decentered image of decision-making as mediated through and dispersed over space and time" (Young 2000, 46). It is imperative that proponents of FPIC should not be content with a "centered" view that narrowly focuses upon a step-by-step sequence of goal-oriented discussions. As explained in the preceding section, restricting the scope of external assistance to micro-level, time-bound social interactions can play into the hands of those capable of shaping "reasoned" arguments. Moreover, as illustrated by the above hypothetical project, rushing through a set of deliberations to determine whether to accept or how to implement a preplanned project potentially blurs alternative possibilities by constricting one's perceptions of existing problems.

Those committed to rights promotion should pay attention to indigenous peoples' self-defined and self-directed struggles over long times and wide distances, and beyond the limited scope of particular projects. In this way, external agents will be able to accord them autonomy in shaping their struggles against oppression and discrimination, and also to assist them to uncover and challenge a particularistic order of norms liable to be inadvertently promoted under the banner of FPIC. Proponents of FPIC, when immersed merely in bringing indigenous peoples' voices to the attention of policymakers within the project cycle, are prone not only to unwittingly get indigenous people to embrace externally conceived agendas, but also to mistakenly position them as a unified entity deprived of dignity. As repeatedly pointed out in this chapter, drawing a dichotomized contrast between an indigenous community and others prone to infringe their rights, such as government and aid agencies or private sector operators, leads us to deny ongoing political activism among "aboriginals," while disregarding the cacophony of perspectives and experiences that coexist within a single community. In many cases, political activism within such communities is only visible at certain points in time.

A downside of this frame of reflection from the viewpoint of external agents is that it is less amenable to outsiders' blueprints, given the absence of a clear-cut beginning and a definite goal. At the same time, there exists ample scope for outsiders to extend support, especially to those segments of the indigenous populace who are more likely to lose out, given their lack of political, social, and economic clout. As illustrated by the case of the Tharus in Majuwa, members of an indigenous community are differently positioned economically, politically, and socially. On the other hand, different subsets of the group continually stake their claims and wage struggles with one another, thus causing continual revisions and transvaluations of intragroup dynamics. Outside actors must therefore realize that external interventions cannot be neutral, and must be wary of tailoring their support strategies to a particular unfolding of events, which do not always proceed in a linear, foreseeable manner. This means that advocates of indigenous rights must accept the impossibility of bringing peoples' struggles under decision-making control. It is imperative to learn to live with this unmasterable reality, and thus to abort a "straightjacket" FPIC strategy, if we are truly to act in accordance with the principle of indigenous peoples' self-determination—supposedly the backbone of the emerging FPIC agenda.

References

Bhabha, H. K. 1996. *The location of culture.* London: Routledge.

Butler, J. 2005. *Giving an account of oneself.* New York: Fordham University Press.

Cooke, B. and U. Kothari, eds. 2001. *Participation: The new tyranny?* London: Zed Books.

Dreyfus, H. L. and P. Rabinow. 1982. *Michel Foucault: Beyond structuralism and hermeneutics.* Brighton: Harvester Press.

Hachhethu, K. 2000. Nepali politics: Political parties, political crisis and problems of governance. In *Domestic conflict and crisis of governability in Nepal,* edited by D. Kumar, 90–116. Kathmandu: Centre for Nepal and Asian Studies.

Hickey, S. and G. Mohan, eds. 2004. *Participation: From tyranny to transformation? New approaches to participation in development.* London: Zed Books.

Masaki, K. 2007. *Power, participation, and policy: The "emancipatory" evolution of the "elite-controlled" policy process.* Lanham, Maryland: Lexington Books.

Mouffe, C. 2000. *The democratic paradox.* London: Verso.

United Nations. 2005. Legal commentary on the concept of free, prior and informed consent. http://www.tebtebba.org/tebtebba_files/ipr/ECN.4Sub.2AC.420052.pdf.

University of Minnesota Human Rights Center. 2003. Study guide: The rights of indigenous peoples. http//www1.umn.edu/humanrts/edumat/studyguides/omdogenous.html.

Uvin, P. 2004. *Human rights and development.* Bloomfield, Conn.: Kumarian Press.

Young, I. M. 2000. *Inclusion and democracy.* Oxford: Oxford University Press.

Notes

1. For a more comprehensive study on how development intersected with ongoing local politics in Baridiya (and in Majuwa), see Masaki 2007.

2. Twenty-five of the thirty-eight Pahadi households were of high caste, while the rest of the Pahadis were either Matwalis (Alcohol Drinkers) or of untouchable caste. The latter two groups of Pahadis were not well off, since they earned their livelihoods from a combination of livestock rearing, backyard farming, and working as day laborers in nearby towns. In this chapter, the term "Pahadis" denotes the high-caste households, since the marginal Pahadis hardly figured in the power contestation around the Pahadi–Tharu divide.

3. For a detailed case study of how the "naked power struggles" among political leaders at the center impacted village politics, see Masaki (2007).

4. In the 1990s the land distribution program, referred to in the preceding section, had been "politicized" by successive political parties in power at the center that used the government's *Sukumbasi Ayog* to allocate land so as to dispense patronage to their respective support bases. Part of the land used by the disadvantaged Tharus had accordingly been condemned by the *Ayog*, in 1994, when the CPN-UML was heading a coalition government. The political party was said to have intended to arrange land grants for its supporters.

5. See note 1.

PART THREE

Do Rights-Based Approaches Offer a Pro-Poor Route to Development?

CHAPTER 6

Property Rights and Rights-Based Sustainable Livelihoods

Leonith Hinojosa-Valencia[1]

Introduction

Property rights are central to people's rights of access to the resources and assets required for their livelihood strategies. They therefore resonate with rights-based approaches to development in all their myriad forms, whether expressed via the international human rights framework, by autonomous movements, or through citizenship approaches. Moreover, both the right to property and the rights-based approach more broadly have increasingly been viewed in terms of their specific relevance to issues of poverty and poverty reduction. For example, it has been argued that rights-based approaches can be credited with

> bringing a much needed focus on accountability to development discussions, underscoring the legal as well as moral obligation to guide public policy towards the fulfilment of all dimensions of human well-being. To governments they provide a normative framework for their efforts to tackle deprivation and marginalization; to those condemned to living in poverty and exclusion, an empowering avenue of redress (CESR 2007).

Meanwhile, as theoretical elements of institutional economics have been mainstreamed into development studies during the past decade, issues regarding property rights have been increasingly linked to the underlying institutional factors that determine economic development. Indeed, in the wake of pioneering contributions (Lewis 1955; Coase 1960; North and Thomas 1973; North 1981) and recent influential commentaries (Knack and Keefer 1995; Rodrik 1999), there is some consensus around a positive association between clearly defined property rights and good economic performance, at least at the macroeconomic level. Less is known, however, about the links between property rights and people's livelihoods and how these influence the exercise of economic and social rights.

This chapter explores the relationship between property rights and the formation of livelihood strategies, and the implications of that relationship for the rights-based approach to development. The starting point is to acknowledge that property rights are a social construct that denote the way in which a particular society organizes the allocation and distribution of resources and assets. Based on the study of peasant communities in the Southern Peruvian Andes, the chapter presents an analytical framework that links peasants' livelihood strategies to their corresponding access to assets and established property rights, particularly concerning natural and physical assets. The Peruvian case is useful to illustrate the connections between property rights, the rights-based approach, and livelihoods. As will become clear, even where constitutional law recognizes citizen rights, as with the right to property, formal tenure over land and other forms of natural resources is not easily achieved, particularly for the peasant population in the Andean regions of the country.

In the rural territories of the Peruvian Andes, the absence of an institutional framework capable of supporting secure property rights coincides with a high level of vulnerability facing rural households as they seek to improve their livelihoods and maintain an adequate standard of living. The case studies of rural Peruvian households explored here show that a stronger regime of individualized property rights in rural Andean areas should have significant benefits for the rural population when compared to current regimes of communal ownership. This conclusion, although valid for all cases and all individuals in each case discussed here, entails different types of benefits depending on the composition of livelihood strategies. Individualized property rights enable households that are more articulated to the market to increase their income derived from productive activities. For those households less articulated and for which livelihood strategies are mainly based on temporary migration and noncommercial agriculture, the benefits derived from individualized property rights are related to an increased sense of security and self-value that property ownership brings. In both cases, in a society where ownership regimes differ in relation to geographic location (e.g., the highlands or the coast) and rural status (peasant or individual farmer), the right to individual or communal property allows rural peasant populations to participate in broader society on more equitable terms. For instance, small farmers in coastal areas—where the legal requirements for individual ownership are less stringent than in highland communities—have been more able to develop commercial and export agriculture than their highland counterparts (Cavassa and Mesclier 2007).

This chapter has implications for development analysis as well as policy. In particular, it suggests that the popular livelihoods framework needs to be extended to specifically include issues of property rights, particularly in considering institutional influences and the tensions of private versus communal or state ownership of capital assets. Tensions over property rights can undermine attempts to improve the conditions within which rural peasant communities develop their livelihood strategies, and can reduce the ability of a governance regime to incorporate a rights-based approach to development.

Incorporating Issues of Property Rights into Livelihoods Analysis and Strategies

The sustainable livelihoods approach offers a holistic analytical framework for understanding the situation and dynamics of the rural poor, and has directly informed development policy and practice since its emergence over a decade ago. The framework defines a livelihood as the capabilities, assets, and activities required for a household to develop a sustainable means of living (DFID 1998). It also assumes that access to capital assets—natural, financial, physical, human, and social capital—precedes the adoption of livelihood strategies, and suggests that institutions and social relations mediate both the adoption of livelihood strategies and access to capital assets (Scoones 1998; Bebbington 1999; Ellis 2000). As yet, livelihoods analysis has paid little attention to the significance of property rights in these processes, despite growing evidence that they are central to the formation of livelihood strategies.

A property right, as originally defined by Irving Fisher, is "the liberty of permit (under the sanction and protection of custom and law) to enjoy benefits of wealth—in its broadest sense—while assuming the costs which those benefits entail" (1923, 27). As such, property rights ought to be understood as "abstract social relations among individuals that arise from the existence of scarce goods and that pertain to their use" (Pejovich 2001, xiv). They should also be taken as subordinate to the institutional framework—the legal rules, organizational forms, norms of behavior, and enforcement mechanisms (North 1990)—that orders the governance of any society. The right of ownership contains three elements: exclusivity of ownership, transferability of ownership, and constitutional guarantees of ownership (Pejovich 2001). These can be organized under three different legal institutional frameworks—private, communal, and state ownership (Pejovich 2001)—with all three systems operating alongside each other in some contexts. The adoption of a private, communal, or state ownership framework occurs in response to the time and effort needed for establishing and enforcing the selected option, and the relative scarcity of the resource to be recognized as property. In so far as many resources are relatively scarce, the usefulness of communal regimes of ownership and the establishment of private property become controversial. While resources are vital for local populations' livelihoods, outsiders can claim direct access based on principles of economic efficiency or even an indirect access recalling "environmental rights." Customs and traditional norms as well as the particular political economy of each place influence the adoption of a property rights regime, and therefore the private allocation of resources can happen on a universal or a discretionary basis. It is in this respect that the discussion about property rights and livelihood strategies connects with the rights-based approach to development.

Among other things, the rights-based approach advocates universal access to the means that ensure survival and facilitate development. This presupposes that resources are abundant and that there is no competition for them; in that case, as stated by Platteau (2000), private property neither is useful nor is economically justifiable. However, when scarcity occurs and externalities or spillover effects arise—by arrangement or by law—restrictions over ownership are imposed and private forms of property rights arise. As Demsetz (1967) suggested, private property rights emerge whenever "the gains which can be internalized individually by enforcing the rights exceed the costs of doing so" and "the net gains from private property exceed those which can be individually realized under communal or state ownership." Although sound in economic terms, this reasoning may be counterproductive to rights-based approaches to development if other factors are not also considered, such as the initial endowments and the distributive effects that one arrangement or another will possibly imply. Indeed, Platteau suggests that "as far as heterogeneity and inequality characterizes a community, the regulated outcome [private or collective ownership] turns to be less efficient and to amplify the distributive effects of regulation, thereby increasing the likelihood that some agents will be hurt in the process" (Platteau 2000, 79; interpolation is my remark).

Consequently, the institutionalization of a particular property rights regime will affect the livelihoods and the livelihood strategies of those who share resources and assets. However, a discussion about the relationships between institutions and livelihood strategies, and particularly about property rights and the rights-based approach, is largely absent from livelihoods analysis and from particular frameworks such as the UK Department for International Development's Sustainable Livelihoods. Although different regimes of property rights are nominally included within the "structures and institutions" dimension of the Sustainable Livelihoods framework—defined as "a sphere in which policies, institutions laws and culture together affect livelihood strategies" (DFID 1998; also Bebbington 2004; Carney 2003)—applications of the framework have reflected little on the issue of the rights-based approach and property rights. Importantly, no efforts have been made to measure the specific influence of institutions and property rights on the livelihood outcomes and economic performance of household livelihood strategies. The need to understand the link between property rights and economic performance at a micro level (the nanoeconomy of a rural household), and to examine its locus within an institutional framework, inspired the research presented in this chapter (Hinojosa 2006).

Figure 6.1 presents a framework for analyzing these relationships. It takes as its departure point the way in which the livelihood strategies of rural peasant households are formed—that is, how property rights determine access to capital assets and the benefits that can be derived from them. Understanding this process reveals both the set of capital assets that makes possible the adoption of livelihood strategies and the outcomes derived from those strategies. Property rights are related to each of these elements: they determine access to and the use of assets and they also influence the control of livelihood outcomes.

In this framework, property rights and the institutional framework that supports them are factors in the constraints faced by rural populations trying to widen their access to assets and to influence their immediate

Figure 6.1 Livelihoods and property rights

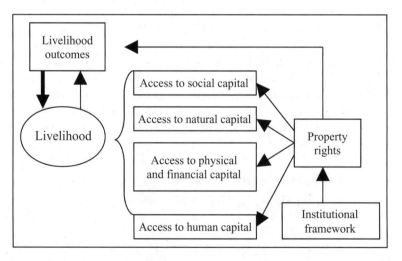

institutional context. The implication of treating property rights as emerging from a defined institutional framework is that the ways in which households construct their livelihood strategies do not respond only to the amount of assets they have access to, but are also based on how laws— and social, communal, and familial norms—define the property rights on those assets. In other words, institutions affect people's livelihood strategies through the property rights over capital assets. The extent to which property rights affect the formation and change of livelihood strategies will depend on how significant the asset is.

This resource-centered framework is underpinned by Hardin's "tragedy of the commons" analysis (1968) and complemented by a discussion about the degree of formality or legal recognition that property rights regimes get in contexts where private and collective property coexist (such as in the Andes). In those contexts, controversy exists between those who advocate formally recognized private property rights—on the grounds that these would improve people's abilities to exchange and derive profit within capitalist economies (De Soto 2000; World Bank 2002; Barbier 2004)—and those (including some governments and many NGOs) who support communal regimes of property rights as the best means of facilitating broad access to resources, in part to keep vulnerable rural people secure from the grip of dominant capitalist economic agents.

In the following section, cases located in rural communities of the Southern Peruvian Andes are used to illustrate this framework and its implications for a rights-based approach to development. Livelihood strategies are perceived through the development of farm, nonfarm, and off-farm activities; livelihood outcomes are measured by the amount of production and the income obtained; and access to assets is operationalized by a set of variables that give account of the current stock of capitals that households possess and that are combined to produce livelihood outcomes. The main difference between livelihood outcomes and livelihood strategies is that the former focuses on *results* whereas the latter emphasizes *processes*. Data used to estimate the relationships between livelihoods and access to assets come from a survey carried out in 2003, in which 400 households are grouped by their degree of inclusion in a market economy, their affiliation to economic organizations, and their location.

Livelihoods and Property Rights in Peasant Communities in the Peruvian Rural Andes

The rural Andean region of Peru extends longitudinally throughout the national territory. It is largely populated by the Quechua indigenous population who have settled either as individual farmers or as peasant communities. Evidence from the Southern part of this region (Cusco) on the linkages between livelihood strategies and access to assets shows that peasant households have been progressively diversifying their livelihoods in an attempt to improve their living conditions and the future of their children. Such a process of diversification follows a parallel process of successive changes in access to resources and assets, due to decisions that households make in regard to their use or to constraints imposed by institutional structures. This study agrees with others (Gonzales de Olarte 1994; Zoomers 1999; Reardon et al. 2001; Bebbington 2004) that: (i) rural livelihoods clearly incorporate farm and off-farm activities; (ii) agriculture plays a double role in facilitating household survival and, under particular conditions, household accumulation; (iii) human capital plays an essential role in the level of livelihood diversification; and (iv) certain social networks and development interventions have played an important role in improving such diversification, but at the same time have deepened a process of differentiation across rural populations.

Table 6.1 presents the study results concerning the relationships between livelihood outcomes and access to assets introduced by Figure 6.1. All variables representing a capital asset are positively related to production and income, with the exception of "age" (implying that older households are likely to make less income). Schooling years of the household head, membership in grassroots organizations, land extension, and the value of physical assets display the most significant positive relations with both total net production and income.

Natural Capital and Property Rights on Land

Land tenure, defined as "the mode by which land is held or owned, or the set of relationships among people concerning land or its product" (Payne 2002, 5) is subject to continual change and renewal in relation to broader forms of social change. The exercise of rights involves several domains, and the right to property can be seen as a domain distinct from the right to its use and from the right to enjoy the benefits that tenure produces. Nonetheless, the introduction of property rights in the rights-based approach to development ensures the exercise of economic rights in all three of these domains.

In the Peruvian Andes, where collective property rights predominate over the land used by peasant households, the plots that households invest in are accessed under the usufruct form—that is, communities legally own the land and, relying on customary norms, give to their household members the right to "privately" use it. Although historically grounded and institutionally reinforced by the 1969 Land Reform law, this type of arrangement has stimulated discussions among developmental

Table 6.1 Relations between livelihood outcomes and access to assets

CAPITAL ASSETS		TOTAL NET PRODUCTION	INCOME
Human Capital	Household size	Insignificant	Insignificant
	Age of household head	Negative	Negative
	Age of partner (c)	Insignificant	Insignificant
	Schooling years of household head	Positive and important	Positive and important
	Schooling years of partner (c)	Insignificant	Positive
	Total training hours per household per year	Positive	Positive
Social Capital	Membership in grassroots organizations	Positive and important	Positive and important
	Number of benefits due to membership	Positive	Insignificant
	Leadership	Positive	Insignificant
Natural Capital	Total land extension	Positive and very important	Positive and very important
	Crop land extension	Positive and very important	Positive and very important
	Grazing land extension	Positive	Positive
Physical Capital	Value of productive physical assets	Positive and very important	Positive and very important
	Value of physical assets	Positive and very important	Positive and very important
	Crop lands with irrigation infrastructure	Insignificant	Positive

Note: "Insignificant," "negative," and "positive" are qualifications based on correlation analysis; "important" and "very important" are judgments made on the basis of regression analysis. (See also Hinojosa, 2006.)

actors about the need of clearer and more efficient property rights regimes, particularly after high rates of rural population growth were noticed. Since 1990, such discussions have revealed disagreements between those who view individualized property rights as merely part of the neoliberal package, and those who see that increased individual ownership among peasant households is part of a long-standing process of change that is in part the result of their own agency.

According to census data, land is a scarce resource in the Andes, and is clearly scarcer for some than for others (INEI 1994). In the area studied, the range of landholdings among groups varies between zero and 45 hectares with a mean of 1.9 hectares, suggesting that land and land ownership may be differently valued by each individual. Taking this together with the fact that most of the land with higher added value is under individual possession, landholding appears to be particularly important for households in which livelihood strategies include more market-oriented activities, for which changes in landholdings catalyze higher change in income compared to total output. This explains why changes in land ownership over time have been caused mainly by peasants, whose farming activities increasingly rely on a market economy and whose need for a more efficient property rights regime seems to be pressing. Conversely, for households whose livelihood strategies focus on off-farm and nonfarm activities or whose connection with the market is mainly for labor supply, private property over land appeared to be less important, though still justified by the sense of security derived from private landholding.

Despite differences on the preference for private ownership, a common feature to almost all households studied is that where property rights regimes display tension between legally imposed communal ownership and the informal practice of individual private ownership, this tension has had a negative impact on peasants' economic performance. The reproduction over time of communal access to land and other natural resources, which aims to guarantee the right of access to these resources to all community members, has encountered considerable restrictions due to three factors. First, given population growth, the decreasing availability of productive land has meant that younger peasants (mostly male) are nominal community members, but have no rights to land other than those inherited within the household. Second, the initial distribution of resources, if ever egalitarian, is now highly unequal, and reflects the abilities of each household to develop market activities and "negotiate" within the community for improved access to land and other resources. In so far as communal norms and the formal institutional framework lock peasant communities into communitarian property rights and governance regimes, market-oriented development has only been possible at a limited scale and without significant opportunities to generate changes in livelihood strategies. Third, investments that are required to increase land factor productivity (notably irrigation and soil conservation), and which are mainly made in response to temporary and conditioned incentives offered by development interventions, have been undermined by a lack of attention to the securities expected by individuals regarding full control of the returns their investment would produce (a conclusion also found by Wiener and Hinojosa et al. 2003).

Under these conditions, and given that the law applicable to highland rural territories constrains individual private ownership within peasant communities, arrangements for land exchange between households have been fully based on informal agreements underlined by traditional norms and intracommunity power relationships. This has opened space for discrimination and eviction among community populations. For instance, given the extended practice of male-based community membership, women are less entitled to participate in informal land markets. Similarly, wherever processes of communal grassland redistribution have been observed, households with bigger livestock endowments have benefited more than those poorly endowed.

Physical Capital and Property Rights

Access to and control of physical assets reflect the rights of people to enjoy the fruits of technology, growth, and development. The contribution of physical capital to the formation and adaptation of livelihood strategies is made through public infrastructure provided by development interventions (e.g., roads, electricity, and water), and through the households' investments (vehicles, machinery, irrigation, and other productive investments). As Table 6.1 shows, the contribution of such assets is valuable for output and income creation; hence, secure access to these assets and the warranties needed to privately invest on land are important.

It is noteworthy that considerable change in the stock of physical capital held by individual households would be needed to produce a significant increase in income (Hinojosa 2006). Furthermore, given peasants' limited income and access to financial resources, households have invested in physical capital if and only if the new assets were expected to contribute considerably to the development of their selected livelihood strategies; peasants are highly rational in an economic sense. In household economies where agriculture accounts for at least half of the income, a weaker link exists between physical assets and farm production than that observed between physical assets and total income (derived from farm and nonfarm activities). The contribution of physical capital to the generation of output and income becomes significant only for households that have developed intensive commercial farming or a combination of farm and nonagricultural activities (e.g., processing of dairy products). Among these households, claims for privatized property rights are justifiable. In all other cases, where a mix of staple agriculture and temporary migration is predominant, investments in physical capital made at the community level are unimportant, and private property rights are therefore apparently not an issue.

Having said that, the case studies show that ill-defined ownership of capital assets has undermined households' ability to take advantage of the opportunities opened by development interventions in order to increase their access to markets and improve their livelihood outcomes. For instance, given that land is the most important form of collateral available to local households, the lack of titling and the constraints derived from the ambiguity of legal norms and registration systems has reduced rural households' access to credit—confirming what Wenner and others found on the national scale (2003). For 17 percent of the households presented in this chapter, access to microcredit was restricted to the NGO sector. Furthermore, in so far as some forms of physical capital are attached to land (e.g., housing and productive installations), they are subject to the same forms of property rights that apply to land. Under customary norms, peasants "own" their properties, but given the informal possession of the land, these attached possessions have no market or even quasi-market value. In addition, given that rural land and housing have been categorized as "essential assets" for rural households, such possessions could not be fully used as collateral for accessing credit. Therefore, despite its apparent purpose of protecting rural populations from eviction, the law prevents individuals from fully exercising their property rights over investments they have legitimately made. The implication of this finding is that private possession is not enough. Formalization and titling appear as important conditions for converting households' goods (land, estates) into market assets.

A second set of implications of unclear property rights over physical capital derives from the provision of community-level infrastructure under a mix of communal and state ownership regimes. This mode of provision has consequences for the generation, management, and maintenance of such infrastructure. The "public good" nature of public infrastructure produces problems of low maintenance, and entails "open access" with concomitant risks of overuse, abuse, and free riding (Ostrom and Ostrom 1977, quoted by McCay 1996, 79). Additional problems arise from the fact that some of these public assets are in reality "club assets," that is, assets that can only be used by selected groups of peasants. Many development interventions have invested in the construction of communal barns, greenhouses, installations for animal sanitation, or marketing infrastructure, that are then transferred to community assemblies for their use and management. All such investments thus become part of the community's stock of capital assets, with access theoretically guaranteed to each community member. In practice, intervening factors such as the location or skill set of particular households means that inclusive access is nominal and that only some groups are able to use a given facility. For instance, marketing infrastructure is only used by those who do commercial agriculture; animal sanitation pools are overused by those households with bigger animal stocks and less used by households that have few; seeds barns have brought problems of distrust after the loss or deterioration of seeds. Ironically, when intracommunity conflicts arise the erstwhile dominant group is often no longer able to conserve or to use the good concerned, because the infrastructure is then reclaimed as communal and no forms of private use exist that could lead to more efficient arrangements. This has often led to the abandonment of communal infrastructure, as can be seen along the Southern Peruvian Andes (and as has also been documented in several development project evaluations, with my participation).

In these circumstances, a communal regime for ownership and management is ineffective unless the asset in question is essential to the development of shared livelihood strategies. Hardin's "tragedy of the commons" (1968) is exacerbated by conflicts between individuals and groups, with the unfortunate consequence that peasants constrain their own opportunities to achieve a cooperative positive outcome based on communal property. This problem has increasingly been recognized within NGO and state development programs, which have started to invest more in lower-level, targeted forms of infrastructure (e.g., barns and stables tailored for one household or a small producers association). Nonetheless, ownership problems still arise in cases of group dissolution. This highlights the fact that peasants, as well as the development organizations working with them, need to develop institutional arrangements that may promote a good balance between universal rights and access, efficient management, and sound economic use.

Finally, Andean peasants' lack of awareness of the benefits of private or communal property rights extends to other forms of physical assets. For instance, protections of their unique natural resources (e.g., the alpaca) or of some forms of cultural heritage (e.g., traditional medicine and natural tints) are almost nonexistent in domestic and international markets. Instead of being interpreted as an expression of peasants' cultural preference for open access, this lack of awareness about the right communities or individuals have to enjoy the benefits of their unique capital can be seen as the result of having negligible information about the world market economy where these resources are highly valued—and privately appropriated by large companies. This reduces opportunities for the indigenous populations that originally "own" such capitals.

Implications for Governance and Change

Open access, communal, and private property rights regimes are all associated directly with broader and corresponding forms of governance regimes—namely state governance, communal governance, and market regulation respectively (McCay 1996). All regimes emerge from arrangements between individuals competing to use and control scarce resources and defining to whom resources will be allocated under what conditions. Such processes of resource allocation embody complex relationships between individuals, in which economic rationale, power, and culture become interlinked to produce an agreed upon—or perhaps imposed—set of rules that govern the use of the resources in question. Consequently, property rights regimes both reflect and reinforce different governance regimes, and any changes to property rights regimes also require broader change within and between the broader governance regimes—change that may be difficult to realize despite the economic rationale for doing so (see Smith 2002 on governance and exclusion strategies; see Polanyi 1944 and Campbell and Lindberg 1990 on how the state manipulates property rights in order to shape the economy).

The imposition of property rights changes by legislators, bureaucrats, political coalitions, ideologues, and pressure groups has frequently entailed conflict with the prevailing informal rules, often with adverse consequences for less empowered individuals (Pejovich 2001; Platteau 2000). This has raised concerns regarding the efficacy and legitimacy of top-down institutional change, but it is worth noting that endogenous change can also produce perverse effects. A valuable example of the latter case is the establishment of discretionary property rights, which threatens the efficiency of any form of governance and restrains the implementation of a rights based approach to development.

Discretionary Property Rights and Rights

The principle of universality embodied in the rights-based approach is restricted in practice when discretionary property rights are established, due either to scarcity of resources or to political decisions. In the Peruvian rural scenario the sources for discretionary property rights emerge from above, but also from below. Since the Land Reform in 1969, legislators and ruling political groups have defined and reinforced the adoption of communal ownership of natural and physical capital from above. This discretionary system has a geographic focus, because the communal regime is mainly reinforced in Sierra (highlands) peasant communities. That long-term determination reflects the understanding among some policymakers and development practitioners that "peasants" in the Sierra are intractably communitarian, reflecting the romantic discourse around peasant communities (Gonzales de Olarte 2004). Communitarian forms of property rights have also been justified for the sake of reducing transaction costs: given the current tendencies to partition and disperse land, shifts toward individual ownership would be economically unaffordable and would eventually produce conflict. While these concerns are fairly understandable, it is also true that with newly available technology for land demarcation, there is no strong justification for maintaining a dual regime between coastal and highland communities.

From below, sources for discretion in property rights are found in the communities themselves. Communal lands and other resources have been redistributed to community members following uncoordinated processes of property rights redefinition, via arrangements framed by ad hoc communal forms of governance and encompassing the community members' demands for private ownership. These internal arrangements, however, are far from a universal recognition that all members have the right to access communal resources in the same way. The institutional arrangements—the social contracts—underlying changes in access to property have responded to the imperative of improved economic efficiency in the management of resources, but they also reflect the communities' internal politics. For instance, while in some communities an equal extension of land was redistributed to each household, in others discretionary changes have simply legitimated successive appropriations by well-endowed members to the detriment of the less advantaged, in terms of either assets or bargaining capacity. The situation of women in these processes of redefinition deserves particular attention, as women's real access to land is often highly constrained, a situation accepted as natural inside peasant communities. While under customary norms individual property rights over land are guaranteed to all qualified members and there is no gender restriction on eligibility, in practice men, as household heads, attain the actual access to resources (see Cleaver, Chapter 8; Drinkwater, Chapter 9).

These issues have barely been addressed by development organizations, which have been inconsistent in their approaches to peasant communities. NGOs and state programs of bilateral cooperation have repeatedly fostered communal ownership and governance at the same time as advocating universal access to assets for all community members; an example of this is the work done to include women in the community membership registry. However, the same organizations have implemented programs and projects susceptible to private ownership, and recently some are reorienting their vision to developing market economies, without much attention to the potential impacts on communal forms of governance, either positive or negative.

Although communal property rights are still advocated by development practitioners, politicians, and academics, it is hard to deny the fragility of communal arrangements in economic and political contexts where privatized property rights are dominant. While the modern sectors of the economy are ruled by private property rights and titling, customary

forms of common-pool and private possession have little or no connection with any other section of the governance system at local, regional, or
national scales. Consequently, there are no legal means by which communal forms of governance can generate secure property ownership
either for individuals alone or for specific communal groups. In such
circumstances and given imperfect or absent markets, enforcement
mechanisms within communal territories must rely on collective understanding and on the deployment of onerous individual efforts to get
acquired rights respected, frequently by means of costly negotiation.

The implications of discretionary property rights are several. First, if
we accept the fact that peasants are already part of a market economy—
no matter how imperfect the terms of this incorporation—then it is
clear that communal ownership for Sierra communities ruled from
above creates uneven conditions for peasant households to enter and
compete in local, regional, and national economies. This places the
Sierra peasants at a disadvantage relative to other (rural and urban)
producers, whose private regime over capital assets enables them to
participate in markets more easily. For instance, nonpeasant producers
who are able to exchange and buy land within their own producers'
association have been able to increase their scale of production and
thus improve their opportunities to compete. Second, adverse conditions are reproduced inside communities, where processes of land
exchange and concentration must pass through nonmarket mechanisms that are susceptible to manipulation at the time of negotiation
and that result in insecure agreements afterwards. For instance, peasants' agreements on land distribution are registered only in the Community Association minutes book. Finally, discretionary property rights
divide local societies into groups (e.g., "the peasants" versus "the small
holders") according to how they access assets or relate to state agents or
NGOs in determining such access.

Conclusion: Implications of Privatized Property Rights for Community-Based Governance

In practice, multiple forms of property rights tend to coexist wherever
and whenever hybrid modes of governance are in place. In the Andes, the
mixture of formal communal property and informal private property
regimes—ruled by a combination of formal law, customary communal
norms, and quasi-market regulation—has influenced the governance
forms implemented in each community. This has produced a regime that
combines communal institutions that oversee community affairs—
notably the modes of allocation of natural and physical capital, and the

establishment of community members' social and economic rights and duties—with state institutions that administer both natural resource allocation and individuals' human and political rights.

According to the theory of property rights, private property assures management efficiency when population density and market integration have increased enough to make natural resources a scarce asset. Privatization is then undertaken on the grounds that individualization will foster growth while also minimizing internal governance costs (Lewis 1955; Demsetz 1967; Platteau 2000). Such change to property rights regimes may also involve the redefinition of governance regimes toward decentralized modes (Ostrom 1990). However, in order to take into account particular contexts, cultures, and technologies, to avoid undesirable effects of unfair redistribution and loss of social capital, and to produce the conditions for sustainable change, community-based solutions accompanied by selective government intervention should also be observed (Platteau 2000). These challenges suggest that the efficiency of community-based property rights and governance regimes as a basis for the rights-based approach to development is, at least, debatable.

On the grounds of the evidence presented here, it can be said that in addition to the failures associated with market and state governance, community governance is not free of problems itself. Indeed, community-based solutions can be excessively time-consuming and less efficient than is often assumed by development agencies. If there is concern that an alternative market-based regime will negatively impact traditional rural societies (i.e., the potential loss of social capital raised by Platteau), it should noted that, in the Andes, the main purpose of membership and conservancy within peasant communities to protect access to natural capital. In that context, fostering the creation and strengthening of social capital based on communal ownership can be destructive when change is promoted from inside by emergent groups of peasants. Although communal ownership may ensure secure tenure for some community members—and in that sense gives support for maintaining current livelihoods—it does not by itself provide a reliable base from which to promote livelihoods change at the level of either individuals or the community. The state has a crucial role in complementing whatever is advanced through communal governance, whether by backing up community institutions legally or by modifying its own institutional structure governing the property rights. Both of these state contributions could certainly help to accelerate and improve opportunities for peasants to participate in market-based processes of change.

Livelihood strategies in the rural Andes are presently so diverse in terms of sectoral and geographic coverage that a single definition of what a peasant community is, and how it relates to the broader society, is challenging. The survival of peasant communities in the Andes can be largely explained by the fact that individuals need to reinforce a communal property rights regime to secure their access to resources. Appropriate and legal tenure security is an evident stepping stone for a rural highland population that needs to establish themselves as citizens with the same rights of those in rural coastal areas or in the rest of the national territory. By this means, individualized property rights can be reconceived in more flexible ways that combine the need for private property over land, communal infrastructure, and the equipment to develop market rural economies with the aspiration of conserving basic elements of a communal life. Hence, the fear among communitarian advocates that the privatization of natural and physical capital will erase peasant communities from the rural landscape should be alleviated. Instead, given other elements of common identity among peasants, one could expect that clearer, more formal property rights will enhance their opportunities inside and outside rural areas to improve their position in the broader economy and society by means of a more efficient use of resources and the enlargement of the social networks that their livelihoods strategies may require. As Arthur Lewis (1955) stated a long time ago, since capital is the scarcest factor in rural environments, secure access to land and free mobility of land and labor is essential for survival and growth.

Well-defined property rights entail more than the classical liberal idea of private ownership. They ought to be interpreted as an indicator of the efficiency of a governance regime that facilitates the change of livelihood strategies. It should also be taken as an unavoidable condition for reducing disparities in access to assets and for countering the factors that underlie such disparities. Transparency on the definition of property rights would also help to clarify the implications of the rights-based approach to development. Analytically, the incorporation of property rights into the livelihoods approach can improve its ability to represent the constraints and opportunities that households face in changing their livelihood strategies. At the same time, the livelihoods approach can be a useful analytical tool to operationalize some of the concepts developed by the property rights school and in the rights-based approach more broadly. Further research could also usefully explore the potential for understanding human capital and intellectual property in terms of rights.

References

Barbier, E. B. 2004. Agricultural expansion, resource booms and growth in Latin America: Implications for long-run economic development. *World Development* 32, no. 1:137–157.

Bebbington, A. 1999. Capitals and capabilities: A framework for analyzing peasant viability, rural livelihoods and poverty. *World Development* 27, no. 12:2021–2044.

Bebbington, A. 2004. Livelihood transitions, place transformations: Grounding globalization and modernity. In *Latin America transformed: Globalization and modernity*, edited by R. N. Gwynne and C. Kay, 173–192. London: Edward Arnold.

Carney, D. 2003. *Sustainable livelihoods distance learning guide.* Brighton: Institute of Development Studies.

Campbell J. and L. Lindberg. 1990. Property rights and the organization of economic activity by the state. *American Sociological Review* 55, no. 5:634–647.

Cavassa A. and E. Mesclier. 2007. Actividades agropecuarias en el campo peruano: ¿Reforzamiento duradero o punto de quiebre? Lima: Mimeo.

CESR [Center for Economic and Social Rights]. 2007. CESR letter to the editor of *The Economist*. April 2nd. http://cesr.org/node/772.

Coase, R. 1960. The problem of social cost. *Journal of Law and Economics* 3, no. 1:1–44.

De Soto, H. 2000. *The mystery of capital: Why capitalism triumphs in the west and fails everywhere else.* New York: Basic Books.

Demsetz, H. 1967. Toward a theory of property rights. *American Economic Review* no. 57 (Papers & Proceedings):347–359.

DFID [UK Department for International Development]. 1998. *Sustainable rural livelihoods. What contributions can we make?* London: DFID.

Ellis, F. 2000. *Rural livelihoods and diversity in developing countries.* Oxford: Oxford University Press.

Fisher, I. 1923. *Elementary principles of economics.* New York: Macmillan.

Gonzales de Olarte, E. 1994. *En las fronteras del mercado, economía política del campesinado en el Perú.* Lima: Instituto de Estudios Peruanos.

Hardin, G. 1968. The tragedy of the commons. *Science* 162:1243–1248.

Hinojosa, L. 2006. *Livelihoods, markets and economic development in the Southern Peruvian Andes.* PhD Thesis. University of Manchester.

INEI [Instituto Nacional de Estadística e Informática]. 1994. *III Censo Nacional Agropecuario* (CENAGRO). Lima: INEI.

Jochnick C. and M. Green. 1998. *Economic and social rights violations in Peru.* Presentation before the Inter-American Commission for

Human Rights (2/24/98). Center for Economic and Social Rights. http://cesr.org/peru.

Knack, S. and P. Keefer. 1995. Institutions and economic performance: Cross-country test using alternative institutional methods. *Economics and Politics* 7, no. 3:207–227.

Lewis, W. A. 1955. *The theory of economic growth.* London: George Allen & Unwin.

McCay, B. J. 1996. Common and private concerns. In *Rights to nature. Ecological, economic, cultural and political principles of institutions for the environment,* edited by S. Hanna, C. Folke and K-G. Maler, 111–126. Washington DC: Island Press.

North, D. C. 1981. *Structure and change in economic history.* New York: Norton.

North, D. C. 1990. *Institutions, institutional change and economic performance.* Cambridge: Cambridge University Press.

North, D. C. and R. P. Thomas. 1973. *The rise of the western world: A new economic history.* Cambridge: Cambridge University Press.

Ostrom, E. 1990. *Governing the commons: The evolution of institutions for collective action.* Cambridge: Cambridge University Press.

Payne, G., 1997. *Urban land tenure and property rights in developing countries: A review.* London: Intermediate Technology Publications.

Payne, G., ed. 2002. *Land, rights and innovation: Improving tenure security for the urban poor.* London: ITDG Publishing.

Pejovich, S. 2001. Property rights: Definition and economic significance. Introduction to Chapters 2, 3, 4 and 5 in *The economic foundations of property rights: Selected readings,* edited by S. Pejovich, 3–6. Northampton: Edward Elgar.

Platteau, J-P. 2000. *Institutions, social norms, and economic development.* Amsterdam: Harwood Academic Publishers.

Polanyi, Karl. 1944. *The great transformation: The political and economic origins of our time.* Boston: Beacon Press.

Reardon, T., J. Berdegue and G. Escobar. 2001. Rural nonfarm employment and incomes in Latin America: Overview and policy implications. *World Development* 29, no. 3: 395–409.

Rodrik, D. 1999. Institutions for high-quality growth: What they are and how to acquire them. IMF Conference on Second Generation Reforms, Washington, DC.

Scoones, I. 1998. Sustainable rural livelihoods: A framework for analysis. IDS Working Paper no. 72. Sussex: Institute of Development Studies.

Smith H. 2002. Exclusion versus governance: Two strategies for delineating property rights. *Journal of Legal Studies* XXXI: 453–487.

Wenner, M. D., J. Alvarado and F. Galarza. 2003. *Promising practices in rural finance: Experiences from Latin America and the Carribean.* Lima: Centro Peruano de Estudios Sociales, Inter-American Development Bank and Academia de Centroamerica.

Wiener H., L. Hinojosa, W. Fernández and T. Steeb. 2003. *Análisis costo-beneficio de las prácticas de conservación de suelos en Cusco y Apurímac.* Cusco: Proyecto MASAL y Centro de Estudios Regionales Andinos Bartolomé de Las Casas.

World Bank. 2002. *World Development Report 2002: Building institutions for markets.* Washington DC: World Bank.

Zoomers, A. 1999. *Linking livelihood strategies to development: Experiences from the Bolivian Andes.* Amsterdam: Royal Tropical Institute and Centre for Latin American Research and Documentation.

Notes

1. I am thankful to Sam Hickey and Diana Mitlin for insightful comments and questions which have improved this chapter.

CHAPTER 7

Reinterpreting the Rights-Based Approach: A Grassroots Perspective on Rights and Development[1]

Sheela Patel and Diana Mitlin

Introduction

There is widespread agreement among development practitioners about the importance of recognizing the rights of low-income and otherwise disadvantaged citizens to development opportunities. However, there is less agreement about how such recognition can be achieved. The present chapter draws on the strategies and experiences of one grassroots network, Shack/Slum Dwellers International (SDI), to offer a perspective on the rights-based approach to development, and an elaboration of what it might mean for the lowest-income and most vulnerable urban dwellers.

Shack/Slum Dwellers International is a network of federations of landless and homeless people and their support NGOs; it works with low-income communities to secure access to land, services, and housing in southern towns and cities. The network is now active in more than fifteen countries in Africa, Asia, and Latin America. At the core of its activities are local savings schemes in which the overwhelming majority of members are women. These savings schemes provide an organizational platform for residents to explore and determine their development strategies to secure land tenure, basic services, housing, and local economic development. The empowerment of the poor is central to SDI's development activities.

Given this orientation it may be surprising that SDI affiliates have generally distanced themselves from the rights-based approach to development. Few groups have been as controversial in this regard as the National Slum Dwellers Federation and their support NGO, the Society for the Promotion of Area Resource Centres (SPARC), both of which refused to join the National Coalition for Housing Rights in India. However, there is a general reluctance within SDI to engage with rights-based approaches as currently defined by many international development assistance agencies, or to identify strongly with this perspective. This reluctance is expressed in SDI strategies and is rooted in the experiences of federation members, who are predominantly low-income women struggling to secure tenure and access to services. Why is there such a lack of interest among these women in associating with what is termed the "rights-based approach," when their focus is so clearly on realizing their rights? A central reason is their understanding of how power operates at the settlement and city levels, and hence of the strategies that are likely to be successful in furthering their interests. The premise within many "rights-based" interventions is that the development needs of such low-income women can be resolved by claiming recognition, rights, and entitlements from the state (Molyneux and Lazar 2003, 26–28). This premise is not borne out by the experiences of SDI groups. Their objections to the rights-based approach do not appear to be conceptual or ideological, but rather are structural and pragmatic. They know that to persuade the state to recognize rights, they must mobilize large numbers of people around solutions that work for them. Their experience suggests that for this to be effective they have to avoid antagonizing the state in ways that would increase their vulnerability to adverse state action, and must instead encourage the state to view their ideas positively.

At the same time, these SDI groups cannot ignore the rights-based approach. It influences the broader discourse in development and poverty reduction programming, including how problems are perceived and solutions developed. This affects the way in which development solutions are conceptualized and the frameworks and programs that donors fund. The SDI network is asked to report on activities using frameworks designed around the rights based-approach, regardless of its relevance to their strategies. Hence, for SDI and its affiliates, it is critical to debate the relation between the rights-based approach, the realization of rights, and pro-poor development strategies.

The present discussion begins, in the following section, with a summary of the key characteristics of the rights-based approach as they relate to the arguments explored within this chapter. The subsequent section describes the development strategies of SDI and discusses how affiliates use these strategies to further their interests and address their needs, including the recognition of their rights. The section then looks in greater depth at how SDI affiliates seek to make the relationship between low-income citizens and the state more advantageous to the poor. Three specific themes are considered in this regard: first, the issues of power, vulnerability, contestation, and compromise as they relate to pro-poor development activities; second, the importance of collective approaches in promoting the rights of the poor; and third, the nature of urban neighborhood development, and the approaches through which outcomes might be more favorable to the poor. A final section concludes.

Rights: Strategies to Engage the State

This section examines three themes that emerge from SDI's experience with the rights-based approach in relation to pro-poor politics and outcomes. The first of these themes is the relative effectiveness of confrontational and collaborative strategies, and their respective mechanisms of protest and negotiation, when used by citizens seeking a more responsive state. A second theme is the relative significance of collective and individual strategies in addressing the lack of development options for the urban poor. While the rights-based approach does not explicitly favor individual approaches over collective solutions, its location within the present neoliberal political and economic context means that, both theoretically and in practice, it tends to reinforce the trend toward individualism (Gledhill, Chapter 3). This is particularly true with respect to the provision of secure tenure and services, a major interest for the urban poor. The third theme is the current lack of effective urban development solutions that offer low-income residents routes into secure tenure and basic service installation. This lack of solutions means that, practically speaking, clear demands regarding rights can seldom be made on the state.

The first theme emerges because the rights-based approach relies heavily on legal processes in claiming and realizing specific laws and entitlements through engagement with the state (Introduction and Archer, Chapter 1 and Chapter 2). Kabeer (2002, 20), considering situations in which those seeking development are in extreme need, argues that "the formal guarantee of rights is likely to be irrelevant, since seeking redress for the violation of even the most basic of civil rights entails unaffordable costs." Moreover, disadvantaged groups—which lack the means to protect themselves if their protest is deemed unacceptable to political elites—are unlikely to make explicit complaints. The scale of prejudice and discrimination toward the poor is highlighted by Igoe's (2003, 878–879) discussion of the failure of Tanzanian pastoralists to gain land rights through legal means.

The tendency toward legal confrontation in the rights-based approach also entails potentially counterproductive methods. The approach often involves a media campaign presenting externally validated, professionally managed documentation to the world, and sometimes to some international agency that arbitrates the information and confronts the nation-state or other violator. A recent example is the campaign against low pay in farms and factories supplying products to supermarkets and clothing stores.[2] Campaigners use surveys, case studies, and objectively verifiable data to prove to the global arena that there have been rights violations documented by third party observers; they then seek to confront the violator on behalf of the victims. The global rights norms invoked here are invaluable, and form an important part of frameworks for promoting local change. Yet rights campaigns based on such norms maintain the position of the poor as perpetual victims, offering them only the roles of supplicant and beneficiary. These campaigns provoke deep frustration and resentment among local grassroots activists, whose roles and contributions are pushed to the periphery of the process.

This frustration is exacerbated by the reality that global actors, however committed to local injustices, cannot "afford" (literally) to remain in a local domain for long; support and media attention soon shift to another local transgression of global rights norms, and the global or national focus moves on. This leaves local actors to deal with the consequences of the campaign, which often include an angry violator whose shaming has made exchanges impossible.[3] The confrontational approach thus ignores the fact that, in the urban arena in particular, all local forces (good and bad) share the space of a city and must deal with each other if progress is to be achieved. Low-income residents, unlike many middle class and professional activists, have few options to avoid hostility.

The second theme concerns the potential conflicts between individual and group rights within the rights-based approach. The association of rights concepts with an emphasis on individualism is a longstanding concern (Ensor 2005; Nyamu-Musembi 2002). Nyamu-Musembi explores this issue in the context of women's rights within certain cultures, focusing on the multiple individual and collective identities that many people, particularly women, hold. As she demonstrates, some rights are only advanced to a group of citizens in light of their collective identity, for example those offered to a group because of their ethnicity or historical experience (e.g., in developing indigenous medicines). Yet for some women, individual and collective needs intertwine; both need to be recognized, and a reconciliation between the two sought, through activities and actions (Nyamu-Musembi 2002, 7–9). This has been true for the women living on the pavements of Mumbai and seeking improved shelter. Collective action has been important in their efforts for multiple reasons. First, it is through their collective identity based around their organizing groups (savings schemes) that low-income women maintain the personal strength to challenge the state and seek the redefinition of their relationship with government. Second, it is the scale of their collective identity that engenders state interest in negotiation. Third, as assets and rights are secured, the collective protects such gains. Ensor (2005, 254–256) argues that the rights-based approach can address such collective dimensions of empowerment, while acknowledging that many rights-based initiatives have not sought to engage with their importance.

The importance of the collective also has relevance for the third theme: the need to develop new programmatic responses to the crises of urban poverty that go beyond simply claiming the right to this or that resource or status, and that create very different kinds of solutions that are more effective in addressing needs. Mageli (2004) reports that the tensions that emerged in the National Campaign for Housing Rights in India, and that campaign's eventual demise, can be partly explained by its failure to deliver tangible benefits to the grassroots groups involved as professional lobbying of parliament failed to produce housing gains (Mageli 2004, 135). One of the problems facing the state was that although housing programs were in place, they frequently did not reach their target groups. As Smets (2002) has described for India, housing programs have allocated benefits in accordance with the political interests of the powerful, rather than reaching groups in need. It was difficult for decisive numbers of politicians and officials to support scaling up housing programs given the evidence of their ineffectiveness. While rights approaches frequently focus on "the interactions between people's 'voice' and the institutional structures that enable their priorities, views and perspectives to be translated into real outcomes" (Moser and Norton 2001, 21), sometimes more than simply the people's voice is needed. Addressing poverty and disadvantage may require new programmatic responses that offer opportunities for the state to implement resource redistribution and service delivery at scale.

This section has raised a number of concerns regarding the rights-based approach as it relates to pro-poor development, particularly its tendencies to favor confrontation over negotiation, to privilege individual rights over collective capabilities and identities, and to make claims without analyzing how needs might best be met. The following section takes up these concerns in the context of Shack/Slum Dwellers International. It describes the strategies of SDI as it seeks new development options for the lowest-income urban residents, and explores the relationship of these strategies to the rights-based approach.

Shack/Slum Dwellers International

SDI was formed in 1996, following five years of exchanges between Indian and South African federations and the emergence of other federations with support NGOs. Many other groups have since reproduced this federation model, and the network now has mature affiliates in the Philippines, Thailand, Nepal, Sri Lanka, Namibia, and Zimbabwe, with emerging federations in Uganda, Tanzania, Malawi, Zambia, and elsewhere.

SDI creates and supports nationwide organizations capable of structuring activism around housing, infrastructure, and citizenship rights in urban areas. The process produces a critical mass of community members able to identify their priority issues, fight evictions, and negotiate solutions. As a result, the urban poor do not simply make demands on the state but seek to create a dialog and then an understanding of what is required, leading to associated agreements with the city and national state authorities about who needs to do what to produce scalable and lasting pro-poor urban development solutions. This people-driven development process reflects the belief among SDI federations that previous development efforts have failed the urban poor because the poor have not had input in shaping state interventions, and that the movement's political objectives can therefore be realized only through the incorporation of poor people's "tried and tested" development strategies into negotiations (Appadurai 2004).

SDI promotes this people-driven approach through mutually supporting strategic activities. Savings groups are foundational here, in that they strengthen self-reliance and organizational skill among members and thus promote a strong local movement with accountable leaders that represent members' interests. Established savings groups consolidate and transform their work by federating, and the federations seek the redistribution of resources by the state in ways that address the needs of their members and strengthen their capacity to negotiate for more.

For most government agencies, accepting the idea that effective solutions may come from and work for the poor is a huge step. Therefore, rather than contesting practices that do not work, federations attempt to secure support from the state by persuading it to review alternative options (SDI 2006; Mitlin 2007). The federation groups call this "precedent setting": collectivities of the urban poor develop innovative strategies to address the need for land, infrastructure, and services, and demonstrate the efficacy of these alternatives, thereby setting clear "precedents" for others to follow.

SDI's strategy and methodology is founded on the capacity of organizations of the poor not only to negotiate their entitlements with local, state, and national authorities, but also to remain involved in implementing the solutions agreed upon. As their organizational capacities have developed, communities of the poor have chosen to play a central role in the planning and delivery of services for the poor, rather than leaving them under the exclusive domain of the state. Both practical and strategic reasoning underlie this preference. On a practical level, the collectives of women's savings schemes are skeptical that the state will deliver the services they need. For example, the traditional approach in India to sanitation in slum-designated areas was for municipalities to design, construct, and maintain public facilities with no community participation. These facilities typically became unusable very quickly due to a lack of maintenance. The model proposed by Mahila Milan, an Indian network of women's collectives affiliated with SDI, has the municipality providing land, capital costs, and water and electrical connections, and NGOs and community-based organizations providing design, construction, and maintenance. This is now implemented in Mumbai and Pune (Burra, Patel and Kerr 2003).

On a strategic level, SDI's experience is that securing and maintaining rights requires the strengthening of organized communities of the poor so they are able to negotiate with state machinery. Communities must be organized to survive evictions and demolitions while putting positive pressure on the state and demonstrating solutions that work for both government and the poor, until the state concedes and enacts protective legislation and legal entitlements. This requires that communities negotiate from a position of autonomy, resisting frequent attempts by local politicians to co-opt and control the process.[4] Equally, it requires that communities use a democratic process to identify preferred strategies and priorities, thereby ensuring that actions have the support of large numbers of members.

The SDI vision for development clearly shares some characteristics with the rights-based approach. SDI aspires to be people-centered, empowering, and redistributive, and to secure pro-poor attitudinal change and regulatory, legal, and procedural reform. Nevertheless, the movement has been wary of aligning with the rights-based approach for fear of its implications. For example, following evictions, the activist-oriented "protest mode" might hit the headlines and provoke mass demonstrations—but what happens afterwards? What concrete alternatives are offered, and what strategies are employed to reorient the state? What proactive steps are taken to change the way things work? How is the genuine anger of people channeled into something more constructive? Our discussion now explores SDI alternatives in these areas.

Rights, Vulnerability and Contestation

The immediate social relations of the urban poor and the location of their (often informal) settlements frequently isolate them from the formal institutions of law and security. Partly for these reasons, federation groups have found that pro-poor laws are often not enforced. Kabeer relates the emergence of a focus on rights in the North to the transformation of social relations in the European states at the time of industrialization—a transformation including a reduced significance of kinship and the increasing mediation of relations through the market. Yet she argues that this transformation happened imperfectly in the South, and that attempts to introduce formal rights there have thus occurred alongside more traditional social relationships. "The highly partial, incomplete and fragmented notions of citizenship which result," she concludes, "often serve to reproduce, rather than disrupt, the socially ascribed statuses of kinship, religion, ethnicity, race, caste, gender and so on in the public domain" (2002, 17–18).

Kabeer's conclusion is broadly in keeping with the federations' analysis of their situation. Vulnerability is a characteristic of poverty, and it is this vulnerability that makes it difficult for the urban poor to press for the implementation of laws that are supposed to protect them (see, e.g., the diverse sources of violence against low-income urban communities reported in Moser 2004). As Cleaver notes (Chapter 8), the capacity of people to claim legal rights depends on the level of agency available to them as they negotiate complex social relations and structures that circumscribe their potential. For example, Agarwal notes that although the Indian Constitution makes provision to protect children from forced or hazardous work, such child labor remains widespread (2003, 247). Similarly, as Roy observes in explaining the lack of tenure and services in informal settlements in Calcutta (2004, 160–163), the gendered relationships that predominate within households are reflected in the leadership of local organizations and the outcomes of clientelist engagement with local politicians and authorities; as a result, changes that would improve women's lives are not secured. Moreover, while rights do exist for those living on the pavements and in informal settlements in Indian cities, differences between policies at the city, state, and federal levels create ambiguities and further reasons for nonenforcement and harassment (Burra 2005). Such factors combine to make those living in informal settlements vulnerable to the partial and discriminatory application of law and entitlement. As a result, residents—particularly women—are reluctant to enter into direct dispute with the authorities.

This reluctance to engage in confrontational contestation emerged early in the life of SDI, as a direct result of the central involvement of women. In India, the grassroots organizations affiliated with SDI are divided into the National Slum Dwellers Federation (NSDF) and Mahila Milan. The former is a network of community organizations that was mainly male-dominated when the partnership was initiated in 1986, but which now has 50 percent female leadership; the latter is a network of women's savings collectives. The NSDF was accustomed to the strategies of the rights-based approach, including vocal and public protest on the streets and pressure for legal reform, but its male leadership had come to recognize that their movement was not progressing beyond marches and demonstrations. The leadership observed that men were generally comfortable with fighting aggressively against eviction and wrongdoing by the state, whereas women—while they passionately sought security of tenure and basic amenities—felt less compelled by confrontational strategies. When women participated it was only passively, because they were asked to support the strategies of their male leadership. These observations brought about a strategic change within the NSDF, accelerated during the 1990s by growing challenges to male dominance of the partnership from Mahila Milan's increasingly confident female leaders.

In 1985, Bombay's city government threatened to demolish pavement dwellings after a petition concerning the right of abode of pavement dwellers was lost in the Supreme Court (Olga Tellis versus the Union of India, 1985). The impulse of NGOs and youth groups in the city was to fight street battles in defense of the rights of pavement dwellers to reside there. SPARC, the NSDF's support NGO, asked women living on pavements in the Byculla area and members of Mahila Milan what they wanted to do. The women replied: "We don't want to fight and we don't want to stay on the pavements either! Go and speak to the municipality and to the state government and see if you can explain to them our situation." Mahila Milan and the NSDF began to work on their rehousing strategy, and in 1995—as a result of many years of pavement enumerations, precedent-setting shelter projects, and related lobbying—were able to ensure that pavement dwellers were included in the groups of slum dwellers entitled to relocation under the Slum Rehabilitation Act. In 2003, a census of all pavement dwellers in the city was started, as part of a plan to relocate 23,000 households in collaboration with the Mumbai municipality and the Mumbai Metropolitan Regional Development Authority.

However, throughout this period the immediate problem of evictions continued. As pavement-dwelling women accepted the need to develop their own defensive strategies, they also began to think about alternatives to existing responses to eviction from their dwellings. Rather than confronting the police, they decided to outwit them. When the police next came, the women offered to take down their dwellings. They dismantled their shacks and neatly stacked their belongings and building materials on the pavement. This left only rubbish on the site where their shacks had stood, which they invited the police to take away. The police were willing to do this, as they could then go back and report that the dwellings had been dismantled. Once the police had left, the women replaced their dwellings. As a result, they kept their material possessions, they and their families were not traumatized by the experience, and the police began to see that they could negotiate with the poor. This showed the group that, when the poor are in a vulnerable position, a collective demonstration of strategic resistance is as powerful as confrontation, and more effective psychologically. Their slogan was *"todna tumhara kam, ghar bandhna hamara kaam"* ("it's your job to break our house, it's ours to rebuild it "): eviction attempts were a challenge to test tenacity.

As this example demonstrates, NSDF members have become very conscious that while the state can be outmaneuvered, they cannot defeat it: the more confrontational their position, the more they risk violence and other forms of repression. Moser and Norton recognize that rights-based approaches may result in short-term conflict, but suggest that this may secure positive outcomes in the long term (2001, 38). By contrast, NSDF and Mahila Milan women working out their strategies in mainly women-led grassroots organizations prefer to avoid such gambles; other southern analysts have similarly suggested that local groups differ from professional NGOs in their assessment of risks (Win 2004, 124). SDI members in India and elsewhere believe their proposals are more likely to be accepted if the state recognizes mutual advantage and if relations are friendly. They also recognize that city governments face many constraints in the present era of globalization. They therefore seek to persuade rather than to threaten, and the use of international exchanges in particular has been very effective in raising issues in a nonconfrontational way.

Related to this model of negotiation is the orientation of SDI affiliates toward positions offering strategic advancement in the longer term. The movement seeks ultimately to control the psychology of the space between citizen and state, so as to advance poor citizens' interests (Appadurai 2001). These strategies resonate with those discussed by Williams in his description of organized groups working to change state policies and actions so as to further the interests of the poor, with a focus on opening up "spaces of empowerment" at the grass roots due to a more supportive "political society" (2004, 100). Such groups seek a virtuous cycle in which grassroots action results in political gains that create stronger grassroots processes. Pal (2006), analyzing the lack of progress in improving metropolitan planning and decision making in Kolkata (Calcutta) as compared to equivalent efforts in Mumbai, highlights the critical importance of local political space in determining prospects for setting precedents and renegotiating state practices.

The Significance of the Collective

The local savings schemes and national federations that make up SDI create an institutional framework that develops a strong political consciousness among members. The groups practice dual strategies, negotiating to secure resources and policy change from the state, while simultaneously promoting community self-reliance. The latter strategy is undertaken both to maintain the groups' autonomy as people's organizations and to enhance their political efficacy.

The savings schemes and federations recognize that priorities are set through political processes rather than managerial or technical capacities, and that therefore—in democratically stable situations—state institutions and other influential actors consent to negotiations only once the local critical mass of the poor persistently and visibly demands them. For this reason, SDI processes are designed to build an internal consensus within the savings schemes and federations as to what are the priorities and "nonnegotiables" in a given dialog between the urban poor and the state. Groups then engage in the dialog and associated negotiations, using externally validated demonstrations to legitimate their claims. These demonstrations may involve exemplar projects that illustrate new processes the state might follow, or they may involve mass events such as life-size model house exhibitions. The organized collective is thus doubly valuable, in that it offers protection for vulnerable individuals but also confers the level of political capital necessary for influencing the state.

However, the federations' recognition of the importance of the collective leads them to go beyond building the organizational consensus needed in negotiating for the redistribution of resources to the poor. In addition, the federations develop community mechanisms for basic service provision that further strengthen collective power while addressing material needs. Collective provision activities develop organizational capacity, thereby enabling groups of the organized poor to bring stronger negotiating ability to subsequent engagements with government. Such collective activities also promote community autonomy.

These goals rest on a model of citizens as engaged actors rather than passive recipients, in which their interests are safeguarded by their own collective capacity rather than by professional legal structures and systems. The enactment of rights that individualize citizens in their relationship to the state may provide short-term benefits, but, in the federations' experience, do little in the long term to address structural inequalities and associated vulnerabilities. For example, the collective is essential in ensuring that the distribution of land to the homeless is completed under terms and conditions that enable the poor to remain on the land they have secured, and that future increases in land taxes and service charges do not force them to sell. Hence federations negotiate for loan agreements and service contracts held by collective groups, which can both organize savings activities so as to aid repayments and support individual households facing repayment difficulties at any time. Likewise, granting the community control of subsidies and developing its capacity to manage finances and construction projects allows even the lowest-income households to participate in service provision—for example, by providing unskilled labor in federation-managed developments (Appadurai 2001; Patel, d'Cruz and Burra 2002; Burra 2005).

The experience of SDI suggests that the ways in which urban poverty solutions are defined and implemented reflect the nature of the process from which they emerge. More specifically, the rights-based approach, with its legal associations, takes the poor firmly into the terrain of professionals and elites, and this terrain influences the solutions that emerge. The formality of the rights-based approach favors those who are able to enter into and articulate within professional discussions, to the disadvantage of the poor. There is a real danger that this formality undermines the strengthening of local organizational capacity, shifting momentum away from mass organizations of the urban poor and toward professional lobbying.

From Claim-Making to Negotiating Alternatives

The interest in developing new, more pro-poor urban development strategies that drives the federation groups' engagement with the state emerges, in part, from frustrations with the development model of the rights-based approach, in which the legal formalization of entitlements impels state-operated service provision. Government is generally involved in development primarily as a resource provider, and may also be involved in reforming the rules and regulations that govern development. In many southern towns and cities, including those in which SDI groups are active, the state has engaged in a process of selling assets and shifting service provision to a cost recovery basis, sometimes with the involvement of the private sector (regarding services, see von Wiezsäcker, Young and Finger 2005). These measures reflect neoliberal pressures for the management of state services and the reduction and reorganization of state budgets. There has been state interest in contracting civil society organizations as service providers, but such plans generally give the organizations little involvement in program design.

Federation groups and their support NGOs are frustrated with these processes, and seek alternative approaches that offer greater development benefits for their members. Pilot "precedent-setting" projects undertaken by SDI affiliates help to define exactly what role the state needs to play. For example, the federation in Namibia has been active in changing the policy of several local authorities so as to enable community groups to install on-site communal infrastructure and increase residential densities, thereby lowering the costs of secure tenure and basic services (Mitlin and Muller 2004). In Walvis Bay, municipal engineering staff have offered technical support to some of these community groups, helping to reduce costs further and build community confidence. The engagement with municipal staff has opened up new possibilities in the search for municipal land for savings scheme members.

A rights-based approach might work for a relatively straightforward claim that involves a simple transfer of financial resources, but its applicability is less evident when there are multiple and complex needs with no solutions that can be implemented using existing resources. The federation groups installing infrastructure face financial, technical, and organizational challenges, and collaboration with the state helps build the political capital groups need to attract flexible and ongoing support. The groups require more than an engineer being sent to their site; they require an engineer who is interested in what they are trying to do, who has the patience to explain the regulatory requirements, who can help to develop cost-saving innovations, who does not mind when they make mistakes, and who is willing to work late. In the experience of federation groups, the capacity to negotiate for this kind of assistance is more important than being able to force through a requirement that there should be a legal right to housing.

A further reason why the federations are interested in reconceptualizing solutions to development is that the legal strategies within the rights-based approach are highly professionalized and formalized. The federations feel that the formal legal approach often fails to address the realities of people's lives. While formal agreements between communities, support NGOs, and municipalities arise regularly among SDI affiliates, most believe that such formalization follows rather than precedes pro-poor change. There is also a concern that the professional/legal discourse itself excludes the poor. Exclusion reduces confidence, and this increases the disengagement of the poor from the processes being considered. SDI affiliates seek a social process for development that avoids this danger.

Critical Concerns

The aim of SDI affiliates is to use exchanges with the state to build experiential learning and local knowledge that help affiliates determine the effectiveness of particular strategies and alliances. The design of SDI processes aims to ensure that such knowledge becomes embedded within institutions of the urban poor, who are constantly restrategizing to advance their interests. In a study of the SDI affiliate in India, McFarland is broadly supportive of the strategy of the Indian Alliance between the NSDF, Mahila Milan, and the support NGO SPARC: he suggests that it constitutes "a more plausible general approach for poverty alleviation than the more oppositional approaches of some other NGOs in the city." However, he notes that some other NGOs criticize SPARC for its uncritical stance toward certain government policies (2004, 908–910).

Similarly, Molyneux and Lazar suggest that too close an engagement with the state might result in civil society losing its distinctive character; they conclude that "rights-based work has, for these reasons, renewed calls for NGOs to take a more independent stance from government" (2003, 84–85). In both India and South Africa, SDI has received criticism for its strategy toward the state, including allegations that affiliates are supporting the withdrawal of the state and the shift toward the free market, or otherwise working within neoliberal policies. For example, it has been suggested that the South African federation's emphasis on self-help has been "diverting attention from traditional movement demands that the state increase its commitment to solving social problems" (Bond 1996, 3). More recently, Kahn and Pieterse (2004, 168–173) have suggested that while the South African SDI affiliates have sought to avoid predefined political "boxes" and to negotiate for new opportunities, the consequences may be to enable the state to shift shelter responsibilities onto low-income groups.

SDI affiliates do not believe that their position favors the withdrawal of the state and the shift toward a free market. Rather, they urge the renegotiation of roles and responsibilities between the state and civil society, so that the state accepts its responsibilities and fulfills its obligations. SDI affiliates recognize that the state has little or no capacity to take control of the development strategies that the federation groups require. This is not simply a matter of insufficient resources: the complex layers of informality that make up the life of the urban poor are not easily managed by state bureaucracy. In Mumbai, the state agreed to resettle families living along the railway tracks, enabling the trains to go faster and the transport system to be more efficient (Burra 2005). But the state needed a process to establish individual household entitlements. Existing state processes are subject to corruption, claims, and counter-claims. Believing resettlement to be unmanageable, some politicians and bureaucrats argued for, and then initiated, eviction. However, after discussions with the government (and a legal challenge to the eviction), the NSDF set up community teams to survey each household and verify entitlements. The local communities and national leaders developed a capacity to resolve claims swiftly and fairly as each of the 30,000 families in the designated area were surveyed and enumerated. What drew the state and community together was a recognition of mutual need.

Conclusion

The women leaders in Mahila Milan know from experience that the state rarely acts in the interests of the poor, but that if what the poor want is also good for the larger city, then the solution becomes attractive. Rather than antagonizing politicians and officials, SDI affiliates aim to establish a commonality of interest to further their strategic needs. Negotiations and collaboration are believed to be more effective strategies than more confrontational contestation. They engage both the state and pro-poor actors in the exploration of new policies and the consideration of their legislative implications.

The experience of SDI is that simply claiming a "right to housing"— even when this right is then recognized—does not provide a practical solution for the poor. Most poor citizens do not receive benefits because supply is limited, and some of those who do may sell the house at the first crisis they face. Rather, the experience of SDI affiliates is that they must develop alternatives, build relationships, and then negotiate within those relationships. The process of negotiation must itself build the skills and confidence of the community to negotiate further. New solutions need to be developed and then implemented at scale for multiple aspects of housing provision, including access to appropriate land locations, the development of commercial areas, the formulation of building and infrastructure standards, community involvement in infrastructure installation, and the ability of communities to sell off some land plots for cross-subsidization.

Thus a discussion that started out as a pragmatic critique of the feasibility of the rights-based approach has resolved itself into a challenge to a Northern model of urban development, in which the market provides housing to those able to afford it, while the state meets the needs of the poor and sets the spatial and financial framework within which infrastructure is provided. Molyneux and Lazar argue that the problem with achieving rights-based development is not a lack of resources but a lack of political will (2003, 29). The experience of SDI affiliates suggests that much more than just political will is required. Groups of the poor might choose to be more strategic in their approaches, recognizing that claim-making alone may not result in a desired change.

Such considerations go to the heart of the relationship between citizens and the state, and between civil society and the state. Advocates of the rights-based approach argue that the role of civil society should be to challenge and critique the state, rather than to actually provide for people's rights through the direct provision of services. The experiences of SDI affiliates and others suggest that this position draws a false dichotomy between empowerment and political engagement on the one hand, and service provision on the other. This dichotomy may be particularly misguided when applied to the strategies of grassroots organizations in promoting pro-poor development. A much more open debate about what works for the poor, and why, is required before reaching conclusions on such strategies.

References

Agarwal, A. 2003. Child labour—A threat to the survival of civilization. In *Law and poverty: The legal system and poverty reduction,* edited by L. A. Williams, A. Kjønstad and P. Robson, 247–268. London and New York: CROP International Studies in Poverty Reduction and Zed Books.

Appadurai, A. 2001. Deep democracy: Urban governmentality and the horizon of politics. *Environment and Urbanization* 13, no. 2:23–43.

Appadurai, A. 2004. The capacity to aspire: Culture and the terms of recognition. In *Culture and public action: A cross-disciplinary dialog on development policy,* edited by V. Rao and M. Walton, 59–84. Stanford: Stanford University Press.

Bond, P. 1996. Confronting the ANC's Thatcherism. *Southern African Review* 11, no. 4:25–30. http://www.africafiles.org/article.asp?ID=3881.

Burra, S. 2005. Towards a pro-poor framework for slum upgrading in Mumbai, India. *Environment and Urbanization* 17, no. 1:67–88.

Burra, S., S. Patel and T. Kerr. 2003. Community-designed, built and managed toilet blocks in Indian cities. *Environment and Urbanization* 15, no. 2:11–32.

Ensor, J. 2005. Linking rights and culture—Implications for rights-based approaches. In *Reinventing Development? Translating rights-based approaches from theory into practice,* edited by P. Gready and J. Ensor, 254–277. London and New York, Zed Books

Moser, C. O. N., ed. 2004. Urban violence and insecurity. Special issue, *Environment and Urbanization* 16, no. 2.

Igoe, J. 2003. Scaling up civil society: Donor money, NGOs and the pastoralist land rights movement in Tanzania. *Development and Change* 34, no. 5:863–885.

Kabeer, N. 2002. Citizenship, affiliation and exclusion: Perspectives from the South. *IDS Bulletin* 33, no. 2:12–23.

Kahn, F. and E. Pieterse. 2004. The Homeless People's Alliance: Purposive creation and ambiguated realities. In *Voices of protest: Social movements in post-apartheid South Africa.* Durban: University of KwaZulu Natal Press.

Mageli, E. 2004. Housing mobilization in Calcutta—Empowerment for the masses or awareness for the few? *Environment and Urbanization* 16, no. 1:129–138.

Mahmud, S. 2003. Making rights real in Bangladesh through collective action. *IDS Bulletin* 33, no. 2:31–39.

McFarland, C. 2004. Geographical imaginations and spaces of political engagement: Examples from the Indian Alliance. *Antipode* 36, no. 5:890–916

Mitlin, D. and A. Muller. 2004. Windhoek, Namibia—Towards progressive urban land policies in Southern Africa. *International Development Policy Review* 26, 2:167–186.

Mitlin, D. 2007. The role of collective action and urban social movements in reducing chronic urban poverty. Chronic Poverty Research Centre Working Paper no. 64.

Molyneux, M. and S. Lazar. 2003. *Doing the rights thing: Rights-based development and Latin American NGOs.* London: ITDG Publishing.

Moser, C. and A. Norton with T. Conway, C. Ferguson and P. Vizard. 2001. *To claim our rights: Livelihood security, human rights and sustainable development.* London: Overseas Development Institute.

Nyamu-Musembi, C. 2002. Towards an actor-orientated perspective on human rights. IDS Working Paper no. 169.

Pal, A. 2006. Scope for bottom-up planning in Kolkata: Rhetoric vs. reality. *Environment and Urbanization* 18, no. 2:501–522.

Patel, S., C. d'Cruz and S. Burra. 2002. Beyond evictions in a global city: People-managed resettlement in Mumbai. *Environment and Urbanization* 14, no. 1:159–172.

Roy, A. 2004. The gentleman's city: Urban informality in the Calcutta of New Communism. In *Urban informality: Transnational perspectives from the Middle East, Latin America and South Asia,* edited by A. Roy and N. Alsayyad, 147–170. Lanham: Lexington Books.

SDI. 2006. *Izwe Lakithi.* Cape Town: SDI Secretariat.

Smets, P. 2002. *Housing finance and the urban poor: Building and financing low-income housing in Hyderabad, India.* Amsterdam: Vrije University.

Von Weizäcker, E.U., O.R. Young and M. Finger. 2005. *Limits to privatization: How to avoid too much of a good thing.* London: Earthscan Publications.

Williams, G. 2004. Towards a repoliticization of participatory development: Political capabilities and spaces for empowerment. In *Participation: From tyranny to transformation?,* edited by S. Hickey and G. Mohan, 92–108. London: Zed Books.

Win, E. 2004. "If it doesn't fit on the blue square it's out!" An open letter to my donor friend. In *Inclusive Aid: Changing power and relationships in international development,* edited by L. Groves and R. Hunter, 123–127. London: Earthscan Publications.

Notes

1. This chapter is written on the basis of internal reflections within SDI and its national federation affiliates, as articulated by the NGO scribes who assist them. This is one more contribution to articulating the position of SDI and sharing the views of its leadership in an international development debate.

2. See, for example, www.corporatewatch.org and www.waronwant.org; and Veigh, K., "Asda, Primark and Tesco accused over clothing factories," The Guardian, July 16th 2007.

3. This was the experience of SPARC in 2005 when the pavement dwellers in Mumbai experienced terrible demolitions, involving 90,000 households and provoking considerable international protest. The international NGO, Centre for Housing Rights and Evictions, named the State of Maharashtra as a Housing Rights Violator in their Housing Rights Award 2005. Archer (Chapter 2) acknowledges this problem and suggests that at least some human rights organizations have sought to amend their practice to avoid this situation.

4. Pal (2006) describes the difficulties of decentralized decision making and community involvement in Kolkata due to the inability of grassroots organizations to manage a political process dominated by existing political elites.

PART FOUR

From Voluntarism to Empowerment?

CHAPTER 8

Rethinking Agency, Rights, and Natural Resource Management

Frances Cleaver

Citizens, Rights, and Participatory Natural Resource Management

The relationship between individual citizens and collective action is central to understandings of rights and good governance. This chapter argues that this relationship is nonetheless inadequately understood. There is a need for more rigorous scrutiny of assumptions about citizens' agency and public participation, and of the ways in which individual agency is molded through inequitable social relationships.

The mainstreaming of a rights discourse in approaches to development has influenced thinking about the governance of natural resources. Participatory governance enacted through associations of collective action is seen as the preferred route for citizens to articulate rights to stewardship or use of natural resources. The strong emphasis in rights-based approaches on the potential of associations and participatory spaces as "schools of democracy" for the creation of active citizens (Cornwall 2004) is echoed in the focus in natural resource management on the importance of institutions through which people learn to cooperate, rights are claimed, and effective governance is pursued (Woodhouse 2002).

However, concerns about the efficacy of participatory institutions—about their capacity, power, representativeness, and inclusiveness (Cornwall 2004, Mehta 2005)—lead to a more critical consideration of *which* processes expand individual freedoms and rights, and *how* these processes are achieved through engagement in social relationships (De Herdt and Deneulin 2007). Optimistic expectations of the transformatory effects of enacting rights (Agarwal 2003) are questioned by those who see the claiming of rights as limited by the social positioning of individuals and their bounded capacity to make rights real (Jackson 2003).

The concept of individual agency—the ability of citizens to take action—is central to understanding rights but is often taken for granted rather than discursively analyzed (Englund 2004). The focus in rights-based approaches and natural resource management on individuals, taken as citizens and rights bearers with sufficient agency to make claimed rights real, tends to overlook the complicated relationships between situated personhood and social collectivities. In this chapter I argue that conceptualizations of agency as primarily manifested through public participation in decision making and collective action are unhelpfully narrow. The chapter synthesizes previous work of the author, and draws on a variety of theoretical positions, to outline ways of understanding agency in collective action as deeply relational and based in practice, not just in decision making. Agency so construed has complicating effects on the exercise of rights; we will see below, for example, how the imperatives of social location may cause people to choose not to exercise rights for fear of damaging their social and livelihood networks. This chapter addresses questions of how rights work out in practice—how they become "real" (Pettit and Wheeler 2005)—and deepens explanations of how the mainstreaming of rights-based approaches has failed to improve the position of many marginalized people (Mehta 2005).

This chapter evolved from thinking about the nature of individual and collective action for the management of communal resources (especially water), much of it informed by critical engagement with common property resource management (CPRM) theory. In CPRM theory individual participation in collective decision making institutions is assumed to positively influence rule making and resource distribution. Individuals are seen mainly as "resource appropriators" cleverly deploying social and cultural norms and positions to maximize their access to resources (Ostrom 2005). Concerns about inequality in decision making are not prominent in CPRM theory; such theories are largely concerned with the choices people make rather than with their ability to make those choices (Agrawal 2005). Similarly, equity of outcome is not a major concern, the emphasis being on the sustainable management of the natural resource. Nonetheless, institutions are thought to work best when all those affected by their rules are involved in decision making.

This last assumption dovetails neatly with the premise in rights-based approaches that freedom of citizens can only be achieved if they participate in the decisions that affect their lives. In development policy and practice, resource-managing institutions are increasingly seen as vehicles of local governance, as manifestations of community, and as the channels through which equity goals can be pursued. In the water sector, for example, local water user associations are thought to foster the instrumental involvement of users in management, and to facilitate the articulation of needs and the negotiation of claims to rights and resources. The concept of water governance is thus being widely applied, linking levels of analysis from the international to the individual, but there is relatively little understanding of *how* good water governance expands people's ability to claim their water rights at the local level (Franks and Cleaver 2007).

Recent "post-tyranny" thinking about participation holds that the micropolitics of participation must be linked to good governance more broadly and to the workings of the state. Indeed, the turn to a rights agenda can be seen as an attempt to respond to this need by repoliticizing the excessively instrumental approach to participation in development (Cornwall and Nyamu-Musembi 2005). The interest in post-tyranny thinking in contextualizing participation politically has produced a concern with promoting radical participatory forms of engagement, in which citizenship and the rights associated with it can be claimed from below (Hickey and Mohan 2004). While asserting that such participatory citizenship works best within the context of a wider societal project of social justice, the "post-tyranny" perspective also takes a very positive view of individual agency as comprising the range of sociopolitical practices through which people can increase control over resources and extend their status. Important to such post-tyranny thinking are concepts of "new spaces" and "new rules" for the promotion and articulation of empowering citizenship and rights (Cornwall 2004; Kesby 2005).

Theorizing the Individual in a Social World

In this chapter I draw on a range of theoretical insights to explore the numerous ways in which individual human agency is shaped and exercised with respect to collective resource management. In so doing I touch upon dilemmas posed by participatory and rights-based approaches to development: How are diverse individual and collective rights negotiated and balanced within social contexts? Within institutions for collective action, what is the relationship between hierarchy and interdependence, between autonomy and co-optation? Critically, how do we understand the balance between individual capacity for autonomous action and the essentially relational nature of exercising agency in the social world? And finally, what are the links between the capacity to exercise agency and the effects of that agency on the realizing of rights to natural resources? Although eclectic, the theoretical perspectives outlined here commonly emphasize the need to place understandings of agency in wider contexts, and to think beyond the assumption that agency equates to empowering action.

Enablement and Constraint

In social theory, agency is often seen as the capability to be the originator of acts, and is taken to be comprised of self consciousness, reflection, intention, purpose, and meaning (Rapport and Overing 2000). Yet agency is also conceptualized as relational: it does not exist in a vacuum, but is exercised in a social world in which structure shapes the opportunities and resources available to individuals—in which appropriate ways of being and behaving are not simply a matter of individual choice. While most social theorists embrace this duality, there are varying emphases on the balances between enablement and constraint, and between conscious and deliberative action and taken-for-granted practice.

Giddens (1984, 1996) and Long (1992) emphasize the variable outcomes resulting from the exercise of agency. They recognize the structural constraints within which agents operate, the unreflexive nature of much everyday practice, and the intended and unintended effects of action. However, they are largely optimistic about the possibilities of individual agency, assuming that the individual's exercise of reflexive agency and conscious deployment of various forms of capital can overcome societal constraints (Greener 2002). For Long agency, though constrained, is about the ability to choose levels of "enrollment" in the projects of others and to exert influence to enroll others in one's own project (1992, 22). Thus even the compromise of "partial enrollment" is seen as a strategic positioning of actors in response to conflicting priorities and critical events (Arce and Long 2000, 3). For Giddens (1996), agency centers on the ability of agents to respond to the challenges society throws at them, to confront and deal with risk.

By contrast, Bourdieu (1977) emphasizes how strongly agency is shaped by "habitus"—a set of dispositions that incline agents to act and react in different ways, which is itself shaped by hegemonic elites. For Bourdieu culture, social institutions, habit, and routine shape agency (Greener 2002). Assumptions underlying mainstream development discourse tend to adopt the optimistic approach to agency, emphasizing the instrumental and empowering effects of individual participation in claiming rights. This chapter tempers such optimism by exploring some of the interlinked constraints that limit the exercise of agency for many people.

Allocative and Authoritative Resources

The collective management of natural resources, favored in rights-based approaches to development, works by invoking various sources of authority and legitimation. In particular, it requires representative local institutions for resource management that are vested with authority in the name of the collectivity. Rights-based approaches further emphasize the importance of effective representation of citizens through democratic institutions (Gaventa and Jones 2002).

The individual exercise of agency within such management scenarios is therefore tied into relations of power and authority. Individuals effect action by deploying various sorts of resources; for Giddens, "resources are the media through which power is exercised" and are "drawn upon and reproduced by knowledgeable agents in the course of interaction" (1984, 15). Giddens distinguishes between the deployment of *allocative* resources (raw materials, means of production, produced goods) relating to command over *things,* and *authoritative* resources implying command over *people* (organization of social time and space, chances for self-development). Human agents make rules that structure the deployment of resources; the patterning of command over resources in turn shapes the actions of agents. Inequitable social relations ensure that some individuals, by virtue of their class, gender, ethnicity, and so on, are better placed than others to deploy resources, to shape rules, and to exercise power and rights.

This concept of "resources" as adapted to the collective management of natural resources encompasses general relationships of power, structures of inequality, "rules" of social life, and unequal levels of access to the physical resource in question. This leads us to ask: Who is able to access resources to the benefit or detriment of others? How are rights to natural resources articulated and affected through the deployment of allocative and authoritative resources?

Governance and Regimes of Practice

Recent writing on governmentality highlights the need to analyze the relations of power and authority implicated in the exercise of agency (Dean 1999, Agrawal 2005). For these writers, who draw heavily on Foucauldian notions of government as "the conduct of conduct," power is often exercised in everyday interactions through embodied "regimes of practice." Such regimes comprise layers of institutionalized practices— the routine and ritualized ways in which we do things in certain places and at certain times. "Governmentality" thus refers to the organized practices through which we are governed and through which we (consciously and unconsciously) govern ourselves. From this perspective participation can become a "technology of government," or potentially a strategy for channeling claims to rights, and the exercise of rights, through governance arrangements.

As one example of recent work along these lines, Agrawal's study (2005) of the collective governance of forest resources in India attempts to uncover how "the conduct of conduct" is taken for granted. He places individual agency in context by illustrating the linkages between the policies of decentralized local government, the emergence of new localized "regulatory communities" (village-level forest councils), and the transformation of how "environmental subjects" who participate in community decision making perceive and respond to the regulatory communities' claims on the forests.

Plurality

Agency is exercised in a variety of ways and in multiple arenas. The concept of governmentality implies that governance and self-governance involve multiple governing agencies and authorities and act on diverse aspects of behavior, and that the practices involved may invoke multiple norms, seek various purposes, and produce a range of effects (Dean 1999, 19). This plurality may further encompass pluralities of scale (as in Agrawal's study) and multiple arenas of overlapping networks within which interactions around governance and self-governance are formed.

The concept of plurality finds direct echoes in current thinking in natural resource management, and has relevance for both the opportunities and the constraints within which individuals may enact their rights. Taking the example of water, Merrey and colleagues (2006) identify three interrelated aspects of plurality: *polycentric governance* (a variety of actors and organizations), *institutional pluralism* (a multiplicity of rules such as congruent traditional and modern water "laws"), and *multifunctionality* (a range of uses and values of water to different users). Similarly, Slaymaker and Newborne (2007) illustrate how the plurality of types of legal water rights that can be claimed or exercised—human, property, and contractual—presents complex possibilities for the balancing of outcomes for differently situated people.

Such analyses of plurality indicate the complexity of the arenas in which the individual agency of rights bearers is exercised. In previous work on the collective management of water and land I have outlined the concept of institutional *bricolage*: the piecing together of institutional arrangements from existing norms, practices, and relationships, through conscious action and unreflexive practice (Cleaver 2002). The concept of *bricolage* implies that individuals may draw on a multiplicity of potential resources, and that different individuals will experience different capacities to act as bricoleurs.

Positions vary regarding whether plurality in governance offers opportunity or constraint. Ostrom (2005) and Merrey and colleagues (2006) seem to imply that the existence of plural and polycentric channels for resource governance provides scope for more negotiability, flexibility, and room for maneuver—a point reinforced by those noting the potential of "new spaces" to provide sites for the renegotiation of norms and inequitable social relationships (Kesby 2005; Cornwall 2004). However, research into plural systems for the governance of land and water resources in Tanzania suggests that these systems reinforce the rights of the powerful and reproduce the marginalization of the weak (Maganga 2002).

Effects of Exercising Agency

The workings of power through plural institutional settings shapes the ability of individuals to effect significant difference in their lives. Power may be exercised and accepted both consciously and unconsciously, and the "self disciplining" of agents—their acceptance of relations of inequality— ensures the reproduction of power through everyday acts and relationships: "[s]elf-disciplining actors often enrol themselves into the projects of others" (Kesby 2005, 2047). While several writers emphasize the entrenchment of such everyday reproduction of relationships of power, a significant strand of thought assumes that the exercise of agency involves not only choice but also the challenging of power relations and accepted practices. This tendency is particularly strong in writing on rights, in which articulation and action are associated with the achievement of equitable social change. In this model of agency, reflexive agents question norms, challenge the inequitable distribution of resources, and claim and extend their rights. Agency is considered empowering, and is potentially transformatory.

However, not all choices are equal, not all agents are equally placed to make them, and similar actions may have very different outcomes. This point has been well rehearsed in arguments about gendered empowerment and change. Jackson (2003), cautioning against overly optimistic expectations of enacting land rights for women in India, argues that women in different subject positions (e.g., relating to seniority in the family, caste, etc.) perceive the importance of claiming land rights variably and differ in their capacity to effect these rights. Kabeer (1999) considers not just an individual's ability to choose to act, but how much power they have to make *strategic* decisions that shape their lives. She distinguishes between first and second order choices, the former referring to decisions fundamental to the shape of a person's life, the latter to choices that affect life's quality but do not constitute its defining parameters. Kabeer is concerned with the real effects these choices can have. In participatory natural resource management, the participation of individuals in itself is assumed to produce benefits for them, although this is demonstrably often not the case.

Exploring Agency and Rights in Natural Resource Management

Let us now draw on some of these debates and insights to explore some examples of how agency is exercised in the context of social interrelatedness. Critics of the dominant human rights discourse question its focus on abstracted individuals located in relationship to the state (Gaventa and Jones 2002). For such commentators agency is not synonymous with autonomy: for most people the claiming of individual rights and freedoms occurs within social relationships, not independently of them (De Herdt and Deneulin 2007). If we accept that making rights operational involves balancing the challenging of structures of power with the need to secure basic sustenance (Pettit and Wheeler 2005; Nyamu-Musembi 2005), then how does this reconfigure our understanding of individual agency?

We might better understand the choices people make in challenging or acquiescing to the status quo if "freedom" is defined as relatedness and belonging rather than "autonomy" (De Herdt and Deneulin 2007). A richer conception of socially located agency can help us to understand the "various intermediate solidarities" that mediate the relationships between individuals and society and between citizens and the state (Englund 2004). The challenge then is to better appreciate the multiple connections between individuals, and between and within collectivities.

Cosmologies Shape Agency

A feature of both rights-based and natural resource management approaches in development is the tendency to err toward purposive and strategic models of decision making and agency. Such approaches place great faith in the ability of people to publicly bargain and negotiate, to strategically respond to incentives, and to position themselves in relation to collective norms. However, work in natural resource management (referred to in Cleaver 2000) documents complex and wide-ranging worldviews within which people, both consciously and unconsciously, understand themselves and their actions. Nyamu-Musembi (2005), writing from a rights perspective, sees people constantly negotiating between an internal moral system (shaped by factors such as culture and religion, and represented by institutions such as kinship) and the formal legal regime of rights offered by the liberal state. Cosmologies matter in the formation of subjectivities and in the shaping of the relationship between individuals, collective action, and social hierarchies (Englund 2004).

Moral worldviews often include strongly gendered and socially strati-fied ideas about proper behavior and the "rightful" place of individuals of different social identities. Such cosmologies cover ideas about sacred places, spirit homes, and the direct relationship of people with ancestors, and one of their notable aspects is that they link "proper" behaviors in the social world (including decision-making forums) with effects in the natu-ral and supernatural ones. For example, in villages where I worked in Zimbabwe, people perceived that rainfall, the associated fertility of the land, and the ability to secure livelihoods were critically affected by the proper observation of custom, the showing of respect to elders, and the mainte-nance of cooperation between people. Patterns of access to resources and the management of land and water were strongly shaped by such "moral-ecological rationality." This influenced individuals' participa-tion in decision making, and their willingness to abide by collective decisions and to broadly comply with unwritten norms of resource use. Moral-ecological rationality was often invoked by elders in criticizing young people for showing insufficient respect. Cosmologies therefore affect understandings of community, participation, and the social order—all integral to "citizenship" (Nyamnjoh 2004). The extent to which people are bound in their perceptions and actions by dominant cosmologies, or are able to renegotiate them, matters for our under-standing of effective participation and the exercise of rights (Dikito-Wachtmeister 2000). Cosmologies may constrain, but they can also be deployed as authoritative resources to vest certain claims to rights and resources with the imprimatur of history, supernatural approbation, and social "rightness."

Crowded Selves and Unequal Interdependence

Our understandings of the ways in which agency is exercised to realize rights are underpinned by assumptions about the identity and autonomy of individuals. Participatory approaches to common property resource management assume that collective action is possible because of some sort of equality of actors derived from common livelihood interests. The liberal suppositions of rights-based approaches reinforce the notion of individual independence, characterized by Englund as the "spectre of dis-crete identities" (2004). These interrelated assumptions of the equality of interests and the autonomy of agents result in the myth that people fol-lowing similar livelihood practices in relation to natural resource use and management are equally placed to exercise their rights. However, indi-viduals do not exercise property rights over natural resources simply as "resource appropriators," but as people with rich social identities. Individ-ual identities and associated motivations are as complex and multilayered as the channels through which resources are accessed. Plurality is thus evident in agents themselves: personhood manifests in "crowded selves" (De Herdt and Deneulin 2007; Jackson 2003), and interdependence rather than autonomy characterizes livelihoods.

For example, evidence from India (Rao 2003; Jackson 2003) suggests the complexity of identities and relationships through which women's land rights are exercised. Women may claim rights to land as legal and equal citizens, but do so also through their subject positions as daughters, wives, mothers, and members of a particular caste or ethnic group. Women inhabit different identities simultaneously, and the aspects prioritized may change over lifecourses (Jackson 2003). To these women living their lives within marriages and kin groups, exercising their politico-legal rights to land through public institutions may be too risky. Jackson sees social relations like kinship and marriage as simultaneously being the major constraints on women securing land rights, and the main means by which such rights may be achieved.

An account of irrigation management in Nepal describes some women drawing on their familial and gendered identities to secure water, rather than using their status as active citizens. These women did not participate in the Irrigation Association, but secured their water through the public participation of male household members, through the patronage of kin, and through stealing and cheating. They justified their nonparticipation by referring to gendered norms: the inappropriateness of them attending meetings held in the evening, the demands of their domestic work, and so on (Zwarteveen and Neupane 1996).

However, Rao (2003) usefully points out that the exercise of agency involves mutuality and interdependence as well as domination and subordination. For many poor and subordinate individuals and groups, access to resources is primarily exercised through inequitable social arrangements. Thus Joshi and colleagues record a *dalit* women from India, excluded from equitable access to water by higher-caste neighbors, explaining why she will not object even in the context of a gender-focused participatory development project: "My neighbours are important to me, no matter what they do. I need their support for my family's daily existence" (Joshi et al. 2003, 2).

Joshi's account also illustrates that while the multiplicity of identity may offer opportunity, the perceptions of others shape the choices individuals are "allowed" to pursue. Social placement matters in the exercise of rights. In a case of participatory forest management in Cameroon, the enactment of laws giving communities rights over forest resources prompted struggles over belonging and representation in villages, particularly over the definition of strangers who could be excluded from claims to forest rights (Geschiere 2004). An individual's ability to exercise agency in claiming rights is partly defined by others and their perception of the individual as worthy of citizenship.

Balancing Belonging and Individuality: Unconscious Motivations and Intended Actions

Assumptions about the nature of individual rationality inform both participatory natural resource management and rights-based approaches. In both schools of thought there has been an overemphasis on the role of reflexive action and deliberative strategizing in people's agency, and a relative neglect of the impact of routinized practices and unconscious motivations. This emphasis produces analyses that overstate the likelihood that actors will consciously and strategically claim and exercise rights. To better understand how and why people exercise their rights, we need to balance assumptions of rationality and autonomy with richer conceptualizations of individual subjectivities formed consciously and unconsciously in engagement with social and emotional relationships.

Social theorists recognize the importance of unconscious motivations for purposive actions, particularly the unconscious self-disciplining of agents and their internalization of hegemonic norms (Bourdieu 1977). For Giddens (1984) not all individual acts are the results of conscious strategy ("discursive consciousness"); some are the product of habit and routine ("practical consciousness") and of the workings of the unconscious mind. Some feminists further critique assumptions of bounded rationality, which take human action to be intentional, reasoned, and goal-directed, albeit "bounded" by the limitations of context and the ability to attain and process information. They suggest that assumptions of bounded *emotionality*, based on a recognition of human interrelatedness, ambiguity, community and relational feelings, and embodied self-identities, may enrich such overly rational models of human behavior (Mumby and Putnam 1992).

Both conscious and unconscious emotions are critical in shaping people's sense of self- efficacy and their social relationships (Myers 1996), and therefore the extent to which they publicly engage and assert their rights. Both Kabeer (2000) and Agrawal (2005) emphasize that for potential courses of action to become real, they must both be materially possible and be understood by the agent to be within the bounds of possibility. "Imagined autonomy" is therefore an important factor in people's conceptualization of their own agency and an essential ingredient of empowering action. The question thus arises of how much the individual perceptions of self-efficacy necessary for the exercise of rights are determined within wider macrosocial patterns of ethnicity, class, and gender (Campbell and Jovchelovitch 2000).

The subjectivities that inform individuals' perceptions of possibility are shaped by the relationships between the individual and the social, the conscious and the unconscious, and exterior and interior motivations. In analyzing the enabling and constraining factors that affect the gendered exercise of land rights in India, Jackson (2003) advocates a stronger focus on understanding subjectivities. She notes the importance of examining the ways in which personal worlds made up of identities, memories, emotions, motivations, and desires impinge upon social action. Relations of interdependence exist alongside structural inequalities; strategic livelihood motivations are entwined with emotional needs for self-realization, relatedness, belonging. Daily livelihood imperatives, unequal command of resources, and placement within networks of emotional relations may push the exercise of agency toward social harmony and conflict avoidance, rather than toward effective resistance or explicit renegotiation of rights.

Structure and Voice

The voicing of needs and claims and their public negotiation is a central focus of rights-based approaches and participatory natural resource management. But if structural placement shapes the ability to exercise agency, and subjectivities constrain as well as enable empowering action, how can we better understand the complexities of exercising "voice"?

Much thinking about the participatory management of natural resources assumes that if the spaces for decision making are local, and the rules for access and distribution fair, then all parties will potentially be able to participate and benefit. We have already seen that this was not the case in some Indian forest communities: despite local decision making arrangements and "fair" rules, patternings of class, caste, and gender shaped the engagement and outcomes of different people (Agrawal 2005). However, the "post-tyranny" literature on participation and gendered empowerment does tackle the perplexing issue of voice. It recognizes that participatory spaces are imbued with power relations that may result in the conscious and unconscious self-muting of disadvantaged people, but is also optimistic about the possibilities of creative participatory methodologies for disrupting "business as usual" and facilitating the articulation of alternative views (Kesby 2005; Cornwall 2004).

The role of power relations in shaping the articulation of rights is reflected in a number of ways. Rights are framed in light of people's own understanding of their entitlements, and under the influence of dominant discourses on rights. There is a need for explicit attention to the rules of debate in participatory forums, and for a critical examination of the potentially alienating discourses deployed by representatives on behalf of others. Ideas about rights may sometimes be the superficial expression of a deeper array of tensions and contradictions (Nyamu-Musembi 2005). A recent case study that used multistakeholder platforms as forums for negotiating multiple claims to water found that public exchange resulted in the "foregrounding" of consensus issues, and the "backgrounding" of potentially more divisive issues concerning the fair allocation of resources (Moreyra and Wegerich 2005). In a lively debate about the exercise (or nonexercise) of land rights by women in India, Agarwal and Jackson (both 2003) differ over how much women's articulated priorities can be seen to reflect their "real" priorities and needs, and how far they reflect preferences adapted to the constraints of power, the exigencies of government policies, the terms of development projects, and social acceptability.

For Jackson in particular (2003), the "politics of speech" has been neglected in analyzing gendered agency. In considering joint forest management, Mohanty (2004) shows how a lack of self-confidence, fears of dependency, cultural barriers, and institutions derived from the colonial state all conspire to make it difficult for women to use their voices and be heard. Hierarchies among women, concepts of proper female behavior, and virilocal marriage arrangements may all constrain women's agency. One young woman explains constraints on her participation in water management to a researcher thus: "I cannot be seen to be taking a lead role at meetings attended by older women as this could be perceived as being disrespectful. I am a young woman who has just been married here for a few years, so I cannot be speaking often and taking a lead in these things" (Dikito-Wachtmeister 2000, 221).

The coexistence of empowerment and subordination in the gendered expression of voice is common and poses challenges to assessing the effects of articulation on empowerment. Cases suggest that there is no simple path from articulation to beneficial effects on rights. For example, Tukai (2005) documents an attempt to empower women in a pastoralist community in Tanzania through a participatory water project. The aim of promoting women's role as active citizens was partially achieved: they increased their representation on the village council, including the water committee, and claimed greater confidence in discussions at the village and household levels. However, within the timescale of the project, the women's increased capacity to exercise agency and voice could not counter the relations of patriarchy in which they were embedded. Despite their gains in individual voice and citizenship, they still could not collectively secure access to water on better terms with men.

The Embodied Exercise of Agency and Rights

Participation in decision making involves embodied presentations of self, and yet the exercising of rights through corporeal human conduct is often neglected in analyses; little attention is given to how embodiment enables and constrains active participation (Jackson 1998). Bourdieu (1977) emphasizes the human body in his discussion of the habitus, taking it as an important signifier in social interaction that expresses social status and power as much as communicative intent. Deportment, ways of dressing, and ways of speaking are produced by and reproduce social structure. So, how far is public participation, the exercise of voice, the assertion of property rights, and the accessing and using of resources shaped by physical capabilities, particularly able-bodiedness?

Research in Tanzania showed that families that suffered multiple constraints on their physical abilities gradually dropped out of associational life and were severely circumscribed in exercising rights to access natural resources. People with reduced able-bodiedness caused by disease and disablement or the physical burdens of caring for others were unable to contribute to collective action, attend meetings and social events, or pay fees to clubs and associations. They were also unable to access distant forest and water resources, and under customary tenure arrangements risked having untilled land confiscated and reallocated within the community. Lack of physical power was a feature of the poorest families, and they were characterized by spatially circumscribed lives (Cleaver 2005).

While embodiment pertains to individuals, not all individuals have equal command over their physical selves. Natural resources are often accessed by deploying the labor of others: children and junior wives sent to fetch water, herdsmen employed to take cattle to grazing lands, youth required to collect and carry firewood for their families. Such people are often the ones who abide or break the "rules-in-use" relating to the natural resource and who exercise the rights-in-practice, and yet they may not be involved in participatory decision making. How far the effective exercise of agency implies command over one's own labor, or the labor of others, is a moot point. Embodiment, agency, and the exercise of rights are recursively linked, though often neglected in analyses of the claiming of rights through public expressions of voice.

Conclusion: A Concern for Equity and Effect

This chapter has raised, and inevitably left unresolved, a number of questions about agency in relation to exercising rights. In thinking about the implications for the collective management of natural resources and the prospects for participatory governance, further questions and dilemmas arise. We need to consider more carefully how far participatory development initiatives require people to exercise agency within the existing rules of the game, within the parameters of the program or project on offer, and according to the prevailing status quo. Which are the factors that discipline people in claiming rights, and which factors are potentially generative of transformatory change? If we are concerned with securing more equitable development for millions, attention to the diverse possibilities of individuals exercising agency and claiming their rights is not enough. Equity concerns and the scale of development goals require us to recognize the importance of structure in patterning inequality and in shaping the likely impacts of interventions. To better understand how the institutions that shape access to rights and resources work, and how effective and equitable their outcomes are, we need better explanations of why and how individuals act, and of the balance between empowerment and constraint in such actions. Critically, we need to expand our gaze beyond visible public forums of decision making to the places where agency is exercised and rights claimed through practice. Analyses that explore the nature of situated personhood, and the ways in which such social placement shapes both the exercise of agency and its effects, are central to deepening our understanding of how rights are made real in natural resource management.

References

Agarwal, B. 2003. Gender and land rights revisited: Exploring new prospects via the state, family and market. *Journal of Agrarian Change* 3, nos. 1 and 2:184–224.

Agrawal, A. 2005. *Environmentality: Technologies of government and the making of subjects.* London: Duke University Press.

Arce, A. and N. Long. 2000. Reconfiguring modernity and development from an anthropological perspective. In *Anthropology, development and modernities: Exploring discourses, counter-tendencies and violence,* edited by A. Arce and N. Long, 1–31. London: Routledge.

Bourdieu, P. 1998. *The logic of practice.* Cambridge: Polity Press.

Bourdieu, P.1977. *Outline of a theory of practice.* Cambridge: Cambridge University Press.

Campbell, C. and S. Jovchelovitch, 2000. Health, community and development: Towards a social psychology of participation. *Journal of Community and Applied Social Psychology* no. 10:255–270.

Cleaver, F. 2000. Moral ecological rationality: Institutions and the management of common property resources. *Development and Change* 31, no. 2:361–383.

Cleaver, F. 2002. Reinventing institutions and the social embeddedness of natural resource management. *European Journal of Development Research* 14, no. 2:11–30.

Cleaver, F. 2005. The inequality of social capital and the reproduction of chronic poverty. *World Development* 33, no. 6:893–906.

Cornwall, A. 2004. New democratic spaces? The politics and dynamics of institutionalized participation. *IDS Bulletin* 35, no. 2:1–10.

Cornwall, A. and C. Nyamu-Musembi, 2005. Why rights, why now? Reflections on the rise of rights in international development discourse. *IDS Bulletin* 35, no 2:9–18.

De Herdt, T. and S. Deneulin. 2007. Individual freedoms as relational experiences. *Journal of Human Development* 8, no. 2:179–184.

Dean, M. 1999. *Governmentality: Power and rule in modern society.* London: Sage.

Dikito-Wachtmeister, M. 2000. Women's participation in decision making processes in rural water projects, Makoni District, Zimbabwe. PhD thesis, University of Bradford.

Englund, H. 2004. Introduction: Recognising identities, imagining alternatives. In *Rights and the politics of recognition in Africa*, edited by H. Englund and F. B. Nyamnjoh, 1–30. London: Zed Books.

Franks, T. and F. Cleaver. 2007. Water governance and poverty: A framework for analysis. *Progress in Development Studies* 7, no. 4:291–306.

Gaventa, J. and E. Jones. 2002. *Concepts of citizenship: A review.* Brighton: Institute of Development Studies.

Geschiere, P. 2004. Ecology, belonging and xenophobia: The 1994 forest law in Cameroon and the issue of "community." In *Rights and the politics of recognition in Africa*, edited by H. Englund and F. B. Nyamnjoh, 237–259. London: Zed Books.

Giddens, A. 1984. *The constitution of society: Outline of the theory of structuration,* Cambridge: Polity Press.

Giddens, A. 1996. Affluence, poverty and the idea of a post scarcity society. *Development and Change* 27, no. 2:365–377.

Greener, I. 2002. Agency, social theory and social policy. *Critical Social Policy* 22, no. 4:688–705.

Hickey, S. and G. Mohan. 2004. Relocating participation within a radical politics of development: critical modernism and citizenship. In *Participation: From tyranny to transformation? Exploring new approaches to participation in development,* edited by S. Hickey and G. Mohan, 159–174. London: Zed Books.

Jackson, C. 1998. Gender, irrigation and environment: Arguing for agency. *Agriculture and Human Values* 15, no. 4:313–324.

Jackson, C. 2003. Gender analysis of land: Beyond land rights for women? *Journal of Agrarian Change* 3, no. 4:453–480.

Joshi, D., M. Lloyd and B. Fawcett. 2003. Voices from the village: An alternative paper for the alternative water forum. University of Bradford. http://www.brad.ac.uk/acad/bcid/GTP/altwater.html.

Kabeer, N. 1999. Resources, agency, achievements: Reflections on the measurement of women's empowerment. *Development and Change* 30:435–464.

Kesby, M. 2005. Retheorizing empowerment-through-participation as a performance in space: Beyond tyranny to transformation. *Signs: Journal of Women in Culture and Society* 30, no. 4:2037–2065.

Long, N. 1992. From paradigm lost to paradigm regained? The case for an actor orientated sociology of development. In *Battlefields of knowledge: The interlocking of theory and practice in social research and development,* edited by N. Long and A. Long, 16–46. London: Routledge.

Maganga, F. 2002. The interplay between formal and informal systems of managing resource conflicts: Some evidence from South-Western Tanzania. *European Journal of Development Research* 14, no. 2:51–71.

Mehta, L. 2005. Unpacking rights and wrongs: Do human rights make a difference? The case of water rights in India and South Africa. IDS Working Paper 260.

Merrey, D. R., D. Meinzen, P. Mollinga and E. Karar. 2006. Policy and institutional reform: The art of the possible. In *Water for food, water for life: A comprehensive assessment of water management in agriculture,* Comprehensive Assessment of Water Management in Agriculture, 193–231. London: Earthscan; Colombo: International Water Management Institute. http://www.iwmi.cgiar.org/assessment/index.htm.

Mohanty, R. 2004. Institutional dynamics and participatory spaces: The making and unmaking of participation in local forest management in India. *IDS Bulletin* 35, no. 2:26–32.

Moreyra, A. and K. Wegerich. 2005. Multi-stakeholder platforms as problems of eating out: The case of Cerro Chapelco in Patagonia, Argentina. Paper presented at the ESRC seminar "Challenging the Consensus" (seminar 3). http://www.splash.bradford.ac.uk.

Mumby, K. and L. Putnam. 1992. The politics of emotion: A feminist reading of bounded rationality. *Academy of Management Review* 17, no 3:465–485.

Myers, D. G. 1996. *Social Psychology.* New York: McGraw-Hill.

Nyamnjoh, F. B. 2004. Reconciling the rhetoric of rights with competing notions of personhood and agency in Botswana. In *Rights and the politics of recognition in Africa,* edited by H. Englund and F. B. Nyamnjoh, 33–65. London: Zed Books.

Nyamu-Musembi, C. 2005. An actor-oriented approach to rights in development. *IDS Bulletin* 35, no. 2:41–49.

Ostrom, E. 2005. *Understanding institutional diversity.* Princeton: Princeton University Press.

Pettit, J. and J. Wheeler. 2005. Developing rights? Relating discourse to context and practice. *IDS Bulletin* 36, no. 1:1–8.

Rao, N. 2003. Only women can and will represent women's interests: The case of land rights. Workshop on "Gender myths and feminist fables," Institute of Development Studies, University of Sussex, July 2–4.

Rapport, N. and J. Overing. 2000. *Social and cultural anthropology: The key concepts.* London: Routledge.

Slaymaker, T. and P. Newborne. 2007. Water rights for water governance. *ID21 Insights* no. 67:5.

Tukai, R. 2005. *Gender and access in pastoral communities: Re-evaluating community participation and gender empowerment.* Paper presented at the ESRC seminar "Challenging the consensus" (seminar 2). http://www.splash.bradford.ac.uk/home.

Woodhouse, P. 2002. Natural resource management and chronic poverty in Sub-Saharan Africa: an overview paper. Chronic Poverty Research Centre Working Paper 14, University of Manchester.

Zwarteveen, M. and N. Neupane. 1996. Free-riders or victims: Women's non-participation in Nepal's Chhattis Mauja irrigation schemes. Research Report No 7. Colombo, Sri Lanka: International Irrigation Management Institute.

CHAPTER 9

"We Are Also Human": Identity and Power in Gender Relations

Michael Drinkwater[1]

Introduction: Into the Heart of Gender Inequity

There are two principal strands of approaches to human rights today. Traditional human rights organizations remain concerned chiefly with the relationship between the individual and the state, and with the state's ability to protect, prevent abuse of, and fulfill the human rights of the individual. However, the rise of rights-based approaches in developmental organizations since the late 1990s has brought a different perspective to human rights. Developmental organizations' use of human rights addresses the perennial question of how to deal more effectively with the endemic social problems of poverty, marginalization, and discrimination, with a focus on the unequal power relations that sustain these inequalities.

The single most important feature of a rights-based approach to development is that it starts from the premise laid out in Article One of the Universal Declaration of Human Rights that we are all equally human. Article One states: "All human beings are born free and equal in dignity and rights. They are endowed with reason and conscience and should act towards one another in a spirit of brotherhood." Sadly, it is one of the most remarkable and persistent aspects of human cultures that among the diverse peoples in every society today there are substantial numbers who inevitably regard other groups as being less human than they are. Wherever people are regarded as less human, they will be discriminated against. And globally, the largest group of all routinely regarded as less human are women. They are thus the largest category of people who experience throughout their lives a variety of forms of discrimination.

Women's movements, and attempts to promote the empowerment of women, have been present for many decades. The debates and discourses around feminism and its interface with development interventions are diverse and intricate (see Cornwall, Harrison and Whitehead 2004). One of the challenges of all continuing efforts to focus on gender equity issues is to avoid "mainstreaming" feminism into a quiet complacency.

My argument is that adopting a rights-based approach to development can further the ability of initiatives seeking to address the more pervasive factors that perpetuate gender inequality. Before the advent of rights-based approaches, practical attempts to empower women often missed an essential starting point and basic matter of social justice: until men accept women as equally human, attempts to promote the empowerment of women will necessarily always be limited in the scope and longevity of what they achieve. Gender and development approaches have stressed the importance of incorporating relational approaches to women's empowerment that require the involvement of men as well as women, but one of the consequences of the mainstreaming of gender equity initiatives has been the depoliticization of gender and development goals in this regard (Goetz 2004).

In moving forward with approaches that aim to further women's empowerment, we must return to questions of how to change the relevant social relations, and thus many of the basic systems, values, and patterns that structure human societies today. At the heart of these relations lies the way in which men perceive themselves and cast their own individual and collective identities. Until men are able to construct their notions of self differently, and change the ways they feel capable of achieving status and respect for themselves and their families, women's status as subhumans and second-class citizens will persist. Women's roles must also be addressed, since as mothers, mothers-in-law, sisters, aunts, and neighbors, they too play a major part in perpetuating the stigmatization and discrimination that affect other women. A change in women's attitudes occurs when they realize that men's portrayal of themselves as superior is not supported by religious doctrines, or most constitutional law, or the international human rights frameworks behind the constitutional codes.

In this chapter it is therefore argued that a rights-based approach is essential to the improvement of the situations of women and their families. Such improvement requires a relational approach to rights that sees us all as moral beings possessing rights and responsibilities equally. For women, especially those who experience daily conditions of poverty and vulnerability, acting to improve their own lives and those of their children requires their ability to advance their status as citizens who regard themselves, and are regarded by others, as having rights equal to those of men and other higher-status social groups. This requires a significant sharpening of our focus on dealing with the culturally embedded factors that sustain the status of women as less than fully human.

This argument will be supported through the use of material drawn largely from analytical and programmatic work undertaken on issues of gender equity within CARE International. For this discussion specific projects are a backdrop, and the commentary engages with some of the learning taking place in the organization as it struggles to come to grips with what an organizational strategic objective to address issues of gender inequity means. In 2004, CARE produced a "unifying framework" that aims to demonstrate the interrelationship of different programmatic approaches the organization has used in its development of a "good programming framework" (McCaston 2004). The unifying framework relates approaches that CARE has used since the mid-1990s—a livelihoods approach, a focus on partnership and civil society, a growing emphasis on gender equity, and now a rights-based approach, which has also led to an expanding focus on themes such as inclusive voice and governance. In essence, the unifying framework states that all CARE's work should be seen as contributing to three outcome areas—changes in human conditions, in social position, and in the enabling environment. Additionally, in contributing to these outcome areas, all programs should be addressing a selected core set of underlying causes of poverty, which the organization believes are critical and feasible targets for its efforts. As one of these underlying causes of poverty, gender inequality is a focus for all of CARE's work.

The Notion of Equity—And Why It Matters

In pondering different ways of starting this chapter, I decided that the best way to do so was by relating the three incidents that most persuaded me of the value in approaching women's empowerment by specifically talking about human rights and the central notion that we are all equally human.

The first of these incidents occurred during a review of the gender component of what was, for its time, an innovative livelihoods improvement project in southwest Zambia—the Livingstone Food Security Project (Turner 2000). Critical to the project's impact was its institutional development strategy based on a simple formula of self-formed village management committees (VMCs) and their constituent cell groups, which spread rapidly through their sharing of drought-tolerant seed varieties. The gender component of the project was initiated as a response to a gender analysis that revealed conflicts between the men and women participating. These had emerged in particular in a meeting at which men accused their wives of "stealing crops" and issues of control over surplus produce and household income became apparent (Sitambuli 1998).

The social roots of men's control over crop surplus decision making lay in the fact that in this matrilineal but patrilocal context, men's families pay dowry, so the man controls income, while children "belong" to the wife who is then responsible for their health, food, clothing, education, and so on. With attention to gender being something new in the project as well as the community, the gender officer decided it was best to tackle practical needs before explicitly confronting gender issues: "Talking about gender in a community was seen as dangerous and provocative."[2] However, the gender officer did work on staff attitudes—for example, some of the Tonga male staff had cancelled meetings if "no one turned up," which meant that no men had showed up, despite women being present. The staff, following the recruitment of additional women, decided that to change attitudes in the community it was better to look at the issues from a male perspective, and persuade men that they would benefit from greater equality. For example, better trained and nourished women would be able to work more efficiently and earn more income, which would benefit the whole family.[3]

The gender program activities focused on raising women's incomes, largely through providing them with financial and business literacy training, then working with the village institutions to create the space for women to engage in income-generating activities more successfully. One area in which women raised their incomes substantially was beer brewing, where they had traditionally "lost" much of their income by giving away free beer for various reasons. By controlling these handouts women were able to increase their profits several times over, and this extra income gave them the ability to meet a range of household needs.

However, this approach to gender was limited: there was no discussion of human rights or dignity, or of the premise that men and women are equally human. The problems with this deficit were borne out in evaluation interviews with some of the main program participants. One woman, the chairperson of an area management committee, was asked about her relationship with her undoubtedly supportive husband, and remarked: "This is just a position, so when I go home I need to remember that I am just a wife. I am married, and so I have to respect my husband, so I am very glad that he has allowed me to accept this position." When asked in a separate interview about the couple's relative equality, her husband responded: "I look at my wife as an equal, because she is able to do what she wants to do, and I can do what I want to do. Other men stop their wives from participating in all these development activities. I can even allow her to go and attend a course (in Livingstone) for a week."[4]

The similarity of a headman and his wife's comments on the subject of feeling equal show how the project had left the underlying factor of women's unequal identity untouched. As the headman's wife noted: "My husband commands a lot of respect, so I have to respect that too and support him. No, we are not equal as people, as he is a headman, and is accorded a lot of respect, and I am just a wife and a woman."[5] The limitations of the Livingstone project in promoting women's empowerment are typical of livelihoods programs of its generation, which perhaps pursued a limited women's group solidarity approach and contributed innovative work on improving gender relations, but did not incorporate a notion of gender equity.

The second incident occurred during a visit to a daytime drop-in centre for sex workers in Bangladesh in January 2002. The centre had been established by a self-help association of sex workers, Durjoy Nari Shanga—the "difficult to conquer women" association. When women were asked how their association had helped them, the first to reply stated, "we realized we are also human beings." Recognizing their innate equality with others had not reduced the risks the women faced, but it had equipped them to deal with these risks more effectively. One example they provided was that they were less afraid to tell the police to stop harassing them, and confident enough to say, "like you, we have an equal right to have an income" (Drinkwater and Bull-Kamanga 2002). Theirs has been a struggle against various forms of male power, and discrimination and stigmatization by both men and women as "bad," "fallen," and "unclean" (Magar 2005).

In its early days CARE's SHAKTI project[6] worked with these women in enormously creative ways, with staff themselves going through a profound change process too. The project was piloted in the Tangail brothel, a community of some 800 sex workers and their children. Interactive discussions with the sex workers late into the night enabled the social analysis and self-analysis staff required to understand the role their own attitudes played in perpetuating the discrimination and stigma against the sex workers (Magar 2005). In one exercise, the sex workers were asked what their priorities were; at the top of their list was the ability to wear shoes outdoors.[7] In the complex network of social relations of the Tangail neighborhood, the *samaj*—modeled after traditional village councils, and consisting of landlords and originally two *sardanis* or madams—wielded tremendous power and control over the sex workers (Magar 2005). *Mastans*—male gangs allied to local politicians and landlords—act as enforcers, regulating local economies and exploiting vulnerable groups through the use and threat of violence. Forbidding the sex workers the right to wear shoes was a way of publicly marking their status as lesser beings and restricting them to the locality.

It was not just the opening statement that marked the day of the visit for me, nor the simple but powerful utterances these women then made while talking about the things they were striving for—education for their illegitimate children, savings for future pensions, and less illegal harassment from the police and the government agencies supposedly responsible for their welfare. It was also the juxtaposition of the courage the women's actions required with the visual evidence in the day refuge of their vulnerability, as well as the understated eloquence with which a woman field coordinator from CARE revealed much of this to me—a hand gesture, or a quiet comment—and the space she created for all the women present to speak from their hearts.

It is extraordinary what these women have achieved—with some guidance, but largely of their own initiative. Their first activity in Tangail, with SHAKTI's support, was to establish a clinic. They contributed money to the clinic's establishment and were part of the management team that ran it (Magar 2005). Years and many achievements later, Durjoy Nari Shanga continues to strive to prevent the exploitation of women, both by fighting the abuse they constantly receive and by preventing them from being forced into sex work against their will.

The third incident occurred during a visit to a *mahila mandal* (women's group) in the Durg district of Chhattisgarh state in India in July 2004. This meeting took place during a reflective practice exercise with a huge CARE India health and nutrition program that worked with some nine million people in ten states. The program sought to expand its emphasis on gender equity issues concerning health and nutrition practices, but as the women noted: "Even in key messages changes are not happening. It is not possible for women to rest during pregnancy, or to improve their diet. Men still think that they are men—they still feel that they cannot get involved with household work."

When asked what changes they would like to see, one of the leaders of the group—a representative on the village's local *panchayat* structure—made her feelings clear:

> We would like to see nothing less than total gender equity . . . we want to be seen as equals, and to know what our rights are. The state should be more responsible for teaching us these rights. Why do we have 33% reservation in the PRI? It should be 50% (since otherwise, men will still make the decisions). Also, whilst we have 33% reservation for women here, this is not the case at [the] national level. We still have very few women there. We need more women who can represent women's interests. We would like to demand equal wages for men and women. . . . We don't have enough information on things, there should be a women's centre in the village, where we can get help if needed.
>
> Some men are really behind times. We would like to challenge traditional roles more. We work both inside and outside the home, yet society still says that men are superior to women. Why does this happen? It really needs to change. It is hard to

think of a program to change men. Men are intelligent enough to know that they should change, but their hearts do not allow them. Men have to make personal decisions to change (Drinkwater, Singh and Hora 2004).

As our discussion continued, case after case emerged of women who had been beaten and harassed by their husbands. So why does this happen? Why do men—and some women—continue to stifle women, to see them as less equally human and hold back their ability to contribute more effectively to their own lives and the lives of those around them? And what does this perpetuation of gender inequality do for men? The women had some answers to their own questions, but more on that later, as these questions are explored in the following discussion.

Women As Less Human

Women are regarded as less than men in diverse ways in different cultures. In many African contexts, the ways in which women are regarded as less than fully human are varied, but most share the common factor of depriving women of their identity as people. First, they do not have names. In cattle owning communities in Zambia, as declaimed by one polygamous Lenje man, "women are like livestock."[8] They can be bought and sold, as cattle can, and they are a productive asset, as cattle are. In a recent interview in a matrilineal Lamba area, an elderly woman asked the name of her daughter-in-law and neighbor of more than 11 years could not supply it. To her she was only *vana* so and so, the mother of her first born son.[9] As commented in a report on a project working with adolescent girls in India, they are often seen only as "temporary people," who will cease to be (at least for the father) once they have disappeared inside a marriage (Mehrotra 2003).

This practice of seeing women only in terms of the men they are tied to has been taken to extremes in Lesotho and Swaziland. In Lesotho, there is an old saying that "[a] woman is the child of her father, her husband and her son" (Goering 2004). It is only recently that the constitutions of both countries have stopped treating women as minors incapable of making decisions of their own. Lesotho women moving to the lowlands in search of jobs in the textile industry have established new forms of household that often lack a "permanent" male and thus previously did not legally exist, further heightening the women's vulnerability (Wason 2004).

This loss of identity, and the resultant devaluation of women's own sense of self, can be traced back to the socialization practices in such cultures—in particular their perpetuation of the social identities of men as sexually dominant and women as sexually subservient. In a study looking at gendered power relations in the Central Region of Malawi, the widespread practice of *Gulu Wamkulu* initiation rites to prepare boys and girls for marriage was reported for the two main ethnic groups in the area, the Chewa and Yao. These ceremonies, it was argued, promote "many of the behaviours and mindsets in households and communities that lead to unequal gender power relations," and also encourage degrading and risky sexual activities and a high prevalence of sex outside marriage. Women "felt their male children were taught bad behaviour and language through the songs of this tradition and that they lost respect for women as a result. Boys are taught that once they have been initiated they automatically become adults and as such deserve respect from their mothers and society." The *dambwe* cult dance, which involves men and boys over nine years of age, encourages violent behavior against anyone not initiated into the institution—which is why there is pressure on young boys to be initiated. Young girls and women caught by the dambwe may be harassed and raped by the dance participants. These traditional institutions are regarded as the training centers for today's youth to become tomorrow's leaders, and the general teaching of these institutions is that a woman should sexually please and listen to her husband—"he knows best" and is head of the family (Chalimba and Pinder 2002).

Whether or not initiation ceremonies are still widely practiced, in most African cultural contexts women remain sexually dominated by men, as now seen through women's ubiquitous powerlessness to protect themselves against HIV/AIDS (Win 2004). Even educated middle-class women are frequently unable to negotiate safe sex and denied a say in decisions about sexual practices. For example, men—taught to prefer dry to wet sex—encourage urban wives to use herbs that will cause dryness and more pain, while preferences for women who have "hot" rather than "cold" vaginas can lead men to prefer women who are HIV/AIDS positive, since they tend to be "hot" As my informant here remarked, addressing these issues is about dealing not just with gender and power, but also with cultural perspectives on sexuality.[10] Yet seeing women as equally human and entitled to their own pleasure, rather than as vehicles solely for reproduction and men's satisfaction, would turn upside down men's conceptions of themselves.

The notions men develop about sexuality go to the center of how they see themselves, to their core concepts of self. Changing sexual practices requires men to reconstitute their identities. This is extremely threatening. The greatest threat of all lies in the requirement that men reevaluate women's status in relation to them. If men are to see women as equally human they are required to understand their own power in the world in a completely different way. Not surprisingly, this poses enormous challenges.

Nowhere are these deeply rooted notions of sexuality and identity clearer than in cultures where notions of honor and shame are paramount. As Rozario notes regarding Bangladesh (and the cultural context within which Durjoy Nari Shanga is struggling for the rights of sex workers):

> Anyone who has any real understanding of Bangladeshi patriarchy will appreciate that making an effective challenge to patriarchal ideologies in Bangladesh is extremely difficult. The ideology that supports patriarchy in Bangladesh centres on concepts such as izzat (honour, focusing in particular on the control of women's sexuality), lajja-sharam (shame) and parda (purdah, restrictions on women's mobility). These concepts pervade the whole society and indeed support the class structure of the society (Rozario 2004).

Beginning to address gender inequality in such contexts means trying to deconstruct the intertwined effects of religion and culture, an exercise that CARE staff in another country office, Niger, developed the courage to undertake. The population in Niger is predominantly Muslim, but the nature of cultural practices is influenced heavily by traditional conservatism. In the south central Maradi Department, a gender equity and household livelihood security project wrestled with whether religion could be used to address some of these gender inequities. The project decided to work with the Union of Moslem Women in Niger (l'Union des Femmes Musulmanes du Niger) to reach the most influential *marabous* (Islamic leaders and teachers) in Maradi. A group of three *marabous* helped to identify two focal point *marabous* per village, and to produce a guiding document summarizing all the *sourates, hadiths,* and verses of the Koran that address the rights of women on issues such as marriage, divorce, inheritance (including of land and other productive assets), cloistering, and access to education and training (Sayo 2002).

Nevertheless, in areas where Islamic practice still lacks women's voices and mixes with deeply conservative cultural environments, women retain a status that is well short of fully human. In late April 2005, the second woman in two weeks was stoned to death in a remote Afghan village, simply for being in the company of a younger man to whom she was not married (IRIN 2005). Although the new Afghan constitution upholds the equal dignity of women, a 2003 Amnesty International report on the justice system in Afghanistan titled itself, "No one listens to us and no one treats us as human beings." The report notes that the widespread violence against women is a result of practices still predominant such as the forced marriage of girl children. The criminal justice system remains too weak to offer effective protection of women's rights to life and physical security, and itself subjects them to discrimination and abuse. Protection for women at acute risk of violence is virtually absent (Amnesty International 2003).

In the focus group discussions held for the production of the Amnesty report, women perceived the difficulty in getting help as rooted in their subordinate status and lesser worth. Even in seeking help from a government body, an abused woman can be seen as "a bad girl who doesn't obey her father or brother." Women participants said, "We just want to be treated as human beings." CARE has long had a focus on girls' education in Afghanistan, and is seeking to effect ways of including women's voices in local decision-making processes, but there remain great challenges concerning how to proceed more broadly with work that addresses deep-seated cultural norms of gender inequity.

Developing Women's Solidarity, Engaging Men and Changing Culture

The final section of this chapter summarizes what some of CARE's more recent experiences have shown about the kinds of approaches needed to address these deep cultural causes of gender inequality. Where successful learning and practice has taken place, it has occurred through three contributions by which rights-based approaches have made a positive difference to the nature and efficacy of projects.

The first contribution is to the nature of analyses. Projects adopting a rights-based approach are beginning to undertake much deeper analyses of why gender inequity and its consequences are so pervasive, and are then addressing the consequences and implications of these analyses. Two brief examples will suffice here, both drawn from Bangladesh.

There is common agreement among all researchers on gender inequality in Bangladesh that the root underlying cause rests in "the overall gender ideology of Bengali patriarchy, with its systematic devaluation of women and its denial of their right to an independent existence without male guardianship" (Rozario 2004, 28). This ideology is held in common by the Hindu Bengalis who comprise 16 percent or so of the population, as well as by the very small populations of Christian and Buddhist Bengalis. It also promotes violence against women, seen by many men and women as a normal part of life, and considered a personal and private affair to be handled within the family or local context. The legal system is distrusted and widely perceived as unlikely to provide unbiased justice in violence cases. Practices related to the patriarchal gender ideology, such as dowry and child marriage, are illegal but almost universally prevalent. Many villagers willingly express unhappiness, particularly with respect to dowry, but see no socially viable alternatives (Robinson 2005, 11).

In the Dinajpur area of northwest Bangladesh, a small pilot violence against women (VAW) project was established to test an approach based on this kind of structural analysis. The pilot was founded on the assumption that "[t]he basic cause of violence is rooted in the gender ideology, which promotes male dominance and superiority and women's subordination and subservience" (Huq and Hassan 2004, 16). Consequently, the pilot sought to take a structural approach in addressing violence, working with a range of institutions in the district context, and linking forums at the village level with legal advice services and the local *salish* (justice) and union *parishad* (government) systems. Using the lessons learned, the country office began further work. From an impact inquiry study undertaken in 2006, the following is concluded:

> In summary, the focus of the project is to raise awareness, stimulate dialog between different actors and change the way in which informal and formal institutions and services work. Attention has been paid to working with men as well as women, recognizing the need to change men's attitudes, particularly those of elite men who wield significant power in local political and social relations. Much effort has been directed at trying to transform social structures to make them more likely to promote women's rights including making space in local institutions for women to participate. The major thrust has been to try to build advocacy and services for women's rights, particularly the right to live in freedom from gender-based violence. Changing highly unequal gender relations is essential to reach the project goal (Kanji 2006a, 8–9).

A second case in which using a relational, rights-based methodology has resulted in a much deeper analysis is the Nijeder Janyia Nijera (We for Ourselves) project, also in northwest Bangladesh. Nijera was initiated through a participatory power analysis that was designed to illuminate institutional arrangements and relationships from the union parishad (district) level downwards. The study sought

> to elucidate the ways in which the practices of local-level elites shape governance institutions and present systematic barriers that prevent marginalized groups from participating in democratic processes. It examines how political networks and alliances between powerful actors are fostered and used to gain access to public resources and how elites use these

resources and benefits to build support within local constituencies (Bode 2002, 2).

Most critically, both elites and nonelites were involved in conducting the
analysis and mapping decision relationships and their implications. This
highlighted various accepted forms of social control through which local
leaders assert their domination, as well as the way in which the alliances
and factions that underpin power relations shift over time.

Consequently, the Nijera project began to build from the increasingly
sophisticated understanding of power relations possessed by the village
residents themselves. Community-led total sanitation has been used as an
entry point for project facilitators who work with men and women to
prioritize initiatives that will have an impact on the social and economic
conditions of the poorest households, the majority of which are female-
headed (Kanji 2006b, 8). In this process, "natural leaders" emerge from
different social economic classes. Kanji concludes:

> Nijera has achieved an enormous amount in a short space of
> time in terms of building women's agency, supporting them to
> change relationships in their locality and to pursue their own
> goals. While there have been fewer changes in the structures
> which disempower women, women's ability to engage with
> more powerful actors has increased. The way in which such
> practices and strategies begin to influence and shape rules and
> norms [is] also evident (Kanji 2006b, 38).

Kanji also noted that, while there have been many tangible improvements
in material well-being, "women and men we spoke to focused on changes
in confidence, self-esteem, better relations between women and men,
poor and better off, and an ability to negotiate with the more powerful as
much as the changes in hygiene, health, hunger and income" (Kanji
2006b, 15). This reflects the difference made in quality of the project's
process by its analytically richer starting point, and the fact that the ongoing commitment in Nijera to participatory analysis for each issue villagers
identify has ensured that this starting point has not been compromised.

The second contribution through which rights-based approaches have
increased the effectiveness of projects in challenging existing power relations and the subordination of women is the explicit use of information
about women's rights within projects. This is a critical part of the process
of conscientization. In learning about their rights-based entitlements as
encoded in national and international constitutions, laws, and policies,
women also learn that their subordination is not part of the natural order
of things, but is imposed by systems of discrimination that are socially

constructed and that can be altered (Martinez 2002, quoted by Robinson 2004). As one of the Tangail sex workers noted, "We are not corrupt, because we get income for the service we provide, and then we use it to buy food and look after our children. But the [government] Ministers, where do they get their money from?"[11] The same speaker noted that with more education they would less likely have become sex workers—and that the government thus bore a responsibility for their situation and for the future expansion of education provision to girls.

Attempts to pursue women's empowerment that start from the "natural order" of things have tended to founder if they come to question the inequities in this natural order more systematically. Because a rights-based approach to women's empowerment requires the challenge to inequities inherent in social and cultural practices to be posed at the outset, it is much more likely that such efforts will confront gender inequity as an underlying cause of poverty and social injustice.

The third contribution of rights-based approaches is a dialogical approach that challenges men to engage with women, viewing them not as passive recipients of men's largesse, but as cocreators of their intertwined (and occasionally not intertwined) trajectories. Such dialog, building on the first and second contributions, is based on the assumption that cultural attitudes and power relations need to change if women's rights fulfillment is to improve. Dialogical processes of this nature also lead to ideas about power itself being reconceptualized, as is noted from the exchange below recorded from a discussion with village forum and union parishad members involved with the VAW pilot project in Bangladesh. The discussion was prompted by a question on power and the way it is perceived:

Man:	I support changing the way power is seen, and the process whereby it is used. Until now men have consumed this power.
Q:	Why don't you transfer this power to women?
Man (continuing):	This would lead to fights . . . this would be war. It is better to change attitudes.
Woman:	It is not a sustainable solution to transfer power from men to women. The rights and dignity of men as well as women require this attitude to change. If men and women respect each other equally this will contribute better to household income. Everyone's potential will be respected equally, and this will lead to the household being better off, not just economically, but also as a family. There will also be happiness and

love. If we respect each other equally, if we value each other, then there will be love and happiness. Rather than taking power away, it is preferable to talk of the empowerment of women so that they have equal power. (Drinkwater 2005, 15).

The learning from rights-based approaches is allowing a more rapid progress toward addressing gender inequity issues than has occurred previously. For instance, in Niger it took half a decade of experience before the project staff plucked up the courage to engage with the *marabous*. In contrast, in the Bangladesh Nijera and VAW initiatives, more deep-seated forms of change have been initiated almost from the outset. Owing to their more insightful analyses, and to the understanding that power relations and structural factors will have to be addressed, these projects have a clearer sense of purpose, pathway, and teleology from the outset.

Noteworthy too in these projects is the awareness that the external dialog seeking to change attitudes and relationships has to be mirrored by an internal one. In the SHAKTI project, for example, the starting point of recognizing the sex workers as equally human was immensely difficult for the project staff to cope with, especially at the outset. SHAKTI staff were themselves marginalized by other staff in CARE and other NGOs, and had to overcome their own prejudices. At first the sex workers did not trust CARE either, but as they felt the process was helping them open their own eyes, they did learn to trust more. The key process was one of interactive, critical reflection, whereby both staff and sex workers learned together (Magar 2005). This mirrors the later experience of Nijera, which has explicitly used dialogical methods internally to bring about changes in organizational culture and to foster a learning environment for the transition to rights-based approaches (Bode 2007, 1).

If gender inequity is to be addressed, we then all face the challenge of having to deal with the definition of self that we grow up with. As was shown in SHAKTI, an effective project requires a mutual exploration process, and an approach grounded in the evolving solidarity and consciousness of the women concerned. Men must be involved in this process, and the key to overcoming barriers to their participation is for them to see themselves too as beneficiaries. In Niger, the breakthrough that occurred was signaled by one woman who commented that it is now the men who are calling upon other men to defend the rights of women (Sayo 2002).

This is not to presume that there is a single appropriate way of addressing women's inequality. Rather, ways appropriate to different cultural contexts need to be found. Since men should not be the sole arbiters of "culture," men and women must find ways of engaging together to explore how women can become fully human. In this process, the building of women's solidarity groups can be valuable in altering power relations so that men do start to listen. For instance, in India CARE worked with social development NGO partners to develop a very efficient microsavings approach in order to build the capacity of women's groups, which the partners then used as a basis to help the women take on an expanding social and political agenda (Drinkwater 2007).

In concluding, I'd like to let Dhanvanti Sohvani, a member of the Chunkatta *mahila mandal* and village *gram sabha*, Durg district, Chhattisgarh, have a last say. In finishing an account of her personal story she said:

> You have to talk about equity before we can talk about health. I would love to become more involved in these things. We would like to learn more about empowerment processes, how these have happened in other places. Women's experiences can be so powerful, and we can really learn from each other, so that we don't need to be educated to be able to generate solutions to our problems. I want to introduce the concept of rights for men and women in my village.
>
> Men have to face certain realities . . . realize that they have to give up some power[12] in order for things to change for the better (Drinkwater, Singh and Hora 2004).

The addressing of gender inequity requires both individual and collective change. Most fundamentally, if we are to address the root causes of gender inequity, we have to address the definition of self that we all grow up with and the resulting social stereotypes. This process has the potential to yield a perspective under which we are all equally human, and which recognizes that the psychological and structural dimensions of change are at least as important as the material.

References

Amnesty International. 2003. *Afghanistan: "No-one listens to us and no-one treats us as human beings." Justice denied to women.* ASA 11/023/2003. London.

Bode, B. 2002. *Analyzing power structures in rural Bangladesh.* Dhaka: CARE Bangladesh.

Bode, B. 2007. *Building a learning culture.* Atlanta: CARE USA.

Chalimba, M. and C. Pinder. 2002. *Gender power relations study and the impact of safety nets in Malawi.* Vol. 1, *Summary of findings, conclusions and recommendations.* Lilongwe: Central Region Infrastructure Maintenance Programme, CARE International in Malawi.

Cornwall, A. Harrison E. and Whitehead. A. 2004. Introduction: Repositioning feminisms in gender and development. *IDS Bulletin* 35, no. 4. Brighton: Institute of Development Studies.

Drinkwater, M. 2005. Women's empowerment in Bangladesh: The emerging story of the SII. Paper presented at the conference "Women's empowerment, impact assessment of development programs, and forms of knowledge: New horizons for cross disciplinary and participative research methods knowledge exchange." Atlanta: Centre for the Study of Public Scholarship, Emory University.

Drinkwater, M. 2007. *Moving towards wide screen approaches: Phase II synthesis report of the strategic impact inquiry on women's empowerment in South Asia.* Atlanta: CARE USA.

Drinkwater, M. and L. Bull-Kamanga. 2002. Giving people a voice: Moving towards participatory governance and the building of a rights based urban program in CARE Bangladesh. Dhaka: CARE International in Bangladesh.

Drinkwater, M., M. McEwan and F. Samuels. 2006. The effects of HIV/AIDS on agricultural production systems in Zambia: A restudy 1993–2005. Lusaka: International Food Policy Research Institute— Regional Network on AIDS, Livelihoods and Food Security (RENEWAL).

Drinkwater, M., A. Singh and G. Hora. 2004. *Change from the heart: Unlocking the potential—report on the Chhattisgarh reflective practice exercise.* Delhi: CARE India.

Goering, L. 2004. In Lesotho, women hope for control of their lives. *Chicago Tribune,* 17 October.

Goetz A-M. 2004. Reinvigorating autonomous feminist spaces. *IDS Bulletin* 35, no. 4. Brighton: Institute of Development Studies.

Huq, N. and S. Hassan. 2004. Violence against women: Report of the needs assessment study for violence prevention. Dhaka: CARE Bangladesh.

IRIN Asia. 2005. *Afghanistan: Woman executed for adultery.* http://www.irinnews.org.

Kanji, N. 2006a. *Partnership for healthy life (PHL): Violence against women (VAW) initiative. Dinajpur district, Bangladesh: Strategic impact inquiry for CARE Bangladesh.* Dhaka: CARE Bangladesh.

Kanji, N. 2006b. *Nijeder janyia nijera (We for ourselves): Strategic impact inquiry.* Dhaka: CARE Bangladesh.

Magar, V. 2005. *Now they look at us as normal: Stigma, violence, sex worker resistance and HIV/AIDS in Bangladesh.* Dhaka: CARE Bangladesh.

McCaston, K. 2004. *Moving CARE's programming forward: Unifying framework for poverty eradication and social justice and underlying causes of poverty.* Atlanta: CARE USA.

Mehrotra, D.P. 2003. *Key learnings and insights for integration of gender concerns in a reproductive health program.* Delhi: CARE India.

Pinder, C. 2002. *Gender empowerment and change processes in CARE Zambia's programming work.* Atlanta: CARE USA.

Robinson, V. 2004. *Responding to gender-based violence: Lessons learned from CARE Tajikistan's PROVAW project.* Atlanta: CARE USA.

Robinson, V. 2005. *CARE Bangladesh's VAW initiatives program assessment.* Dhaka: CARE Bangladesh.

Rozario, S. 2004. *Building solidarity against patriarchy.* Dhaka: CARE Bangladesh, Rural Livelihoods Program.

Sayo, H. 2002. *Gender equity: Involving Islamic leaders. A case study from the Gender Equity and Household Livelihood Security Project.* Niamey: CARE International in Niger.

Sitambuli, E. 1998. *Gender status report 1994–1998. CARE Zambia. Livingstone Food Security Project.* Lusaka: CARE International in Zambia.

Turner, S.D. 2000. *Extension that works: Lessons learned by the Livingstone Food Security Programme, 1994–2000.* Lusaka: CARE International in Zambia.

Wason, D. 2004. *Evolving livelihood strategies of rural Basotho 1993–2002.* Maseru: CARE International in Lesotho.

Win, E.J. 2004. Not very poor, powerless or pregnant: The African woman forgotten by development. *IDS Bulletin* 35, no. 4. Brighton: Institute of Development Studies.

Notes

1. With thanks to Elisa Martinez, who commented on the original draft.

2. "Notes of meeting with former LFSP Gender Officer (Emma Sitambuli)," interview notes for Pinder 2002.

3. "Notes of meeting with former LFSP Gender Officer (Emma Sitambuli)," interview notes for Pinder 2002.

4. Notes from Drinkwater and Sitambuli interviews with Maria and Marron Mungara, February 21, 2002.

5. Notes from Drinkwater and Sitambuli interviews with Amos and Mary Chalaba, February 21, 2002.

6. Stopping HIV/AIDS through Knowledge and Training Initiatives. Established in 1995, originally as a DFID-funded project with sex workers aiming only to increase contraceptive prevalence rates.

7. Magar (2005) quotes one sex worker: "We feel humiliated when we go to the market without shoes on our feet. Everyone looks, hurls slurs and spits on our bare feet in front of all to see."

8. From a 1992 PRA exercise in the Central Province of Zambia.

9. Fieldnotes for research documented in Drinkwater, McEwan and Samuels (2006).

10. Loveness Makonese, in notes on visit to CARE Zimbabwe, November 16, 2004.

11. Fieldnotes for research documented in Drinkwater (2007).

12. Or change the way they perceive power.

PART FIVE

The Operational Implications of Rights-Based Approaches

Rights-Based Development: The Challenge of Change and Power for Development NGOs[1]

Jennifer Chapman[2]
in collaboration with Valerie Miller,
Adriano Campolina Soares and John Samuel

Introduction

Where there is a need, a right is born.
                    —*written on a wall, Bariloche, Argentina*

Many development NGOs have recognized the importance of integrating rights into development work. As a result their use of rights language has increased, though there are disagreements about definitions and approaches.[3] For the present authors "rights-based approaches" integrate the political side of development and change efforts with the organizing, capacity building, and creative dimensions. The political aspect focuses on ensuring that legal frameworks support and advance rights of the poor and excluded. The organizing dimension builds people's organizations, leadership, and synergy for collective struggle. The practical and creative side supports education and innovations that give meaning to rights and lay the basis for challenging oppressive practices and paradigms. Weaving together ideas and action can promote key aspects of change—strong social movements, critical thinking, relationships of reciprocity and mutual support, and the formulation of compelling alternatives to those current development models and ideologies that interact to deny people their rights.

Many economic, social, cultural, and political rights have been enshrined in United Nations conventions and procedures to provide a set of guiding principles. Other rights are not enshrined in law but are moral entitlements based on values of human dignity and equity. Rights are not static but have been articulated, defined, and put into law by the collective efforts of many

Figure 10.1 Illustration of a rights-based approach

The double helix illustrates that values are the core of the processes of rights work, and all aspects are dependent on each other.

Values: justice, equity/equality,

dignity, related attitudes & behaviour,

respect, inclusion, solidarity

centrality of marginalized people

Processes:
Organizing;
Mobilizing;
Enabling participation;
Shared analysis of causes, context and power;
Consciousness-raising;
Joint decision-making/action: private, public, legislative, legal;
Relationship building;
Supporting/accompanying;
Questioning assumptions;
Challenging ideology/hegemony;
Building alternatives.

Characteristics:
Empowering and Participatory–strengthens critical analysis skills, values, leadership, organisation and decision-making of poor/marginalized and NGO support organisations, builds self-esteem, solidarity, political awareness, social responsibility; needs gender and power considerations; iterative; progressive; deals with formal and informal forces (state/government, private sector, communal, cultural, multilateral); long-term process; commitment; requires belief and taking sides; inherent conflict; unpredictable.

people over many years, and they will continue to evolve (or be lost). This collective struggle is a vital element of rights-based approaches: rights can only be made real by the involvement and empowerment of the community at large, in particular those whose rights are most violated.

The values of justice, equity, equality, dignity, respect, and inclusion are at the core of a rights-based approach, as shown in Figure 10.1.

We view rights and participation as connected and see empowerment as being vital to the success of rights. Unfortunately, this connection is often lost. For example, many advocacy approaches exclude those already marginalized from decision making, thus doing little to change power structures or dynamics, and making any change achieved less likely to be sustained. Such approaches instead promote a singular focus on policy reform, which often results in advocates being consumed by lobbying and losing touch with constituencies. A focus on empowerment and partici-pation leads to questions about how power is used and promoted inside advocacy efforts: who sets the agenda and who carries out strategies, on what issues and using what approaches?

Despite the current popularity of rights rhetoric, the massive implica-tions of a development NGO truly adopting a rights-based approach have not been fully appreciated. A rights-based approach is inherently political, and takes power, struggle, and the vision of a better society as key factors in development. It implies that problems cannot be seen "as purely technical matters that can be resolved outside the political arena" without conflict, and that instead they are rooted in differences of power, income, and assets (Harriss 2003, quoted by Dóchas 2003, 8). Rights cannot be truly realized without changes in the structures and relationships of power in all their forms: changes in who makes decisions, in whose voice is heard, in what topics are seen as legitimate, in people's sense of relative self-worth, and in the confidence people have to speak out. This suggests that development NGOs must shift, in their primary role, from being implementers and drivers of development to being allies with people's organizations and social movements in a collective struggle for change. Such a shift means a much more complex mix of roles involving sharing and negotiating power in new ways, challenging assumptions, and taking clear, often risky, political stands in favor of people marginalized by poverty and the privilege of others.

Finding a balance between promoting the leadership and voice of the marginalized and speaking on their behalf can be a challenge. At times it may be difficult or dangerous for the marginalized to speak for themselves; in such cases NGOs may need to intervene directly to try to defend and guarantee rights, while still trying to take the most inclusive approach to making decisions about strategies and roles. We also cannot assume that the poorest and most marginalized always offer the best analysis or proposal. However, in all cases NGOs must be cautious that their actions do not undermine local organizations or place people unduly at risk.

Power and Change

Justice and power must be brought together so that whatever is just may be powerful and whatever is powerful may be just.

—*Blaise Pascal*

Poverty and the denial of people's rights are linked directly with unequal power relations, yet many organizations claiming to adopt rights-based approaches ignore power in their analysis and planning at all but the most superficial levels. This is a fundamental problem, as gains in rights are unlikely to be sustained without the transformation of power relations at all levels and the creation of new relationships based on values of solidarity, equity, dignity, and the common good (VeneKlasen et al. 2004).

Power works at many different levels and in many different ways (VeneKlasen et al. 2004). This means multiple strategies and actions are needed, ranging from lobbying and pressuring governments, protesting unfair business practices, and strengthening social movements and coalitions, to increasing the political awareness, solidarity, and confidence of poor and excluded groups and their supporters. Transforming unequal power relationships and sustaining new more inclusive ones requires change on a number of levels:

- In inequitable and unjust laws and policies

- In the way laws and policies are implemented and enforced and the attitudes and behaviors within the agencies entrusted with these tasks

- In societal attitudes and behaviors that support inequity and discrimination

- In poor and marginalized people's own sense of individual and collective self-worth, entitlement, and access to justice

- In the capacity of the powerless to analyze power, develop a collective identity as rights holders, develop solidarity, and act collectively to gain concrete long-term changes

- In knowledge and acceptance of new practical development alternatives that challenge the prevalent neoliberal model and provide new ways of understanding the world.

These elements are self-reinforcing, and without progress on all fronts gains achieved in only a few arenas will remain vulnerable. Which aspects of change take priority at a particular time will depend on the context and moment. Many organizations adopting a rights-based approach focus on issue-based lobbying of decision makers by advocacy professionals. The weakness of this approach lies in its assumptions that the political system is relatively open and democratic, and that the policy concerns of the powerless can be met through the work of professional lobbyists backed up by adequate resources, solid information, and soundly researched, well-presented arguments. This approach ignores certain realities of power, and is likely to have little impact on areas crucial to ensuring long-term change: citizen participation; community organization; leadership development; political awareness; societal norms; organizational capacity to monitor and enforce policy gains or hold institutions accountable; and people's sense of self-worth.

Strengths of the Rights-Based Approach: ActionAid International's[4] Experience

With the launch of its strategy *Fighting Poverty Together* in 1999, ActionAid formally adopted a rights-based approach defined as "seeking solutions to poverty through the establishment and enforcement of rights that entitle poor and marginalized people to a fair share of society's resources" (1999, 12). In reality a number of ActionAid country programs had been moving in this direction for several years. By 2005 ActionAid was beginning to see a number of positive developments attributable, at least in part, to this new way of conceptualizing its work.[5]

Significant modifications in approach were made possible through changes within ActionAid, including a shift to southern leadership bringing with it more perspectives from the global South, and a related change in governance structures as the organization shifted from being a northern NGO to a more international one.

The ways in which rights-based approaches have been made operational throughout ActionAid have largely depended on the local context and the senior management team in each country. For example, AAIndia places a strong emphasis on redressing the denial of rights of the most marginalized groups. Its efforts often start with building and strengthening local organizations, followed by helping people to create ways to access resources and other basic services to address their immediate livelihood needs. The work includes an education component to assist people to develop relevant capacities, a broader understanding of issues, and a sense of empowerment so they can collectively assert and advocate their rights and dignity (Thomson 2001). In contrast, AABangladesh believes that "prolonged denial of freedom, security and dignity has imposed severe 'natural' limits on the ability and willingness of poor people to reverse the injustices inherent in their institutional environments which impose prohibitively high costs for personal and collective actions" (ActionAid 2001). While working to build poor people's capacities and livelihoods AABangladesh also emphasizes its own "direct advocacy" with broader civil society, aimed at removing the governance and institutional injustices that produce inequity, marginalization, and denial of rights.

More Holistic Thinking in Planning

Before 1999 ActionAid had tended to work on a long-term basis in discrete geographical areas on issues such as education and agriculture, with a focus on meeting people's basic needs in a participatory and empowering manner. These projects frequently led to tangible and concrete benefits for the people directly involved, but often became quite self-referential, working in isolation from other initiatives. Projects did not adapt to changing contexts or seize new opportunities, and their benefits were limited in scope and area. In some cases, by providing services that ought to be the responsibility of the government, they were absolving government of its obligations. Over the first five years of adopting rights-based approaches, ActionAid began to see considerable change in this way of operating:

> To understand poverty, we are increasingly looking beyond people's material conditions and focusing our attention on their position in society . . . on the web of oppressive social relations and deprivations which restrict poor people's access to resources and services, while limiting their substantive and instrumental freedoms (Morago 2004, 4).

Reviews undertaken by ActionAid from 2004 to 2005 reveal more comprehensive understandings of the conditions and factors that create and perpetuate poverty. By focusing on people's position in society, ActionAid found it could better understand local power dynamics and assess the viability of ideas for intervention, recognizing that in some cases certain ideas may be completely inappropriate. For example, when AANepal started work in one rural area, staff envisioned a project that would address poverty by helping tenant farmers increase production and suggested that irrigation would be a good investment. It was only after probing the farmers' opposition to the scheme that staff realized irrigation could actually be counterproductive for tenants who had no enforceable right to the land they farmed. With improved land value and productivity, landlords might find it more worthwhile to evict tenants and farm themselves. The irrigation project was scrapped and instead work began on organizing, education, and advocacy for the defense of tenant rights. ActionAid also supported efforts to build strong local organizations, influence policy, and increase farmers' critical analysis and leadership skills, thereby contributing to the growth of a wider social movement of tenant farmers and peasants (Uprety et al. 2005).

Over this period, ActionAid moved from a focus on discrete projects in particular areas to working in the context of broader processes of social change, particularly by promoting links across programs and strategies to foster short- and long-term change at different levels. This included increased strategic engagement with government agencies at different levels to help guarantee these agencies' capacity and political will to protect the rights of the poor and marginalized—for example, by supporting local and national government entities in negotiations with more powerful bodies, be these national government, multilateral bodies, or other actors.

Simultaneously, ActionAid was undertaking more work on selected global issues through teams drawn from offices worldwide. Critical thinking and reflection, and knowledge about power and change, are vital skills for ActionAid staff at all levels. The attempt to develop these skills was supported by the introduction of a more open accountability, learning, and planning system (ALPS) intended to encourage reflection and learning throughout the organization.

Working More in Partnership and Networks

The critical analysis that led to the adoption of a rights-based approach in ActionAid also resulted in several new types of initiatives, and a broader range of partner organizations. In some countries, Guatemala and Bangladesh among them, ActionAid started to work on capacity building to inform an independent media. In others, such as Kenya and Guatemala, ActionAid started work with lawyers and justice systems to link them with civil society organizations working with the poor. Some ActionAid teams are working with interfaith groups (Kenya, Nigeria) and Muslim groups (Kenya, Ethiopia, Uganda), or forming new partnerships around disability (Kenya) and youth (Ethiopia) (ActionAid 2004). In particular, ActionAid has started to partner more with networks and social movements. ActionAid also initiated discussions on causes of poverty with existing partners, who had been providing services without a wider analysis of power and change. These partners were encouraged to explore and make similar shifts in their analysis and work, though some old partnerships have ended.

In a rights-based approach it is essential to challenge power imbalances. Local organizing, alliance building, and networking are key strategies for this project. ActionAid's work at national and international levels is increasingly carried out in conjunction with national or global networks and coalitions. In a number of countries, providing networking opportunities and links empowered partners and encouraged them to make a shift away from an exclusive focus on service delivery.

Collaboration with Social Movements

Work with social movements grew in priority under ActionAid's new approach. Implementing rights-based approaches was found to be easier and more effective when the community had its own strong social movements. In Brazil, for example, the national landless peasant movement draws its strength from local groups, and from a comprehensive change strategy that integrates support for concrete development initiatives with work on rights, advocacy, organizing, political awareness, and critical thinking. In such situations, a central component of ActionAid's rights-based approach involves support for organizing, consolidating, and strengthening the ongoing work of local social movements.

Another key objective of the approach is to link community-based social movements with each other, as well as connecting them with other regional, national, and international social movements and networks. This integration can increase the power of community based social movements, broaden their understanding of poverty and the denial of rights, increase their capacity to network and build powerful alliances, and provide opportunities for them to learn from the experience of others. The World Social Forum processes have become important opportunities for forging new thinking, building alternatives, exchanging experiences, and forming alliances. ActionAid has been encouraging partner and staff participation in these spaces as a way to learn, connect with, and contribute to increasingly compelling visions of justice and approaches to social change.

Working in alliance with poor people's social movements certainly makes the struggle for rights more sustainable. However, what remains a huge challenge is how to work in poor and excluded communities that lack significant social movements (here understood as movements of people with a common identity and a collective agenda for changing public policies). ActionAid has worked to support the building up of such movements in various countries (e.g., Haiti). In the process of building movements the role of an external facilitator such as ActionAid is crucial for creating an enabling environment in which rights holders can develop a collective identity, elaborate a common agenda for policy change, analyze power, and strategize toward their goals. In many cases service delivery—the addressing of immediate needs—was used as an opportunity to bring the community together and start building up the collective agenda, or as a demonstration of the kind of alternative models that should be implemented by the duty bearers.

A Focus on the Most Marginalized within Communities

ActionAid's new focus led to expanded efforts to assist processes for including marginalized people in the social, political, and economic life of their communities. In Burundi, such efforts contributed to the 2003 inclusion of the marginalized Batwa community in the Bashingantahe, a traditional system of local governance. In Vietnam, ActionAid's program commenced working with unregistered migrant women, and in Haiti, India, and China work began with economic migrants (ActionAid 2004). This ensured that ActionAid's understanding of the political agenda was being opened up to new issues, and perhaps more importantly that new social actors were being supported to engage in political arenas.

It is of course not always strategic to work solely with the most marginalized or impoverished since they can be particularly difficult to organize and mobilize. There are times when the most effective way to challenge inequitable power relations and structures is to work with broader groupings of excluded groups or poor communities. However, it is always important to consider inherent inequities and tensions within any group.

Concrete Results within Longer Social Change Processes

It can take many years to transform deeply entrenched forces of margin-alization and impoverishment, but it is possible to see concrete results as groups organize to identify and claim rights and related services and resources, and to represent themselves and their communities in arenas of public decision making.[6] In Tanzania, ActionAid worked with local farmer groups such as the Tandahimba Farmers' Association in the Mtwara Region, the Liwale Farmers' Association in the Lindi Region, and the Clove Rehabilitation Coalition in Zanzibar, which were influential in obtaining better prices for local farmers in 2003. Additionally, one of ActionAid's local partners, ZAFFIDE, mobilized farmers to form a union. The union began negotiating with hotel owners for guaranteed prices for their produce, and in 2005 were about to sign a deal with the seed sup-plier to make it responsible for bad seeds. "Bringing us together was one of the greatest achievements," explained Jaji Ramadhani, a vegetable farmer. "I feel motivated for being a farmer because we are now going to have one voice" (ActionAid Tanzania 2003). In another recent success addressing a different arena of inequity, ActionAid supported polio patients in Sierra Leone who formed the Disabled Workers' Alliance Movement. The group lobbies government on disability rights and has secured financial support from donors (ActionAid 2004).

New Energy in Work on Gender and Women's Rights

The conceptual shift toward rights offered an opportunity to reenergize work on gender, and restore its political edge, by incorporating a clear women's rights dimension. ActionAid began to look at gender issues out-side mainstream poverty reduction efforts, moving to address violence against women and reproductive and sexual rights. For example, the Mutapola Campaign—a Southern Africa Partnerships Program launched by ActionAid and the Open Society Initiative for Southern Africa—put women's rights right at the centre of its work with a clear statement that the challenge of HIV/AIDS could not be met without a focus on con-fronting the position of women within society as second-class citizens (ActionAid 2005). ActionAid recognizes that it still needs to be bolder in taking sides with women and girls who are marginalized and oppressed in many contexts, but also acknowledges that it is "still afraid of rocking cul-tural and religious boats" (ActionAid 2003, 16).

More Focus on the Organization's Power, Position and Relationships with Partners

When analyzing power it is impossible to avoid looking at its dynamics within one's own organization and between that organization and its partners. Some ActionAid staff have started to think more critically about how they work with others and how they use their power as an international NGO in those relationships. Behaviors and attitudes related to power are a central component of ALPS that all staff are expected to adhere to.

The amalgamation of the ActionAid family into ActionAid International is partly an attempt to address power dynamics within the organization by overturning the typical model for international NGOs, in which the organization's power is situated in the North and most of the operations conducted in the South. ActionAid is now an international NGO based in South Africa and with principally southern leadership. As part of this shift, ActionAid is becoming a federation of affiliated organizations from the North and South, each having equal status. Despite this laudable vision, power issues within the organization will continue to be challenging. Equally, power issues in the relationship between ActionAid and its partners will persist, as the 2007 partnership review indicated.

Work on Building Active Solidarity Constituencies in the North

The concept of development as a right rather than charity, and the understanding that change will only be sustained through organized constituencies, challenges ActionAid to recognize that supporters in the North should not be viewed purely as sources of finance but as allies in a common struggle for justice. Fundraising and campaigning are important parts of the organization's global solidarity, but sometimes other approaches may be appropriate. More work is needed in developing such approaches, but one positive example comes from the efforts of ActionAid UK to engage youth as potential activists while making no attempt to raise funding from them.

Accountability to Poor and Marginalized Communities

Rights-based approaches will ultimately mean little if they have no potential to transform power relations. Thus approaches must be judged against their ability to support and strengthen the capacity of the poor and excluded to articulate their own priorities, take leadership, build organizations, and claim genuine accountability from development agencies. Similarly, they need to be assessed on the extent to which the NGOs themselves become critically self-aware and address inherent power inequalities in their interaction with poor communities (A. Pereira Jr., in Chapman et al. 2006).

ActionAid has made considerable efforts to become more accountable to all its stakeholders, and in particular poor and marginalized people. This is one of the key aspects of ALPS, and among other things it calls for all programs to hold annual participatory reviews and reflections that allow communities and partners to question ActionAid about its work.

Challenges of Adopting Rights-Based Approaches

We may be seeing myth-making in progress . . . all the elements are there—claims based on high moral principles backed by selective evidence, a large army of convinced proponents, eloquent and elegant defenses and even taller claims when the myth is questioned but not much besides.

—*Dzodzi Tsikata (no date, 10)*

Rights-based approaches are very much in vogue among development organizations, at least on paper. Many claims are made about how these approaches will finally solve the intractable problems we have been tackling for such a long time. The present authors are more cautious, and believe that positive outcomes of rights-based approaches depend largely on linking them with what we have learned about the roles of participation, empowerment, and development alternatives in change processes that focus on transforming power relations. There are considerable dangers in construing a rights-based approach as relying solely on policy and advocacy, and as operating exclusively of other development approaches.

Keeping a Balance

While policy change is necessary, it is not sufficient to transform the structures, attitudes and values that are at the root of societal inequalities and injustice.

—*John Samuel (1996, 1)*

Many development NGOs increasingly emphasize rights and policy work led by professionals over local organizing, education, and development initiatives (Miller 2005). To pursue this focus, they often attempt to meet their lack of skills in policy analysis and advocacy by employing lawyers or policy analysts at the expense of those with grassroots organizing and participation experience. The authors contend that the real deficit in NGO staffing is not in either of these areas, both of which are important but not sufficient for effective operation. The need is rather for people who possess cross-disciplinary capacities and perspectives, and who are thus able to make connections with other types of knowledge and practice and build relations of synergy and cooperation with others (VeneKlasen et al. 2004). These are the people who have the vision and potential to bring together the multiple aspects of rights-based approaches so that different strategies can support each other rather than operating in isolation or at cross-purposes.

Lessons gained from women's movements around the world are important to consider here. Some activists are finding that over the last 25 years their increasing, almost exclusive focus in the policy arena has been too narrow, and that in order to address the multiple dimensions of power they need to revisit the more comprehensive and holistic strategies of their initial efforts—including developing and organizing grassroots leadership, as well as pursuing individual reflection and empowerment processes.

Power in Networks and Partnerships

Given ActionAid's organizational size and resources in Africa and parts of Asia, its presence and activism can eclipse the capacity and confidence of local groups to advance their ideas and interests. The way in which large international organizations use their power becomes key to whether participation, empowerment, and rights are fostered, and whether poor and marginalized groups have a meaningful voice in their societies. For large organizations to contribute effectively to such goals requires staff who are aware of, and who continually reflect on, their assumptions and approaches. National alliances, created by international NGOs, often fail when they do not respond to local dynamics and powerfully felt needs and demands on the ground.

The review of the Elimu campaign on education found that the most successful coalitions between ActionAid and local organizations appeared

> to be those where ActionAid staff had time and money . . . to invest heavily in the formation and early development of the network, but subsequently have been able to step back from power. . . . [S]everal country programs said that they played a "facilitating" role within the network: carefully encouraging other organizations to take on leadership functions, helping to establish participatory and democratic decision-making . . . and assisting members to clarify and focus their aims, as well as providing funds and occasional technical support. (Elimu 2002, 9)

The report contrasts this model of partnership with the Global Campaign for Education, under which conflict between international organizations created "intense pressure to define strong positions and achieve 'hits' very early in the campaign." In areas where the campaign had not emerged from the grassroots or existing social movements, this orientation had a tendency "to crowd out the space for the weaker partners in the international network—organizations based at national or local level in the South—to develop and own the campaign's agenda" (Elimu 2002, 17).

One analyst reflecting on the Kamaiya Campaign to eliminate bonded labor in Nepal notes that while the campaign was successful on the legal front, the policy victory itself undermined the campaign and weakened Kamiaya-led organizations moving forward. When the Kamaiya were freed in law, but found themselves with no livelihood options, the campaign was inhibited in reacting and regrouping due to the dynamics between the Kamaiya and the NGOs who, over time, had gained the dominant role. Similarly, a ActionAid study in a different context warned of the risk that rights-based approaches might result in poor people feeling obliged to "sing along with the tune of the professional middle classes to an even greater extent than has previously been the case" (Fiedrich and Jellema 2003, 188).

Internal Investment Needed

While ActionAid has made an enormous shift in the way it conceptualizes and implements its work, ensuring common understanding of this across the organization remains highly difficult. The challenges of moving a large, diffuse organization through a radical change process are immense and were perhaps underestimated. The transition was further complicated by the lack of a coherent change strategy and by insufficient resources and support for staff. As a result one review found:

> There is no general understanding of rights-based approaches (RBA) in the organization and there are many different interpretations of it. Some country programs know little about RBA and others do not have the confidence to put it into practice. A good deal of work needs to be done within the organization to demystify RBA and integrate the different elements of rights-based analysis and practice. (Morago 2003, 2)[7]

ActionAid has also struggled with the challenge of achieving the depth on policy issues necessary to engage relevant regional and international institutions and bring coherence across themes into a visible and viable program of work. While more country offices are now engaged in international campaign work, this has occurred primarily in response to events rather than being determined by a comprehensive long-term agenda for change based on, or strongly connected with, grassroots work. In a related problem, ActionAid has found it difficult to directly engage with external actors on the substance of policies by providing thought-out critiques and suggestions for alternatives. Progress in developing and agreeing on policy positions confronts a number of obstacles:

- The need to support policy positions emerging from the concerns of the poor with solid evidence and developed analysis

- A lack of capacity to analyze policies and integrate this analysis with grassroots education and mobilization work

- Insufficient coherence in advocacy strategies and approaches

- The need to engage more critically in an environment that is dynamic and constantly changing

- Limitations of policy perspectives that focus on international debates without making links to domestic issues or to underlying paradigms and ideologies

- A lack of initiatives to build the policy capacity of social movements.

To meet these challenges, ActionAid staff need to develop more experience in policy analysis and advocacy, and to gain knowledge about how hegemony, ideologies, and government structures work and interact. They also need to learn how to engage people living in poverty in change processes that contest these multiple forms of power. Program officers must be better able to tease out policy issues arising from their field interventions, and the organization needs to break down the barriers to working cooperatively at and across all levels.

One means by which ActionAid has tried to build staff abilities in these areas is through hiring high-profile activists. This has met with mixed success as these hires often find themselves in administrative positions, overloaded with bureaucratic tasks and unable to use their strengths as activists.

Finally, ActionAid's transition to a rights-based approach and international amalgamation has also led to some confusion about the role and identity of ActionAid, as the following quote from AABrazil's country review illustrates:

> Sometimes it is not clear if ActionAid is a civil society organization, an international cooperative organization that supports Brazilian civil society or an agency that supports political strengthening of Brazilian organizations. Sometimes AABrazil is also seen as an organization that assumes a protagonist role whether this be in the campaigns or in an indirect way through local development projects. (ActionAid Brazil, no date)

ActionAid needs to be much clearer about its identity and political positioning. Managing changing perceptions of ActionAid's role requires strong leadership and vision at all levels of the organization. It also calls for strengthened processes for dealing with internal disputes and conflicts over meanings, strategies, and priorities, so that the organization is able to challenge itself without losing collective identity or synergy.

The Political Aspect

The inherently political nature of rights-based approaches can pose problems, since in many countries people's perception of politics is negative, and development is viewed as an apolitical activity. Claiming to be apolitical or nonpartisan has been a survival strategy for many NGOs operating under repressive regimes. Donors have also contributed to NGOs' reluctance to emphasize or even recognize the political nature of development and rights through their own concerns about government backlash. Most donors make it clear to potential grantees that they do not support political activities.

Organizations and individuals may also be unprepared for the conflicts that can arise where rights-based approaches demand taking sides. International NGOs in particular can be unaware of the different arenas in which such political conflicts occur, and of the insidious ways in which opponents may attempt to undermine the legitimacy of activists or threaten and even eliminate them (VeneKlasen et al. 2004).

Hierarchies of power and clashes of opinion are also at work within civil society as groups negotiate on issues and strategies. Some may be willing to take more risks while others prefer less confrontational approaches. Rights-based approaches mean being prepared to deal frequently with conflict both within alliances and with external forces. This can be difficult where the kind of debate entailed is not common:

> The debt campaign was very lucky in that they could pick on foreigners as the bad guys. . . . When the responsibility lies here at home it is much more difficult. There is massive corruption in our education system and our members know who is to blame, down to the names and addresses of the individual officials. But it has taken us a whole year to even be able to discuss such highly political issues in a coded way within our own network, and if we went public with them, we would be at high risk of losing credibility with government, because we would be seen as playing into the hands of the opposition parties. (Elimu 2002, 13)

A widespread weakness in ActionAid in the past has been a lack of attention to the analysis of risk and power in all its forms. The shift to rights-based approaches entails adopting more political positioning in relation to other actors, and requires a more explicit analysis of power dynamics and the potential dangers arising from political engagement—particularly in contexts where there is a high level of social and political violence.

Building on Empowerment and Organizing

ActionAid reviews have highlighted the lack of follow-through in some of the organization's work. Numerous cases speak of poor people coming together, mobilizing, and opening channels of contestation. Yet these processes do not necessarily lead to effective action. ActionAid staff and partners, particularly at local levels, need more support in ensuring that initial processes of training and awareness raising are sustainable and are expanded into broader collective experiences. Very often there is no change in power relations, and people are not able to free themselves from the status of simple "beneficiaries" (Morago 2004). Staff are unsure of what outside knowledge to introduce, of how to do this in an empowering way, and of what skills ActionAid might build in areas such as campaigning or advocacy (Thomson 2004). Approaches that do not lead to tangible progress in people's lives can lead to disillusionment and cynicism.

The False Dichotomy between Service Delivery and Rights

In some organizations that adopted rights-based approaches there has been a tendency to see any type of "service delivery" as outmoded and inappropriate. This ignores the role that service delivery efforts can play in strengthening empowerment processes, local organizations, leadership development, alternative development models, trust building, and concrete changes in people's living conditions. In many cases these types of work are necessary steps before any work on rights is conceivable. Development outcomes are determined less by whether service delivery work is done than by how it is done and by whom, and whether it can build in the long run to more transformative work.

AAIndia's work with homeless people provides a good example of how immediate problems and needs can be used as starting points, and how a range of actions and strategies are necessary for substantive change. AAIndia began by addressing the immediate needs of homeless people living on the streets through a variety of services: health services, shelter, and blankets in freezing weather. This work built trust and laid the basis for subsequent work on leadership, mobilization, and organization. AAIndia made further contributions by studying policies and laws that discriminated against the homeless, such as the policy of night shelter and the law on begging. Raising awareness of homeless issues among the broader population helped to create an environment conducive to policy change (Thomson 2001).

Despite such examples of good practice, ActionAid has made limited progress in integrating service delivery and rights-based aspects of its programs, as noted in a 2004 review:

> In many country programs, there is little relationship between the service-delivery elements of our work and other components of ActionAid's approach (for example mobilization of the poor, political and legal advocacy). Different approaches seem to coexist with program staff often confused about how to link the two approaches and achieve greater synergy and impact in our work. Further work is needed with staff to help them understand the links between different kinds of work. (ActionAid 2004).

Utopian Expectations

Some interpretations of rights-based approaches lead to the assumption that the national government is the sole duty bearer, obligated to provide all rights to citizens regardless of its capacity to do so. This ignores global power dynamics and allows the international community and richer governments to avoid their responsibilities:

> Given the dismantling and disabling of the state under structural adjustment, the proactive role being given to the state under the [rights-based approaches (RBAs)] is unrealistic. Even more significant is the fact that not much is being directed towards the accountability of the [international financial institutions (IFIs)], trans-national corporations, western governments and international NGOs. . . . Given that the site of development policy making has changed from the state to the international arena, the focus of the RBA on national actors—citizens and governments—and the exclusion of the corporate sector, foreign governments and the IFIs from scrutiny makes it a non starter. (Tsikata, no date, 5)

In addition to reexamining the temptation to focus exclusively on the state, development workers must come to grips in particular with what a rights-based approach means in countries with failed, repressive, or bankrupt states, or states whose authority has been crippled by international policy or other factors. Communities in Zimbabwe, for instance, have raised many rights issues with ActionAid that people felt unable to talk about publicly.

Critics have also asked whether rights are the most useful framework for analyzing all issues, from the global to the interpersonal:

> It is . . . doubtful if rights are the best analytical tools for understanding the challenges of globalization, militarism, the rise of the trans-nationals, the impacts of neo-liberal policies, class, gender, race, kinship and other social relations. Does the rights language help us to understand the world trading system, or even marriage and intra-household relations? (Tsikata, no date, 6)

Work is therefore needed to clarify how roles and responsibilities might be divided between government, civil society, and other players. For example, is the government the sole duty bearer in efforts to change attitudes on gender or to respond to domestic violence? Would women's groups want or trust the government to take a lead on changing gender attitudes, or should the state's role be mainly to set the framework for such change—adopting the appropriate laws and policies, providing support programs, and ensuring that school curricula challenge rather than reinforce stereotypes?

Conclusions

Our experience with ActionAid and other development organizations shows that rights-based approaches hold considerable potential for restoring attention to politics and power in development work and encouraging development workers to think more deeply about their actions. Indeed in many cases these approaches have energized staff to make more connections between their work, their own lives, and the larger societies they live in. This deepening of analysis and strengthening of people's power has the potential to help ensure that actions have greater long-term impact, making a genuine difference in the lives of poor and excluded communities. However, this will only happen if rights-based approaches are grounded in careful analyses of power in all its forms, and in a sophisticated understanding of how change is brought about and sustained. In particular, the hard-won lessons of grassroots development work on issues of participation, empowerment, conscientization, organizing, and leadership development must be built upon and integrated into rights-based approaches:

> In the absence of grounding [in people's daily needs and struggles for survival and dignity], RBAs are merely a new form of technical fix that combines expert-driven social and

economic interventions with legal change that may not be relevant to people and communities or engage them as citizens. (VeneKlasen et al. 2004, 4)

There is no quick policy fix to issues of exclusion, powerlessness, and poverty. Considerable dangers exist in the tendency to equate rights-based approaches primarily with policy and advocacy work and to see rights as the sole solution to poverty. This narrow interpretation ignores key fundamentals about how power and change operate in society. It can lead to ineffective strategies, a lack of engagement with the poorest and their immediate concerns, a devaluation of grassroots leadership and organizing skills, and a continuing power imbalance between donors, NGOs, popular organizations, and social movements. Organizations such as ActionAid must develop, support, and critically examine development efforts that include a more comprehensive view of power and incorporate multiple change strategies, and in the process must seek lessons and insights that can be used to improve ongoing programs and collaborations with partners around the world.

References

ActionAid Brazil. No date. Internal document. Brazil: ActionAid.

ActionAid Tanzania. 2003. Annual participatory review and reflection report. Tanzania: ActionAid Tanzania.

ActionAid. 1999. Fighting poverty together: ActionAid's Strategy 1999–2003. London: ActionAid.

ActionAid. 2001. Standing up and speaking out: ActionAid annual policy function report 2001. ActionAid.

ActionAid. 2003. Action Aid in practice: Understanding and learning about methods and approaches of rights and empowerment. Internal review meeting, November 17–22. Addis Ababa, Ethiopia: International Livestock Research Institute (ILRI).

ActionAid. 2004. Global Progress Report 2003. London: ActionAid.

ActionAid. 2005. Mutapola campaign: Making home based care work for women and girls. Johannesburg: ActionAid South Africa.

Chapman, J., A. Pereira Jr., V. Azumah, S. Okwaare Otto and L. Uprety. 2006. *Critical webs of power and change: Resource pack for planning, reflection and learning in people-centered advocacy*. London: ActionAid International.

Dóchas. 2003. "Application of rights based approaches—Experiences and challenges." Report on Dóchas seminar on rights-based approaches to development, Dublin. http://www.dochas.ie/documents/rba_seminar.pdf.

Elimu Campaign. 2002. Preliminary review of the Elimu campaign. Draft 3, May. London: ActionAid. http://www.actionaid.org.uk/doc_lib/136_1_elimu_review.pdf.

Fiedrich, M. and A. Jellema. 2003. *Literacy, gender and social agency: Adventures in empowerment.* Research report for ActionAid UK. London: Action-Aid. http://www.dfid.gov.uk/pubs/files/litgenempedpaper53.pdf.

Miller, V. 2005. Rights-based approaches: Trends and tensions. Just Associates Working Paper. Washington: Just Associates.

Morago, L. 2003. Development as justice: Action Aid's use of rights approaches for poverty reduction. In *Report on Dóchas seminar on rights-based approaches to development: "Application of rights-based approaches— experiences and challenges,"* 8–10. February 12th. Dóchas, Dublin. http://www.dochas.ie/documents/rba_seminar.pdf.

Morago, L. 2004. Will our rights-based wishes let the genie out of the lamp? One tale & seven reflections around rights-based approaches to development practice. Paper for CONCORD's rights-based seminar "Making development for all real," November 2004. London: ActionAid.

Samuel, J. 1996. What is people-centred advocacy? NCAS Working Paper. Pune, India: National Centre for Advocacy Studies.

Thomson, K. 2001. *Standing up and speaking out: ActionAid annual policy function report 2001.* London: ActionAid.

Thomson, K. 2004. Eighteen policy reflections 2003. Personal notes. London: ActionAid.

Tsikata, D. No date. The rights-based approach to development: Potential for change or more of the same? http://www.gwsafrica.org/knowledge/dzodzi2.html.

Uprety, L. P., H. P. Sedain and I. Rai. 2005. People-centred advocacy for land tenancy rights in Nepal: A case study of the community self-reliance centre's grassroots campaign. Advocacy Action Research Project Working Paper 6, London: ActionAid International.

VeneKlasen, L., V. Miller, C. Clark and M. Reilly. 2004. Rights-based approaches and beyond: Challenges of linking rights and participation. IDS Working Paper 235. Sussex: IDS.

VeneKlasen, L. with V. Miller. 2002. A new weave of power, people & politics: The action guide for advocacy and citizen participation. Oklahoma City, OK: World Neighbors.

Notes

1. The Department for International Development (DFID) has partially funded the work on which this chapter is based; however, the views expressed do not necessarily reflect DFID policies.

2. During the development of this chapter, Jennifer Chapman served as the coordinator of ActionAid's three-year action research project and team studying advocacy, evaluation, and learning; Valerie Miller of Just Associates served as special advisor and outside team member to the project; and Adriano Campolina Soares and John Samuel were ActionAid regional directors for the Americas and Asia respectively. This chapter also draws on the work and thinking of ActionAid's research and action team, including Almir Pereira Jr., Laya Uprety, Sarah Okwaare and Vincent Azumah. This chapter is based on a paper that was written for the Manchester Conference of 2005 and doesn't take account of changes in ActionAid since that date.

3. For example, Marks (2003, quoted by Tsikata, no date) has identified seven approaches through which human rights thinking is applied to development.

4. In 1999 the organization was called ActionAid. It has since internationalized to become ActionAid International with headquarters in South Africa. For ease of reading, from this point on it is called ActionAid throughout the text.

5. It should be noted that there is no clear cause and effect relationship in this process. ActionAid is a large, decentralized organization, and many changes were happening and continue to happen simultaneously.

6. While in this chapter we emphasize the support and collaboration provided by ActionAid to these groups, we also recognize that communities often receive backing from multiple sources.

7. These assessments are also backed up by staff audits in India and Bangladesh.

CHAPTER 11

The "Human Rights–Based Approach to Programming": A Contradiction in Terms?

Lauchlan T. Munro

[M]any human rights specialists have little experience in or knowledge of the development world. Issues like budgets, programming, indicators, assessments are foreign to those who have focused on arbitrary detention, torture, fair trials and freedom of speech. . . . [T]he cultures, vocabulary, experience and instincts of the human rights world and the development/assistance/humanitarian worlds are distinct.
—*William O'Neill and Vegard Bye (2002, 19–20)*

Value-driven arguments for social policy must work in tandem with instrumental ones.
—*United Nations Research Institute for Social Development (2006)*

Introduction[1]

The development assistance ("aid") industry is a deeply pragmatic, at times even amoral, business. Especially in recent years, it has adopted a strong technocratic bent, including an obsession with target setting and measurement. The classical planning and programming tools prevalent in the development industry analyze a complex situation, identify big problems, and set priorities. The industry's practitioners recognize that trade-offs and compromises have to be made, given the scarcity of resources. Once big problems have been selected for attention, development planning and programming then break them down into smaller, tractable problems and find concrete solutions to those problems. Development planning and programming combine various inputs (resources such as money, personnel, tools, materials), shape them through various activities (construction, writing, social mobilization, training), and thereby produce the desired outputs that will address or even solve the tractable problems identified earlier. By solving discrete problems in this way, development planning and programming contribute to the overall objective that is "development."

As this classical technocratic, results-based trend in development planning and programming was gaining momentum in the 1990s, many development organizations—UN agencies, NGOs, bilateral donors, even international financial institutions—also started to embrace the discourse of human rights. Indeed, "development" was increasingly seen as the progressive realization of human rights. The modern human rights movement is both moralistic and legalistic, using evocative language such as "violations" of human rights and relying on an increasingly large and complex body of international legal instruments and jurisprudence. This worldview is holistic, since all rights are interrelated. In international human rights law, rights cannot be prioritized or placed in any hierarchy; "there are no small rights" (UNICEF 2000). Until recently, the mainstream human rights community has not been concerned with measurement, and has even explicitly resisted the measurement of human rights (Ignatieff and Desormeau 2005). The human rights–based approach to development is thus in sharp contrast to the thinking and practice of classical development planning and programming, in several ways (see Table 11.1).

Nonetheless, starting in the late 1990s, some development organizations tried to combine this human rights tradition with the classical planning and programming tradition. They embraced a "human rights–based approach to (development) programming" (UNDP 2000; UNICEF 1998), asserting that human rights principles must inform and infuse every stage of the development planning and programming process. Can the holistic and absolutist tendencies of rights-based approaches to development be consistent with the pragmatic and atomizing approach of development planning and programming? Are these compatible or contradictory approaches to development? Or can both schools learn from each other, if only they can assemble the necessary humility? This chapter analyzes and assesses what happens when one tries to combine classical and rights-based approaches to programming and planning. The chapter uses the United Nations Children's Fund (UNICEF) as a case study to illustrate some of these issues.

The Development Planning and Programming Tradition

The planning and programming tools used in today's development industry are modernist tools with several common characteristics. By "modernist" I mean that they are based on the fundamental conviction that humans can change their circumstances for the better. The bywords of this tradition are evidence, analysis, rigor, and technique. Modernist planning and programming techniques are objectives-oriented (NORAD 1992).

Modern planning and programming are also pragmatic. Success or failure is judged by impact, by the degree of achievement of stated objectives, and by efficiency. No moral or legal criteria of success are necessary for such tools to be used. Indeed, planning and programming are amoral; they can be used for good or evil.

Development planning and programming are atomizing. They break big problems down into ever smaller problems and break the solutions down into ever smaller projects combining inputs, tasks, and outputs (Baker and Baker 2000; Haugan 2002; NORAD 1992). Project management, like all planning and programming, starts by analyzing a situation and asking what is wrong or what could be improved. Having identified what can be improved, the planners then assess what their organization can and cannot do about it, and make their choices of what projects to undertake. Verifiable, and often quantitative, indicators of progress toward targets and objectives are routinely monitored.

The conventional project management tools used in the development industry are tremendously powerful over a broad range of issues. They have been used to build whole new cities, put men on the moon, and eradicate smallpox. They have also been used to conduct several genocides. There is reason to doubt, however, whether the conventional project management toolbox is universally applicable. For instance, in "soft" areas with behavior change objectives, where processes are as important as outputs, conventional project management tools may be of limited effectiveness (Earl, Carden and Smutylo 2001). Such areas include projects with objectives related to the changing of attitudes, the empowerment of women, the promotion of democratic norms and practices, and the improvement of governance. This has not, however, prevented the application of conventional project management tools in such areas (Carothers 1999, 255–327; Crawford 2003).

Human Rights: Law and Theory

A huge corpus of international human rights law and theory has emerged since the end of World War II. The first step was the Universal Declaration of Human Rights (UN 1948). It was followed two decades later by two covenants that have each been ratified by around three quarters of all states, namely the International Covenant on Civil and Political Rights (UN 1966) and the International Covenant on Economic, Social and Cultural Rights (ICESCR) (UN 1966a). There have since been other major international human rights conventions, notably the Convention on the Elimination of All Forms of Discrimination against Women (UN 1979) and the Convention on the Rights of the Child (UN 1989); the latter is the most widely ratified instrument of international law in history, having been ratified by all states except Somalia and the United States of America. A key moment in modern human rights law was the UN's Vienna Conference on human rights of 1993. It was there that the doctrine of interdependence or indivisibility of human rights (discussed below) was enshrined, as a way to counteract Western countries' traditional emphasis on civil and political rights instead of, and to the detriment of, economic, social, and cultural rights.

Modern human rights theory and international human rights law rest on four fundamental principles: universality (also known as nondiscrimination or equality), indivisibility (also known as interdependence), accountability, and participation.

The principle of universality asserts that all human beings have rights simply by virtue of being human. People have rights regardless of their race, national or ethnic origins, class, sex, language, religion, or political or other beliefs. The universality principle is also called the principle of nondiscrimination, signifying rights theorists' assertion that all human beings are equally entitled to all rights. This has important implications for the design of public policy, in that programs designed to provide rights-based entitlements must be universalistic (Munro 2002).

The principle of indivisibility or interdependence asserts that "one cannot deal with one specific right in isolation without taking into consideration the whole range of related rights" (UNDP 2000, 6). The rights-based *Weltanschauung* is a holistic one; it envisions a web of interrelated and mutually supporting rights. There are two important corollaries of the indivisibility principle. The first is that there is no hierarchy of rights (UNDP 2000, 6). The second is that one cannot pursue the realization of one right to the detriment of another right. The old argument "bread now, freedom later"—used by Soviet planners and Brazilian generals alike—is banned in a rights-based approach to development.

The principle of accountability asserts that people are active subjects, or claim holders. To have a right is to have a claim against others, whether against other individuals or against organized social units like the family or the state. Thus, for every claim holder there must be at least one duty bearer—that is, someone who has the obligation to support the realization of the claim holder's rights, or at least not to interfere with the claim holder's enjoyment of her rights. If every child has the right to an education, then her parents have the duty to send her to school, the state has the duty to ensure that adequate schooling facilities are available, the school authorities have a duty to ensure that the school environment is conducive, and so on.

The principle of participation insists that humans are entitled to have a role, a voice, in decisions that affect them and their communities. Participation is not an option; it is a must. The embrace of this principle has profound consequences for the design of development projects and programs. Even consultation with those affected by a project may not be enough: participation and accountability imply that those affected must have a measure of control and power.

Most importantly, the proponents of a rights-based approach to development insist that the existence of these international human rights conventions means that development policy is no longer simply a matter of charity, or morality, or social preference, or economic or social benefit. It is a matter of law, of legally enforceable entitlements. The great majority of countries, of all political, religious, social, and other stripes, have voluntarily assumed these obligations when they ratified the international conventions in question. Rights have legal force.

Though rights have legal force, they are obviously not all respected in practice. While the realization of some rights requires only forbearance on the part of other people, the realization of other rights requires substantial resources. This is particularly true of many economic and social rights (for example, the right to an education), but also of many civil and political rights (for example, the right to a fair trial, the right to vote). Since resources are more plentiful in some societies than in others, the question arises of how these resource-intensive rights can be respected, protected, and fulfilled. In a concession to economic reality, the rights discourse invented the concept of the progressive realization of rights (UN 1966a, Article 2). In other words, society or the state may tolerate some cases where rights are not realized, as long as there is a plausible commitment to devoting resources over the medium to long run to improve the realization of those rights.[2]

A Study in Contrasts, and a Synthesis

As Table 11.1 below shows, the contrasts between the human rights–based approach to development and classical development planning and programming could hardly be starker.

What happens, then, when these two very different worldviews are brought together? One possibility is simply mutual incomprehension—even unintelligibility—and a frustrating *dialogue de sourds* (O'Neill and Bye 2002). Another is an attempted synthesis. Several development organizations, especially members of the UN Development Group and some NGOs, have attempted a synthesis, called the human rights–based approach to programming (HRBAP).

Table 11.1 Contrasting two approaches to development

CHARACTERISTIC	HUMAN RIGHTS-BASED APPROACH TO DEVELOPMENT	CLASSICAL DEVELOPMENT PLANNING AND PROGRAMMING
Analytical approach	Holistic; rights are inter-dependent	Atomistic; development challenges can be broken down into tractable problems
Ontology	Individualistic	Agnostic about ontology
View of Participation	Mandatory	Optional, depending on costs and benefits
Moral Framework	Normative, binding	Amoral, pragmatic, cost-benefit
View of Accountability	Accountability for both process and results, especially to the poorest members of society. Accountability is a central pre-occupation	Accountability for results to donors, funders, taxpayers and stakeholders. Accountability is often a secondary pre-occupation
Legal Framework	Universal (international human rights law, international humanitarian law, Natural Law) and local	Local
Attitude to Priority Setting	Rights cannot be prioritized, but actions can be	Priority setting is a central pre-occupation. Some projects are more important than others. Actions within projects need to be sequenced
Attitude to Measurement	At best, measurement issues came as an afterthought; at worst, there is hostility to measurement, especially if it is quantitative	Measurement and quantification are central pre-occupations

HRBAP attempts to move human rights work away from merely identifying and denouncing violations to a new role of promoting rights through development work. For most of the organizations involved, denunciation became one possible tool among many, usually used as a last resort. Increasingly, rights-based development organizations saw their role as building the capacities of individuals, institutions, and societies to respect, protect, and fulfill human rights, especially for those whose rights were least likely to be respected. The explicit incorporation of human rights considerations into development work was meant to add value in five ways: human rights have universal international legitimacy as an organizing framework; states have legal obligations to respect, protect, and help fulfill rights; rights are universal, so their use draws attention to the most marginalized groups whose rights are least respected; human rights, having legal force, bring with them the possibility of legal redress; and finally, the realization of rights is not just of mere instrumental value for the fulfillment of other objectives—rights are ends in themselves (Jolly et al. 2004, 187).

UNICEF and the Human Rights–Based Approach to Programming—Part 1

Early attempts at HRBAP in UNICEF represented a relatively "lite" version in which the rights implications of programs were simply considered and documented. I recall one staff meeting in UNICEF-Zimbabwe in 1996 at which all staff read through both the Convention on the Rights of the Child (UN 1989) and the UNICEF country program document. Staff then identified which rights were promoted by each program component; they thus assured themselves that their country program did indeed promote many of the rights in the Convention. In practical terms, such exercises did not change much, but they at least had the advantage of clarifying the human rights implications of UNICEF's programs.

In the years immediately following the adoption of HRBAP as UNICEF's official programming standard (UNICEF 1998), it was not uncommon for UNICEF offices to give old programs new, rights-based names. Some health programs came to be called the "survival rights program," while some education and child protection programs were renamed as the "development rights program." At least initially, this was HRBAP–ultra lite, since not much changed except the names.

In the late 1990s there arose a serious debate within UNICEF about the value added of the human rights–based approach to programming. It was suggested that all it did was to point out that UNICEF programs not only promoted conventional development goals (such as increasing immunization coverage rates), but also promoted human rights (such as the right to the highest attainable standard of health care). In reply it was argued that HRBAP did add something to conventional planning and programming.

First, it drew attention to *how* programs were implemented, not just *what* they intended to achieve. Development programs have to be implemented so as to secure developmental results and respect, even promote, human rights. Table 11.2 below illustrates this with a 2 × 2 matrix having the quality of development results on one axis and the quality of the process on the other axis. Everyone agrees on the need to avoid the bottom-left quadrant, the "hell" scenario in which a development program neither produces good development results nor respects people's rights. Supporters of classical planning and programming might accept as successful any program in the right-hand column, that is, programs producing "good results," regardless of the methods used. These same supporters of classical planning and programming would reject programs in the top-left quadrant, where development results are absent, but rights were at least respected. HRBAP supporters, on the other hand, would demand that development agencies strive only for the top right-hand quadrant—the "heaven" scenario in which developmental results are achieved while human rights are respected, even promoted and fulfilled. The scenario of the top-left quadrant, describing programs "ineffectual" in promoting rights but respectful of them, might be acceptable as long as it could be moved toward the "heaven" scenario. HRBAP supporters would never accept the "vaccine commando" scenario of the bottom-right quadrant, in which rights are violated to get good results. This is not merely a theoretical debate. In Chad and Burkina Faso in the 1980s, health workers went around immunizing children with support from

Table 11.2 Process and results in development programs

| | | QUALITY OF THE DEVELOPMENT RESULTS | |
		BAD RESULTS	GOOD RESULTS
QUALITY OF THE PROCESS	GOOD (that is, Rights-Promoting) Process	"Ineffectual but well intentioned" Scenario: Rights are respected, but no results obtained.	"Heaven" Scenario: Strong development results combined with promotion of human rights
	BAD (that is, Rights-Violating) Process	"Hell" Scenario: Worst case—neither results nor rights	"Vaccine Commando" Scenario: Strong development results, but with violation of rights

government soldiers, called the "vaccine commandos"; many children were literally vaccinated at gunpoint.

Second, defenders of the human rights–based approach to programming argued that it drew attention to the interconnectedness of development interventions. The human rights worldview is a holistic one in which rights are interdependent. To quote a UNICEF colleague, "a child who is fully immunized and who has access to all modern medical care but who is being physically abused is not a healthy child." Once UNICEF staff began to understand the holistic nature of human rights, the naivety of associating the health program with "survival rights" became evident. The health program should be about more than just survival, important though that is. It should also be about promoting health for those who survive. Similarly, nonhealth programs should (and do) contribute in the long or short run to survival: for example, people who complete primary education are likely to have healthier and longer-lived children. HRBAP pushed UNICEF staff to look at their client, the child, as a whole, not as a being with sectoral needs in health, water, education, and so on. In some offices, this helped break down the unnecessary silos between programs.

Third, defenders noted that HRBAP brought important changes to the situation analysis that precedes project selection. In classical project planning and programming, this analysis usually follows sectoral lines—for example, it may comprise separate chapters attending to health, education, tourism, environment, agriculture, and so on. Furthermore, the situation analysis was typically undertaken by groups of "experts," usually people from outside the communities being examined. Under HRBAP, the situation analysis had to be organized around internationally recognized human rights, and implemented using human rights principles such as participation and accountability.

In UNICEF's HRBAP, the situation analysis takes rights holders as the point of departure, and looks for violations of their rights. For example, suppose that in country X a large proportion of children, especially girls, are not in school. This is a violation of their right to education (UN 1948, Article 28; UN 1966a, Article 13; UN 1989, Article 28). One then looks for duty bearers, those who are supposed to respect and protect girls and help them fulfill their right to education. The rights-based situation analysis asks, "who is failing to respect, protect, or fulfill girls' right to education, and why?" Say that it is the parents who are not sending their girls to school; one then needs to ask why not. Is it because they refuse to do so— or is it due to a lack of resources, excessive distance from school, or perceived dangers?

The job of the development aid organization and its national partners is thus to identify the duty bearers, and to find out why the duty bearers are unwilling or unable to fulfill their duties toward the rights holder(s).

If they are unwilling, they must be cajoled, convinced, or possibly coerced to stop the violation of rights.[3] If duty bearers are unable to provide the support that is their obligation, then the development agency's job is to support them with money, ideas, capacity building, or whatever else is needed to stop the violation. In the case of girls not going to school, an integrated rights-based package of interventions might seek to convince parents of the value of educating their daughters, reduce out-of-pocket costs of schooling, build more schools, and make the schools more girl-friendly. In this way, the situation analysis becomes a tool for accountability. In all this, the situation analysis must involve participation from the groups likely to be affected by the development programs. For UNICEF, this meant involving children in the situation analysis, as well as other rights holders and duty bearers such as parents, health workers, and teachers.

Thus far, UNICEF's HRBAP is not at all inconsistent with good classical planning and programming. In fact, in line with recent thinking on how to improve the delivery of public services, UNICEF's HRBAP put the focus on "the client," that is, the rights holder. Schools should be run in "the best interests of the child" (UN 1989, Article 3), not in the interests of the principal, the teachers' union, or the local pedophile ring. Though it should be a no-brainer, this focus on the rights of the client has been strikingly absent from the public services of far too many countries for far too long. The rights-based approach adds value, because it provides development planning and programming tools with the moral and legal basis they otherwise would lack. And the human rights framework provides the situation analysis with the legitimacy of (virtually) universally acknowledged standards and norms. Properly used, HRBAP promotes accountability, good results, and good process.

UNICEF and the Human Rights–Based Approach to Programming—Part 2

If this were the end of the story, there would not be much controversy. But this is not the end. UNICEF's shift to HRBAP brought at least four problems. The first was only transitional, but significant nonetheless. It was the noticeable downturn in UNICEF program activity in each country office as it embraced HRBAP. UNICEF staff spent enormous amounts of time absorbing and debating the new HRBAP way of operating. They spent even more time trying to work things through with their sometimes skeptical partners in governments and NGOs. Program implementation suffered. In one of the early-adopting UNICEF offices, Zimbabwe, program expenditures dropped from an average of over 90 percent of available core resources in the three years before the introduction of HRBAP to under 70 percent afterwards. In several countries, UNICEF's national partners quietly moaned that an organization previously known for its effectiveness was turning into a talking shop; similar grumblings were heard from some donors at UNICEF's Executive Board.

The second problem that HRBAP brought to UNICEF was the addition of a thick layer of human rights jargon on top of the dense layers of planning and programming jargon to which UNICEF, like the rest of the aid business, was already prone. This rights-based language was an obstacle to communicating with nonspecialist audiences, since it tended to be highly legalistic. With his tongue only slightly in his cheek, a wise UNICEF staff member wrote: "Some years ago, we were training technicians to repair refrigerators for the national Immunization Programme. Now we are building the capacity of 3rd level duty bearers, identified through participatory processes, . . . to facilitate the enjoyment by children of their right to good health and access to vaccines delivered in temperature-stable environments" (Detlef Palm, personal communication). The rights-based language also created a number of cross-cultural communication problems, since the notion of rights in general, and of child rights in particular, does not exist in every culture and language.[4]

The third problem was that the dense jargon and holistic worldview of HRBAP often got in the way of identifying the essentials of a problem. Being holistic and taking a comprehensive approach in line with human rights theory became *de rigueur*. Every analysis became more exhaustive: every facet of a problem was dissected, explicated, and connected to other problems, while being grounded in the sacred legal texts of the international human rights treaties. But the results often overlooked the most salient points in a situation. For example, it was no longer good enough in UNICEF for children to go to school and for UNICEF to help measure gross and net enrolment rates for primary school-aged children. The school had to be a "rights-based, child-friendly" school. In principle, this was an advance; schools should be places where children's rights are respected and promoted. But in practice, UNICEF's definition of a "rights-based, child-friendly school" was over a page long and textually dense (UNICEF, no date). It is doubtful whether any school anywhere meets all of the criteria. I showed UNICEF's definition of a "rights-based, child-friendly school" to an educational expert with extensive experience in both industrial and developing countries and asked her opinion. "It's fine," she said, "but they missed out one thing." What was that? I asked. "Are there teachers in the classrooms? Do the teachers actually show up for work?" (Joan O'Donoghue, personal communication).

The fourth problem that HRBAP brought to UNICEF was a paralyzing internal debate on whether a rights-based organization could set priorities and, if so, how. This debate took place around the development of

UNICEF's Medium-Term Strategic Plan for 2002–2005 (UNICEF 2001). Classical planning and programming are consistent with the fundamental insight of mainstream economics, namely that resources are scarce and desires are infinite. Therefore organizations must allocate scarce resources among competing ends: "to plan is to choose" was the aphorism of Julius Nyerere. Organizations can either choose priorities explicitly, for example in a strategic planning document, or they can do so implicitly, as a result of the accumulation of unrelated, decentralized decisions. Either way, there will be priorities.

This is where the human rights tradition finds itself in full-blown contradiction to the classical planning and programming tradition. The human rights–based approach to development denies that any prioritization of rights is possible: "[t]here are no small rights" (UNICEF 2000) and "all human rights are equally important" (UNDP 2000, 6). This is the principle of interdependence or indivisibility of human rights. But if there can be no hierarchy of rights, can a human rights–based organization choose its strategic priorities? The question became acute as UNICEF professed to be a rights-based organization while at the same time embracing "results-based management," the latest version of the classical planning and programming tradition.

Some members of the rights-based tradition within UNICEF stated flatly that to set priorities or development goals was simply incompatible with a rights-based approach. One Deputy Director told me, with a straight face, that UNICEF's next Medium-Term Strategic Plan should be "one line long: Implement the Convention on the Rights of the Child." I do not think he was joking. Obviously, this was a political nonstarter, especially since the United States, UNICEF's largest donor, had not ratified the Convention on the Rights of the Child and had expressed its doubts about HRBAP at UNICEF's Executive Board. More importantly, if UNICEF's strategic plan had been that one sentence long, it would have been the least informative and least useful strategic plan ever written, for it would have given UNICEF staff no guidance on how to allocate the scarce resources put at their disposal.

The official UNICEF line tried to meet the reality of scarce resources halfway, while still respecting human rights logic. Time and time again it was repeated that while rights themselves could not be prioritized, actions to promote rights could. In fact, this was just fudging the issue. No one has yet been able to explain how actions to promote rights could be prioritized without (implicitly) prioritizing certain rights over others. Yes, rights are indeed interdependent, but not symmetrically so. A given action will inevitably have a greater or more direct impact in promoting certain rights rather than others, and this will be largely predictable in advance. Immunizing a child against measles promotes the right to health most directly, by protecting the child from a preventable disease; measles immunization may also promote the right to education, by preventing measles-induced blindness for children living in areas where schooling for the blind is decidedly second-rate. But measles immunization will do little or nothing to stop violations of the child's right not to be trafficked into commercial sex work. When you choose to use scarce UNICEF funds to run the immunization project rather than the antitrafficking project, you have a good idea which rights will be protected most.

Some in UNICEF also argued that the key to prioritizing lay in the doctrine of progressive realization of rights. The international human rights treaties all accept this doctrine. In other words, they accept that economic scarcity is a problem, but insist that governments and other duty bearers must make a concerted effort over time to allocate resources toward the fulfillment of their duties to various rights holders. The International Covenant on Economic, Social and Cultural Rights asserts that "[e]ach State Party to the present Covenant undertakes to take steps . . . to the maximum of its available resources, with a view to achieving progressively the full realization of the rights recognized in the present Covenant" (UN 1966a, Article 2). In strategic planning terms, however, invoking the doctrine of progressive realization was also something of a fudge, for two reasons. First, there is the question of "how much effort is enough?" What are the defining characteristics of "the maximum of . . . available resources"? What are "the standards and processes for monitoring . . . [the] core minimum obligations of State parties and the progressive steps required" (O'Neill and Bye 2002, 29)? Even those sympathetic to the rights-based school admit that neither the statute law nor the subsequent case law—both the findings of the various international human rights and the case law created by various national courts—has helped to clarify the issue much (O'Neill and Bye 2002, 31–32; Robertson 1994). Second, progressive realization cannot handle trade-offs between rights competing for the same scarce resources. It may be argued that rights are interdependent and that therefore promoting one right promotes other rights as well. As explained in the last paragraph, however, this interdependence is not symmetrical. A given action promotes some rights more than others, and more resources for one set of actions means less resources for other actions and the rights they support, at least in the short and medium run.

Those in UNICEF coming from the classical planning and programming background (including the author) responded to the prioritization debate by arguing that a rights-based organization could of course set priorities, and that a certain conception of results-based management could be made compatible with human rights; the key was that development results had to be understood as the realization of human rights

(UNICEF 2001, paras. 5 and 28). Admittedly, there were measurement issues to be resolved, and the short-term focus that plagues much of modern results-based management had to be guarded against, since the promotion of human rights is a long-term venture (UNICEF 2001, para. 107). By studying the life cycle of the child, key points could be identified where interventions could have long-term, even lifelong, impacts on the child's quality of life and prospects for enjoying rights in the future. Preventing micronutrient deficiencies in early childhood, for example, can help prevent blindness, cretinism, and other forms of subnormal mental development; children with such disabilities are likely to suffer multiple violations of their rights over the course of their lives, and therefore UNICEF opted to include micronutrient deficiencies in its list of corporate priorities.

This was the approach adopted in the UNICEF Medium-Term Strategic Plan for 2002–2005 (UNICEF 2001). While many in the organization embraced this combination of pragmatism and rights, many others were unconvinced or even hostile. These critics openly stated that UNICEF had turned its back on child rights. The accusation gained force in 2001 and 2002, when UNICEF's then Executive Director watered down the rights language in several key UNICEF documents as the new Bush administration in the United States—especially the Secretary for Health and Human Services—made known their opposition to the Convention on the Rights of the Child.

In any event, the degree of consensus within UNICEF was not sufficient to make the Medium-Term Strategic Plan stick in any meaningful sense. The organizational structure of UNICEF added to this problem. The Medium-Term Strategic Plan was developed at headquarters, albeit after substantial consultations with the field. But the country offices, where programs were designed and implemented, were supervised not by headquarters but by the Regional Directors in UNICEF's seven Regional Offices. At least three of the then Regional Directors were openly skeptical about the new Plan; the Regional Director for the region alleged to be the most advanced in HRBAP declared that following the Medium-Term Strategic Plan was "optional." The heads of country offices tended to follow their Regional Director's lead. The proponents of the Medium-Term Strategic Plan won the battle in getting the plan approved, but then lost the war in getting it implemented systematically throughout UNICEF.

The reaction was not long in coming, and it came from no less a figure than the editor of one of the world's leading medical journals, *The Lancet*. The editor, Richard Horton, and his journal had previously collaborated with UNICEF on various health issues, and Horton was clearly sympathetic to UNICEF and its mandate. But Horton (2004) felt that

UNICEF's newfound obsession with child rights—and, implicitly, its strict adherence to the principle that there could be no hierarchy of rights—got in the way of setting clear priorities. Horton's view was that child survival was being sacrificed to child rights. Many others agreed: "The deepest error [is the] . . . argument that everything matters. If everything matters, nothing does. Priorities must be set" (Bhagwati 2004).[5]

Heterodox Reflections on HRBAP

Horton's specialty is medicine and public health, not human rights theory. But his arguments do have some grounding in rights theory, albeit from the heterodox end of the spectrum. This perspective starts with the assertion that there *is* a hierarchy of rights, and that the first right is the right to survival, followed closely by the right to security of the person. Other rights flow logically and temporally from these two rights. Such a view has a long pedigree in human rights theory going back to Thomas Hobbes (1651; see Munro 2000).

This heterodox view does not deny the principle of the interdependence of rights, but radically reinterprets it. Rights are indeed interdependent, but interdependence does not imply indivisibility. In other words, the interdependence of rights does not lead logically to the conclusion that there is no hierarchy of rights. Anyone familiar with systems modeling knows that some variables in a system simply have bigger and/or more direct effects than others, even in cases where all variables are interdependent to some degree.

The key distinction to be made is between a rights-based approach such as UNICEF's HRBAP and a rights-based perspective (Ljungman and Forti 2005) on development and public policy. A rights-based *approach* insists that everything the organization does must be based on human rights. Rights literally form the basis of all actions. A rights-based *perspective* is less absolutist and much more helpful in the pragmatic game of running an organization and setting goals. A rights-based perspective accepts that human rights provide only a partial framework for action; that is, there can be more than one perspective on, or more than one way of looking at, a given problem. As important and vital as rights are, the human rights framework cannot provide answers to all questions about human conduct. Other frameworks are at times needed. In particular, the mainstream human rights framework is ill-adapted to certain tasks, notably to the selection of priorities and the allocation of scarce resources between competing ends. A human rights–based approach emphasizing the sacred equality of all rights is not merely unhelpful in such tasks; it leads to organizational paralysis via a morass of relativism. A rights-based perspective allows a pragmatic union of the promotion of rights with the exigencies of managing the inevitable scarcity of resources.

Conclusion

In the quotation at the head of this chapter, O'Neill and Bye point out the great differences in experience, knowledge, culture, vocabulary, and instincts between the "human rights world" and the world of classical planning and programming. They go on to conclude that "[t]he gaps must be bridged and each side needs to move away from its traditional and therefore comfortable positions into territories that are unfamiliar and perhaps unsettling" (O'Neill and Bye 2002, 19–20). This is good advice. This chapter has dealt only with the deficiencies of the standard human rights approach from the standpoint of good planning and programming. The flip side, namely the deficiencies of classical planning and programming in domains where measurement is more of a problem than it is in bridge-building or vaccination campaigns, is another subject. Suffice it to say that classical planning and programming address a large swathe of problems only imperfectly, especially those related to issues such as democratic development, good governance, and the empowerment of disadvantaged or marginalized groups. The way out of this maze is beginning to appear, though many of the elements have been in the literature for decades, notably the notion of adaptive administration (Rondinelli 1993; see too Pressman and Wildavsky 1983). A little humility from the absolutists on both sides would greatly facilitate progress.

The challenge in integrating human rights into the everyday slogging of planning and programming is to adopt the good and the useful elements of the approach while avoiding the pitfall of organizational paralysis and the morass of relativism. Integrating human rights principles into project management is relatively easy. UNICEF, NORAD, and others have done it, and it adds value by clarifying the raison d'être for development objectives (that is, the promotion of human rights) and by emphasizing the need to pay attention to both process and results. A rights-based situation analysis and a rights-based perspective on project management add value by identifying rights holders and duty bearers, and by focusing interventions on supporting the rights holders to help themselves and the duty bearers to do their part as well. The use of human rights contributes key insights into how development programs, indeed all public policies, should operate. Furthermore, human rights provide a moral and legal compass; without such a compass, the amoral tendencies of classical planning and programming can land to an awful mess, as the story of the vaccine commandos shows.

Conversely, moral and legal strictures without practical effect are mere hot air, and tend to discredit the whole human rights project. The human rights community does itself no favors in its use of dense, legalistic jargon and in its propensity to talk for so long before getting around to practical action. But the real Achilles heel of the mainstream human rights community lies in its interpretation of interdependence as implying indivisibility. The idea that there is no hierarchy of rights flies in the face of common sense and of the exigencies inevitably imposed by the stark reality of scarce resources. If no rights are more crucial or more basic than others, how does one begin to plan or prioritize in a rights-based fashion? Refusing to set priorities is mere foolishness. The standard interpretation of interdependence and indivisibility as propounded by the mainstream human rights community is a terrible basis for strategic planning, and the classical planning and programming school lands a knockout punch on the human rights crew when it comes to the question of priority setting.

We need both idealism and pragmatism. A human rights–based perspective is morally and legally correct. Leavened with humility and an admission that human rights provide only a partial framework for human conduct, a rights-based perspective yields practicality as well. Philosophers and jurists may talk about the human rights situation differently; the point for development workers, however, is to change it.[6] We are here to improve human rights, not to talk endlessly about them and then flail around futilely. For if we flail around futilely, we are not only wasting our time, but also risking discrediting the whole human rights project. That would be a sad, and unnecessary, result.

References

Baker, S. and K. Baker. 2000. *The complete idiot's guide to project management.* 2nd ed. Indianapolis, IN: Alpha Books.

Bhagwati, J. 2004. Ambitions that led to an avalanche of failure. *Financial Times.* London. October 1.

Carothers, T. 1999. *Aiding democracy abroad: The learning curve.* Washington, DC: Carnegie Endowment for International Peace.

Crawford, G. 2003. Promoting democracy from without—Learning from within (Part I). *Democratization* 10, no. 1:77–98.

Doyle, L. and I. Gough. 1991. *A theory of human need.* London: Macmillan.

Earl, S., F. Carden and T. Smutylo. 2001. *Outcome mapping: Building learning and reflection into development programs.* Ottawa: International Development Research Centre. http://www.idrc.ca/en/ev-9330-201-1-DO_TOPIC. html.

Gautam, K. 2006. We can beat child mortality. *Ottawa Citizen,* September 21.

Haugan, G. T. 2002. *Effective work breakdown structures.* Vienna, VA.: Management Concepts.

Hobbes, T. 1651. *Leviathan.* London. (Many modern editions available, e.g., http://www.gutenberg.org/dirs/etext02/lvthn10.txt.)

Horton, R. 2004. UNICEF leadership 2005–2015: A call for strategic change. *The Lancet.* 364, no. 9451:2071–2074.

Ignatieff, M. and K. Desormeau. 2005. Introduction. In *Measurement and human rights: Tracking progress, assessing impact.* Cambridge, MA: Carr Center for Human Rights Policy, John F. Kennedy School of Government, Harvard University.

Jolly, R., L. Emmerij, D. Ghai and F. Lapeyre. 2004. *UN contributions to development thinking and practice.* Bloomington and Indianapolis: Indiana University Press.

Ljungman, C. and S. Forti. 2005. Applying a rights-based approach to development: Concepts and principles. Paper presented at conference on "Winners and losers in the rights-based approach to development." University of Manchester, February 21.

Munro, L. T. 2000. Is there a liberal case for the comprehensive welfare state? Discussion Paper no. 61. Manchester: Institute for Development Policy and Management, University of Manchester.

Munro, L. T. 2002. Social protection. In *Handbook on development policy and management,* edited by C. Kirkpatrick, R. Clarke and C. Polidano, 182–192. Cheltenham, UK and Northampton, MA, USA: Edward Elgar.

NORAD [Norwegian Agency for Development Cooperation]. 1992. *The logical framework approach (LFA): Handbook for objectives-oriented planning.* 2nd ed. Oslo: NORAD.

NORAD. 2001. *Handbook in human rights assessment: State obligations, awareness and empowerment.* Oslo: NORAD.

O'Neill, W. and V. Bye. 2002. From high principles to operational practice: Strengthening OHCHR capacity to support UN country teams to integrate human rights in development programming. Geneva: Consultancy report to the UN Office of the High Commissioner for Human Rights.

Pressman, J. and A. Wildavsky. 1983. *Implementation.* 3rd edition. Berkley and Los Angeles: University of California Press.

Project Management Institute. 2000. *A guide to the project management book of knowledge.* Newton Square, PA: Project Management Institute.

Robertson, R. E. 1994. Measuring state compliance with the obligation to devote "the maximum available resources" to realizing economic, social and cultural rights. *Human Rights Quarterly* 16, no. 4:693–714.

Rondinelli, D. 1993. *Development projects as policy experiments: An adaptive approach to development administration.* 2nd ed. London and New York: Routledge.

UN [United Nations]. 1948. *Universal declaration of human rights.* New York and Geneva: UN. http://www.un.org/Overview/rights.html.

UN. 1966. *International covenant on civil and political rights.* New York and Geneva: UN. http://www.ohchr.org/english/law/ccpr.htm.

UN. 1966a. *International covenant on economic, social and cultural rights.* New York and Geneva: UN. http://www.ohchr.org/english/law/cescr.htm.

UN. 1979. *Convention on the elimination of all forms of discrimination against women.* New York and Geneva: UN. http://www.un.org/women-watch/daw/cedaw/text/econvention.htm.

UN. 1989. *Convention on the rights of the child.* New York and Geneva: UN. http://www.ohchr.org/english/law/crc.htm.

UNDP [United Nations Development Programme]. 2000. *The application of a human rights–based approach to development programming: what is the added value?* UNDP, mimeo.

UNICEF [United Nations Children's Fund]. 1998. *Guidelines for human rights–based programming approach. A human rights approach to UNICEF Programming for children and women: What it is, and some changes it will bring.* April 17. New York: UNICEF, CF/EXD/1998-2004.

UNICEF. 2000. *Poverty reduction begins with children.* New York: Division of Evaluation, Policy and Planning, UNICEF.

UNICEF. 2001. *Medium-term strategic plan for the period 2002–2005.* New York: Economic and Social Council, E/ICEF/2001/13.

UNICEF. No date. "Characteristics of a rights-based, child-friendly school." Internal document. www.unicef.org/lifeskills/files/CFSchecklist.doc.

UNRISD [United Nations Research Institute for Social Development]. 2006. Transformative social policy: Lessons from UNRISD research. *Research Policy Brief* 5. Geneva: UNRISD.

Notes

1. The author would like to thank Diana Mitlin, Asha Jalan, the participants at the February 2005 Manchester conference on "Winners and losers from rights-based approaches to development," and the students

of Scott Streiner's class on human rights at Carleton University for incisive comments and questions that have improved this chapter. Responsibility for the contents of the chapter, however, rests entirely with the author. The views expressed in this chapter are strictly personal, and do not represent the policy of any organization with which the author is or has been affiliated.

2. One of the failings of the international human rights mechanism is that it has not well defined the standards for the "progressive realization" of economic, social or cultural rights (Robertson 1994).

3. Laws enforcing compulsory schooling of children are among the possible coercive measures the state could take.

4. UNICEF has recently toned down the rights language in its communications, and gone back to the more straightforward and easily understandable language that it used in the 1980s and early 1990s. The Deputy Executive Director of UNICEF, in a recent commentary for a major Canadian newspaper, did not use the word "rights" at all, but used the simpler language of reducing child mortality (Gautam 2006).

5. Bhagwati was writing about the World Bank and its expanding list of priorities.

6. With apologies to Marx.

PART SIX

Conclusions and Ways Forward

CHAPTER 12

The Potential and Pitfalls of Rights-Based Approaches to Development

Sam Hickey and Diana Mitlin

Introduction

Clearly, there is no single rights-based approach to development. The experiences discussed in this volume have ranged from the deliberate efforts of development agencies to formalize and implement a specific "rights-based approach" to the inevitably messier tasks facing popular actors who may use the language of rights in their struggles for dignity. What it means for rights to be claimed and obligations to be met may involve highly diverse processes, depending in part on whether the rights concerned involve access to resources, protection against exclusion and discrimination, or social inclusion, and on which actor or group is claiming or being claimed against. The meaning of rights, and the strategies most effective for realizing them, differs from place to place and time to time; despite the universal tenor to debates over rights, context clearly matters.

Given this complexity, it is no easy task to draw concrete conclusions on whether rights-based approaches are working. In any case, this question can never be answered conclusively—certainly not through a simplistic cost-benefit analysis conducted for a limited time period. Some writers have argued that we should judge rights-based approaches as much by the processes they catalyze as by their outcomes (Ball 2005). Our concern here has been to neither praise nor damn rights-based approaches to development, and to instead work toward a more balanced understanding of both the potential and the pitfalls of such approaches. We hope that this measured assessment will avoid the antagonisms within other new approaches to development (e.g., social capital, participation), in which reasonable disagreements have become running battles—entrenching increasingly polarized positions, clouding attention to facts on the ground, and preventing the productive synergies that should develop between opposing views.

Nonetheless, our glance back at the last decade or so of efforts to promote rights-based development does suggest that patterns are emerging, some positive and some harmful. This ambiguity can be considered an intrinsic quality of rights-based approaches to development at present, and it reflects the hard questions that confront any approach promising a comprehensive way forward for development theory and practice. Such questions include: What are the underlying ideological or philosophical assumptions and objectives of the approach? For whom and for what does it stand? What strategies and methods might development organizations use to work toward its objectives? What forms of politics and social change are required to achieve its aims? Finally, does it offer a clear conceptualization of key development processes and challenges? The contributions to this volume in each of these areas—conceptual, organizational, political, and ideological—offer different and often opposing responses to each of these challenges. These differences are articulated in short-hand in Table 12.1, and elaborated in more depth thereafter. Our conclusion to this chapter offers our own perspectives for moving things forward along each plane.

Do Rights-Based Approaches Offer a Coherent Means of Conceptualizing Development Processes and Challenges?

Adopting a rights-based perspective to development changes the way in which development actors conceptualize the problems and solutions of development. For example, thinking of development in terms of rights rather than needs necessarily shifts debates over development to a different, more political frame of reference. Within this frame, development problems arise not so much by accident, or through people being "left out" of development, but rather through more direct acts of omission or commission that in turn impose obligations on certain actors and institutions to respond. For example, some agencies such as UNICEF have developed rights-based contextual analyses for identifying violations of rights, detailing their origins, and—as a result—working out who is responsible (Munro, Chapter 11).

Rights-based approaches tend to reposition development as a genuinely universal project, and also to ensure that analysis focuses on the underlying causes of poverty and exclusion, rather than on more contingent issues. The framing of development as a universal right involves an assertion that development should be about everyone, not only those who are worst off (Archer, Chapter 2). This offers an important counterbalance to the poverty agenda that has come to dominate development debates and

Table 12.1 The potential and pitfalls of rights-based
approaches to development

DIMENSIONS OF DIFFERENCE	PROGRESSIVE POTENTIAL	PITFALLS
Conceptual	Offers politically informed insights into development problems and solutions. Legal perspective offers a high degree of analytical rigor and discipline to development debates. Repositions development as being for all (not just the poorest).	Offers analysis by analogy, not history or process. Suggests idealistic and "western" solutions for development problems. Simplifies complex development problems. Non-negotiable stance makes it difficult to think through trade-offs, for example short term costs vs. long-term benefits of progress. Individualistic focus distracts from the relational basis of poverty and social change.
Organizational and strategic challenges	Brings clarity and rigor to development planning. Generates new partnerships and brings natural allies together. Holistic approach enables development agencies to break down false internal barriers (e.g., governance and social development). Encourages development agencies to engage with the political challenges that are central to development. Offers new resources and approaches to local organizations.	Generates wish-lists; very difficult to prioritize actions as all rights are equally important. Generates uneasy bedfellows (for example formal agencies and popular actors). Does not resolve the divide between social and economic tendencies in international development. Greater political engagement is often contrary to institutional statutes and the foreign policy requirements of bilateral agencies, may compromise 'neutrality' and dilutes the humanitarian imperative, endangering local staff and partners.

Table 12.1 (*Continued*)

DIMENSIONS OF DIFFERENCE	PROGRESSIVE POTENTIAL	PITFALLS
Political	Imposes clear obligations on duty-bearers. Brings the state back in as an empowered but responsible and responsive actor. Strengthens local struggles for democracy and development, promotes sense of equality and citizenship. Repositions aid recipients as active claimants rather than passive recipients.	Risks overburdening the state weakened by decades of neoliberal reform; reinforces particular modes of governmentality. Individualistic focus may undermine collective struggles; support for minority rights may empower difference and deepen inequalities. Might be too confrontational a strategy for vulnerable groups and could undermine/obscure the search for other approaches to negotiation. Sense of voluntarism exaggerates the agency commanded by poor and marginal people. Ignores the different and strategically useful "subject positions" that people may wish to adopt, other than "rights-bearing citizen"; may adversely incorporate citizens into dominant political formations.
Ideological	Helps to reposition development as a progressive struggle against discrimination and exclusion that involves redistributive measures. Could help reposition development within a broader struggle for social justice.	Can reinforce the existing neoliberal agenda through its focus on individualism, property rights and the right to participate in markets. Associated with Western ideals and ideas that may not be appropriate in all contexts. Rights left only as ends in themselves, therefore open to co-optation within any broader project.

policy over recent years, which inevitably relies on creating a distinction within global and national societies between the poor and the nonpoor. Although morally persuasive and an essential antidote to the apparent ignorance of distributional issues within dominant approaches from modernization to neoliberalism, this poor–nonpoor binary creates an inevitably arbitrary distinction between two categories of people, and may facilitate the stigmatization of those deemed to be "poor" while also obscuring the causes of deprivation by focusing on the poor themselves rather than on underlying structural factors (O'Connor 2006, Hickey 2008). As an alternative to the poverty frame, analyzing development in terms of the fulfillment of basic rights demands a deeper engagement with the causes of poverty and exclusion than is often undertaken (Green and Hulme 2005).

However, reconceptualizing development as a problem of rights or their lack can also be seen as putting the cart before the horse—and a rather Eurocentric cart at that. Viewing development in these terms alone leads analysis of development issues down a certain path, whereby all problems are essentially failures to realize a certain set of rights. This risks imposing a particular view of progress—namely that associated with industrialized countries in Europe and North America—and thereby practicing what Mamdani (1996) has called "history by analogy," rather than "history by process." Surely it makes more sense as a method of analysis to leave open the question of how current problems of uneven development have emerged, rather than to frame them from the outset as reflecting a particular type of institutional deficiency.

The chapter by Archer suggests that rights-based approaches bring a more disciplinary and uncompromising language to the messy, malleable, and essentially faddish world of development ideas and discussions. This argument has genuine strength: there is a moral and political force to the language of rights that is not easily matched within development thought, and the language of rights may well be able to offer this cloak of resilience to more malleable discourses such as participation (see Holland, Brocklesby and Abugre 2004). The ethical and political universalism of the rights perspective, which insists on every person having the same entitlements, is highly persuasive for development thinkers who seek to move beyond the often disabling relativism of contemporary thought.

In other respects, however, this blunt insistence on certain absolutes in rights-based approaches inspires concerns about their unexamined extension across the field of development thinking and practice. It seems clear that the language of rights might simplify and obscure certain concrete problems of development, as suggested in this volume by Cleaver's discussion of development thought concerning access to natural resources, particularly gendered access to land. As Jackson (2003) has argued, to frame the debate over women's land access solely in terms of rights is to ignore the roles of relationships as a means of gaining access to resources, as tools in negotiating for alternative outcomes, and also as constraints on achieving access (see Cleaver, Chapter 8).

Additionally, when development interventions are reframed in terms of rights it can become even more difficult to think through the compromises and trade-offs such interventions involve (Munro, Chapter 11). To state that no abuse of rights is acceptable is to rule out development interventions and processes that may have adverse impacts in the short term but which, in the medium or long term, may offer considerable benefits to a large number of people. Such trade-offs are the basis for frequent debates in development work over the construction of dams and pipelines, and over the links between growth and inequality, to give just two examples. Although this rigid quality of rights-based approaches could be seen by some as valuable and progressive, we identify it as a problem here given the extent to which development involves struggles between competing interests with often contradictory goals, and often requiring compromises between second-, third-, or fourth-best solutions. In this context, implacable bargaining positions may offer little room for maneuver.

The potential and pitfalls identified above often involve the more extreme scenarios that may emerge from a wholesale reconceptualization of development interventions in terms of rights, in order to draw attention to the underlying logic of such a shift. Real life is of course less black-and-white, and there may well be a middle ground that could be usefully exploited here. For example, as Hinojosa argues in this volume (Chapter 6), it is possible to integrate a rights-based focus within existing frames of development analysis, including the popular sustainable livelihoods approach.

What Organizational and Strategic Issues do Rights-Based Approaches Raise?

Adopting a rights-based approach tends to lead development organizations into a series of difficult trade-offs across a range of important strategic issues. Decisions must be made regarding how to program and prioritize activities and resources, how to overcome boundaries between different tendencies within development, how to maintain or rethink working partnerships, and how to approach issues of positionality arising in particular from the political character of rights-based approaches. It is in confronting such challenges that the ambiguous implications of rights-based approaches become most apparent, as nearly all of the pros and cons identified above are two sides of the same coin.

For example, proponents of rights-based approaches would argue that development organizations that adopt them make considerable gains in the level of coherence and rigor they bring to their processes of planning and prioritization (e.g., Archer, Chapter 2; also Jonsson 2005). However, the insistence that *all* things matter, that all rights are not only equal but also interdependent, can tend to complicate rather than enable such processes, leaving agencies unsure of where to start or how to sequence or prioritize their activities (Munro, Chapter 11). For example, Munro has elsewhere compared the challenges faced by development agencies seeking to approach social protection programming from either a rights-based or a "risk-based" approach. He found that while there is a growing range of rights-based programming, the fact that human rights doctrine refuses to accept a hierarchy of rights means that "such project-level tools are of little use in deciding which violation(s) of rights are the most serious. The risk-based thinkers, with their concepts of welfare losses and opportunity costs, have much less difficulty" (Munro 2008, 34).

Advocates of rights-based approaches argue that their adoption forces or enables organizations to develop synergies between areas of engagement traditionally treated as distinct; for Moser, "[t]he originality of a rights perspective is that it highlights the linkages between different arenas" (2005, 41). Such synergies might operate across lines ranging from the division between "governance" and "social development" foci within bilateral and multilateral aid agencies, to the gulf between the "human rights" and "development" communities more broadly (Archer, Chapter 2). However, it is not clear that a rights-based approach will be able to transcend what is often the most consequential and intractable divide within development institutions, particularly large aid agencies— namely that which persists between economic and more socially-oriented actors (e.g., Kanbur 2001). In particular, the utilitarian perspective of most economists leaves little room for rights issues to be included in calculations of the optimal allocation of limited resources. The conflict here is similar to that described by Munro (2008): while economists are familiar with optimizing within politically determined constraints, solutions may not be possible under the added constraints of rights concerns (e.g., where all rights must be met fully). This is significant: the economic tendency remains the dominant force in international development, and if actors within this tendency cannot be persuaded of the feasibility of adopting rights-based approaches, these may well be doomed to playing the more marginal role to which other social concerns from gender to participation are consigned.

Looking beyond individual organizations to the broader partnerships that rights-based approaches tend to catalyze, our sense is that rights-based approaches have promoted new alliances within civil society between traditional "development" and "human rights" actors (Duni et al., Chapter 4). NGOs seem more likely to develop closer partnerships with popular and often political actors within civil society, including the types of social movement that have historically been at the forefront of struggles to secure rights for marginalized people (Chapman et al., Chapter 10). At the same time, NGOs that align with social movements are more likely to find themselves working with rights. A greater concentration on rights has been associated with some significant successes in holding the state to account and providing ideological and financial resources to local actors in their struggles. However, formal development institutions need to be sensitive to the consequences of such support if they are not to create new problems. For example, professionally oriented advocacy programs can undermine nonprofessional actions and perspectives that are of more fundamental value in strengthening grassroots movements. The issue-based lobbying of decision makers by advocacy professionals rarely engages with certain realities of power, and tends to sideline popular actors. It is critical that NGOs are able to respond to the perspectives of grassroots movements regarding what works for them within processes to reclaim and further rights. Strategies to realize rights cannot be imposed from outside; they must instead be negotiated from within (Masaki, Chapter 5; Patel and Mitlin, Chapter 7; Chapman et al., Chapter 10).

This increased partnership with social movements reflects a wider shift of development agencies adopting rights-based approaches into more politicized thought and practice. For example, "[a] development agency that has embraced [a rights-based approach] fights for civil and political as well as economic, social and cultural rights. It seeks structural change and just power relations rather than, or in addition to, technical fixes and service delivery" (Ball 2005, 281). More broadly, "[g]iven the close linkages between rights and power, mainstreaming rights-based approaches means that such [development] institutions are also incorporating issues of power and power relations into their dialogue and practice" (Moser 2005, 46).

This has clearly been the case for those NGOs that now engage more closely and critically with the state, as well as with thorny issues of political exclusion (Duni et al., Chapter 4; Chapman et al., Chapter 10) and, to an extent, patriarchy (Drinkwater, Chapter 9). We would encourage this closer political engagement as a welcome move away from approaches that tended to frame development problems as subject to purely technocratic solutions.

While some observers note that NGOs' political engagement invites risks of overreach, insufficient institutional capacity, and deficits in skills such as advocacy and human rights education (Ball 2005), our contributors suggest that the challenges are somewhat trickier again. Adopting a rights-based approach may necessarily compromise the position of neutrality that many humanitarian agencies in particular have adopted in line with wider principles (Ball 2005, 282–283). Moreover, promoting the rights of marginal groups is a dangerous business in certain contexts, and in some cases may endanger staff (Duni et al., Chapter 4; Rafi and Chowdhury 2000). Rights efforts may also endanger grassroots movement participants themselves, leading to suggestions that unreflective actions to support rights pay insufficient attention to the messy realities of politics (Patel and Mitlin, Chapter 7; Kabeer 2002). Finally, agencies that fail to fully mainstream a rights-based approach may find that they end up contradicting themselves in practice—witness the UK Department for International Development's promotion of water privatization alongside its insistence that affordable access to water is a basic human right.

The Politics of Rights-Based Approaches to Development

Of the issues raised by rights-based approaches, political challenges are perhaps the hardest to define clearly, since politics cuts across each of the other dimensions (conceptual, organizational, and ideological) we have identified. We will focus on politics in terms of what rights-based approaches mean for the roles of and interactions between key actors within the state and civil society. Broadly speaking, we suggest that rights-based approaches to development tend to reinforce what we see as the current mainstream paradigm for understanding and acting on the politics of development. This paradigm emphasizes the nexus between higher levels of citizen voice and higher levels of state responsiveness. It is increasingly influential throughout international development work, as reflected in the publications of international financial institutions such as the World Bank (e.g., World Bank 2000, 2004) and international NGOs such as OXFAM (Green 2008), and in development policy research (e.g., Gaventa and Goetz 2001). Here we critically examine the role of rights-based approaches in promoting this wider paradigm, first in terms of the implications for the state, and secondly in terms of how rights-based approaches join up with local political struggles for rights, resources, and recognition.

Toward a More Responsive State?

Rights-based approaches help to place the state back at the forefront of development debates. Language mandating equality and dignity requires the implementation of widespread redistributive and protective measures that only a strong state can legitimately undertake. A strong state is also required to protect people from the vagaries of markets and traditions alike (e.g., Harriss-White 2005; Mander 2005). However, it is also clear that citizens have often needed protection from the state's own tendency to curtail and abuse their rights. States are therefore charged not only with being strong and responsive, but also with acting constitutionally and legitimately. However, it is not clear whether the state in many southern countries is able to fulfill this role, or whether the promotion of a rights-based approach can assist in reforming the state to be an effective duty bearer and protector of citizens' rights.

On the one hand, we do find some evidence that the state and its agents can be made to act more accountably toward the claims made on them by citizens (Duni et al., Chapter 4), and to accommodate citizens' right to be involved in negotiating solutions (Drinkwater, Chapter 9; Patel and Mitlin, Chapter 7). However, Gledhill's contribution (Chapter 3) raises serious doubts about the capacity of the state to respond to claims in meaningful ways—not least because of long-standing efforts under neoliberalism to reduce the state's public role (Manzo 2003). Others affirm that we should not expect the state to have the right answers regarding how different rights should be met in practice (Patel and Mitlin, Chapter 7). In facing these limitations, a pragmatic approach—based less on vocal demands for rights than on longer-term strategies of building relationships and revealing alternative models for development—can be a more effective strategy for promoting the just allocation and protection of rights. It seems that the dominant voice/responsiveness paradigm for development neglects a series of questions concerning the messy power relations that mediate engagement between states and citizens. This paradigm may need supplementing with strategies that seek to alter those power relations that ensure some voices are both louder and listened to more clearly than others.

One way of understanding the importance of the field of power relations between citizens and the state is to examine how rights-based approaches rely on and reinforce forms of governmentality. For Foucault, any set of new laws that is adopted needs to be seen as an extension of the disciplining process through which the state intervenes in the lives of its subjects (Dean 1999, 17–18). For example, rights-based approaches have brought the legal system and its associated actors more clearly into play within development contexts and in so doing have strengthened the state and an associated discourse of explicit entitlements and obligations that it may enforce. As Burchell argues, "[t]he impossibility of reconciling law and governmental order without subordinating the former to the latter remains" (1991, 145). Rights enable the state to produce and reinforce the individuation of its subjects, thus restricting the extent to which they can consider alternative forms of social organization that might better address their needs. Masaki (Chapter 5) suggests that rights approaches risk "legitimizing the proliferation of state intervention, rather than allowing [subjects, in this case the indigenous group] to shape and pursue their own strategies." Individuals are to realize legal rights via state-controlled legal institutions, even if they hold these rights by virtue of belonging to a group. This can weaken counter-hegemonic challenges to the state, particularly those involving mass organizations and collective action, to the extent that citizens are subjugated into passivity and dependence on a higher authority.

Even from a more sanguine point of view, the achievement of rights through improved legal status can be seen as a strategy dependent on the successful extension of the formalized modern world into the lives and locations of low-income communities. This draws subalterns into one more form of supposedly neutral relationship in which both ideology and outcomes are stacked against them. Moreover, legal solutions are in themselves often highly technocratic fixes, and may involve exclusive processes and even outcomes. The closer incorporation of poor and marginal people into the legal realm may therefore have its downsides (Masaki, Chapter 5; Patel and Mitlin, Chapter 7). Chapman and colleagues suggest that the nature of this realm can in fact make it harder for low-income and excluded citizens to participate in development, as compared to better educated and more "professional" groups.

Against this fairly negative reading, it is also clear that lawyers and the law can be powerful allies for poor and marginal groups (Duni et al., Chapter 4), and that much can be achieved by insisting on the application of existing legislation and due process. Rights can provide a powerful ideological perspective from which to challenge outcomes and propose alternatives, inspiring rebellion and insurgency as well as less dramatic forms of protest and negotiation. Gledhill points to some of the difficulties in drawing simple conclusions in this debate. Rights are not fixed or given but become real by being selected as an arena of struggle by social actors (Gledhill, Chapter 3; Duni et al., Chapter 4; Masaki, Chapter 5; Patel and Mitlin, Chapter 7; Drinkwater, Chapter 9). Laws, regulations, policies, and even constitutions often reflect rather than precede social activism, and legal reform cannot be seen as an entirely top-down phenomenon.

Clearly, the law is only one of the arenas that needs to be addressed if rights are to be recognized. The state in many contexts has a partial and often weak commitment to supporting the law, especially when the law seeks to protect those who are disadvantaged and exploited. In such situations, an active citizenry is important not simply to push for pro-poor laws but also to provide the scale of follow-up necessary to ensure such laws are operational. This need to promote rights through arenas outside and around laws themselves is emphasized by several of our contributors. Drinkwater in particular argues (Chapter 9) that rights laws, whether legally enforced or not, should be considered a starting point—a perspective for analysis and consideration—rather than an outcome. Rights perspectives help to catalyze socially transformative struggle, triggering a range of changes in behaviors, relationships, and agencies that may help to address needs and interests. It is to this more bottom-up perspective that we now turn.

Toward Citizenship?

> "Rights-based approaches are inspired by autonomous movements such as those of women, the landless and indigenous peoples which often include demands for participation in decisions which affect their lives. A [further] trend . . . emphasizes an historical evolution from clientelism to citizenship." (IDS 2003, 1)

The key questions we want to explore here concern the ways in which rights-based approaches converge or clash with new and ongoing struggles around development at local levels, and whether or not rights-based approaches help ensure that claims by previously excluded groups are heard and have influence. Under a rights-based approach the "recipients" of development are reframed as rights-bearing actors with legitimate claims on duty bearers, rather than as supplicants standing bereft before their patrons. This is largely a positive shift—on paper, a rights-based claim to recognition or resources involves a more empowering exchange than one made within the rubric of development as patronage or charity. However, a more rigorous assessment of this reframing of "recipients" as actors requires looking beyond legalistic and state-led solutions to development problems, to instead examine the everyday and organized struggles of poor people themselves, as located within a broader historical transition toward citizenship.

Some of our contributions offer evidence that rights-based approaches can indeed contribute to these struggles toward citizenship—most notably Gledhill's analysis of the historical transition to democratic forms of rights in Latin America (Chapter 3), and also the account by Duni et al. of the success of a struggle for rights by a combined NGO-legal-social movement in Cameroon (Chapter 4). In some cases, especially where politics is particularly elitist, exclusive, or repressive, the language of rights can offer one of the few progressive discourses available for local groups seeking to make their claims (Duni et al., Chapter 4; Masaki, Chapter 5). However, Gledhill, Duni, and Masaki also emphasize the absence of any simple, teleological, or swift movement between clientelism and citizenship. Even where rights are nominally established, patronage and violence will often remain integral elements of the political and social relations that define access to rights and status in a political community. As Nyamnjoh (2004) has argued regarding "democratization" in Africa, Africans are currently both citizens and subjects, even if some are more citizens than others (Mamdani 1996). Masaki (Chapter 5) expands this line of analysis to suggest that actors in local struggles for citizenship rights inevitably become complicit with the system of ideas and norms that previously excluded or subordinated them. Such bottom-up movements are unable to alter the contours of the political community in ways that reshape the terms of citizenship and inclusion, and must rather submit to at least some of the exclusive and disempowering tendencies that exist therein. In addition to such divisions within communities, citizenship rights are invariably limited to the membership of particular political entities, an exclusion that tends to deny migrants recognition and that runs counter to the universalism preached within the more general rights-based approach to development.

The emphasis on bottom-up struggles in rights-based approaches reflects a broader trend in international development toward emphasizing issues of participation, empowerment, and improved livelihoods, as well as longer-standing debates around self-emancipation. There is a danger in this trend of slipping into an attitude of voluntarism and "responsibilization" when framing poor and marginal people: efforts to cast them as powerful actors can lead to an exaggeration of their capacity to cope and progress under structural constraints, sometimes to the point that they are effectively framed as responsible for both their plight and their recovery (Cleaver 2004, and Chapter 8 of this volume). A significant degree of agency is required on the part of local actors if they are to engage with rights-based strategies, and this is often definitively missing in the case of poor and marginal people and communities.

For Patel and Mitlin (Chapter 7), the confrontational strategies of the rights-based approach are simply too blunt to work within the complex and personalized world of urban politics; here agency is limited in that working relations between local groups and politicians are essential to advancing a range of development aspirations including rights. Local people who seek to push the boundaries of what is politically possible may be keenly aware of the dangers of doing so in too confrontational a manner, lest they provoke a violent backlash at the hands of political and security actors, or foreclose the possibility of building positive relationships across state or civic boundaries. In addition, Gledhill warns (Chapter 3) that we would be wise to avoid exaggerating or romanticizing the civic character of local people living in (often extreme) conditions of inequality and deprivation. The apparently growing tendency toward violence as a means of settling disputes suggests that the liberal norms and expectations of rights-based approaches are often dislocated from everyday life.

Finally, the introduction of rights-based discourses and practices may also underpin other, less progressive tendencies within local and national level politics. Disparities in agency can in fact subvert the progressive goals of rights-based approaches, allowing powerful groups to dominate the process of seeking to secure rights. Indeed, the very universality of rights concepts guarantees their availability to all, and the story of democratization across the developing world has often involved the capturing of opportunities by elite rather than popular political actors. Even among popular actors, efforts to challenge marginalization by promoting minority rights may further empower the discourse of difference that prevails within many political arenas today, and that easily slips into fractious conflicts between groups along ethnic and religious lines. In such circumstances, a rights-based approach may exacerbate the problem that "the current aesthetic of recognition allows little other than discrete individuals, groups and communities pursuing their own agendas" (Englund 2004, 12). There is sometimes a political economy to this problem: struggles for recognition and against political marginality may be valid on their own terms, but at the same time may reinforce material inequalities in wealth and access to secure livelihood resources (again, see Gledhill, Chapter 3; Duni et al., Chapter 4). The discourse of rights seems to work better for powerful groups who are more able to stake and defend their claims against perceived wrongs.

This raises a familiar but often unresolved concern that counterposes the politics of justice with a politics of difference (Fraser 1995, Young 1997), and it remains to be seen whether rights-based approaches are more likely to consolidate one or the other. For Englund (2004, 12–13), an "alternative aesthetic must do more justice to the relational field in which the politics of recognition emerged," and must recognize that groups reflect each other and are mutually constitutive rather than distinct. We would go further and argue that the challenge in reconciling universal rights with group differences is to ensure that struggles for rights do not become detached from the struggle against material inequality that lies at the heart of a broader project of social justice (see conclusion below). Finally, internal differences also complicate collective action, through both intragroup and intergroup divisions. Groups seeking to promote a particular agenda (e.g., workers' rights, minority rights) will often downplay important differences between members, especially those along lines of gender and class. Several of our contributors emphasize the importance of such internal differences, and caution against the simplistic promotion of rights for a "uniform" group (Gledhill, Chapter 3; Duni et al., Chapter 4; Masaki, Chapter 5).

Ideological Issues: What Do Rights-Based Approaches Stand for?

The final dimension of development that we address here is ideology. Although the ideological differences that once pervaded debates over development and politics more broadly have become less distinct since the apparent impasse of the late 1980s (Booth 1994), important tensions remain—most notably those between state-led and market-led, and between neoliberal and redistributive, approaches to development.[1] It is important to ask where a rights-based approach might fall in these debates, and toward which visions of the good life it might contribute most strongly. Once again, our contributors suggest that—at least in theory—a rights-based approach is resolutely ambiguous, and might be mobilized in support of each of the apparently contradictory tendencies drawn out here.

Regarding the state versus market debate, we have already indicated that a rights-based approach identifies significant duties for the state in providing for, including, and protecting its citizens.[2] However, we have not yet examined the potential relevance of the market to these duties. In particular, we have not considered whether adopting a rights-based approach to development involves complicity with the prevailing neoliberal agenda, or a challenge to it in favor of an alternative. For many advocates of rights-based approaches, it is clearly the latter. The underlying thesis of a rights-based approach, whereby all people are equal and thus have equal claims to make, inevitably opens up politically contentious issues such as the redistribution of assets to poor people and the extension of citizenship to excluded groups (see Duni et al., Chapter 4; Masaki, Chapter 5).

However, at least one contributor (Hinojosa, Chapter 6) argues that the market can provide an empowering institutional arena within which people may realize their rights, at least when compared to the "community." Indeed, the market is significant as a means of organizing the distribution of economic resources and opportunities, and may provide a route of emancipation from the retrograde and patriarchal tendencies (as well as more modern forms of discrimination) that may exist within "traditional" approaches to resource allocation (Friedman 1962; also Cleaver, Chapter 8). Under certain economic theories, market-led societies tend to promote the development of rights by valuing the right to participate in the market on a "level playing field," and by taking certain property rights to be essential preconditions for growth (de Soto 2000). For some, a market-led society also has a clear interest in avoiding social discrimination to prevent anomalies and asymmetries inimical to the functioning of markets; this argument has recently been promoted by some within the World Bank (WDR 2006). From these perspectives, there would appear to be a strong degree of convergence between rights-based approaches and free-market economics.

Now, it might be clear to many (including ourselves) that the operations of power in actual markets tend to undermine moves toward such equalities between citizens. As some of our contributors suggest (Hinojosa, Chapter 6; also Duni et al., Chapter 4), accessing rights via the marketplace works best for those with a capacity to benefit from market exchanges. The move under neoliberalism whereby the market rather than the state or civil society becomes the arena in which citizenship rights are to be negotiated and attained (Dagnino 2007) has often had disastrous consequences—not only deepening processes of impoverishment and marginalization, but also relegating the key duty-bearing institutions of the state to minor roles, and casting citizens as consumers in a highly unequal, competitive, and profit-driven arena. Therefore, it seems unwise to expect too much from an institutional sphere unfamiliar with and often hostile toward the philosophical and operational logic of the "claims and duties" rubric.

However, the convergence between rights-based and neoliberal approaches to development is contextual as well as theoretical. Rights-based approaches are currently promoted in an environment in which capitalist enterprise and liberal forms of democratic politics are broadly dominant. This may mean that certain forms of rights will be more easily accepted and institutionalized than others, because the "fit" is better. Hence rights to property are more easily recognized than rights to services, because the former adds to the market while the latter is a shift away from commodification. As pointed out earlier regarding the Department for International Development's approaches to water issues, agencies that claim to be promoting a progressive rights agenda on the one hand may find themselves undermining this agenda on the other. Witness also the role of NGOs whose piecemeal efforts to deliver services further the privatization agenda and undermine the role of the state.

This raises serious dilemmas for those who would adopt a rights-based approach in pursuit of an alternative, more progressive process of development. It is not at all clear that "a rights-based approach is democratic and pro-poor: its antithesis is 'free' market" (Ball 2005, 286). Rather, rights-based approaches must be explicitly and rigorously elaborated as part of a wide and robust alternative to the prevailing neoliberal order, and as a project around which appropriate strategies can be devised: it cannot be taken for granted. For us, this challenge exists at the level of philosophy as much as praxis. In the closing section we elaborate a potential way forward.

Final Thoughts

Both the promise and pitfalls of rights-based approaches are substantial and very real. Considering the impacts of rights-based approaches on the political space in which development is contested enables us to offer some cautious conclusions about future potentials. For example, rights-based approaches might offer a means of relocating development actors and debates onto more political terrain; they can ensure that key obligations are imposed on certain institutions, and in so doing help underpin the revival of the state as a central development actor; and they can provide a valuable ideological resource to local groups struggling against exclusion and discrimination. At the same time, rights-based approaches may deepen socioeconomic inequalities and political grievances between groups; help embed the neoliberal commodification of natural resources and social relationships; and facilitate disempowering forms of governmentality. Rather than attempting to weigh these pros and cons, our final thoughts will aim at offering a few suggestions for how rights-based approaches might most usefully be taken forward with the goal of securing more progressive forms of development. We restrict ourselves to four key ideas, one for each of the dimensions that we have elaborated in this chapter: the first two are strategic (including conceptual and organizational elements), the third political, and the last ideological.

First, the suggestion that rights-based approaches may not offer development agencies a particularly useful way of organizing their day-to-day activities does not imply that the approach is somehow strategically irrelevant. It indicates rather that realizing rights is a difficult challenge, and development agencies need to consider and undertake a strategic repositioning if they are to take rights seriously. To recap, we are not persuaded that rights-based approaches can directly assist with the more detailed activities of development agencies, such as prioritization and planning— and there is little to be gained from torturing rights-based approaches to play this role while other more appropriate approaches abound. Nor can rights-based analysis realistically yield the informational base that agencies require to operate. Even if such analysis might usefully supplement other approaches (as Hinojosa argues regarding livelihoods analysis), it is surely better to address problems of exclusion and impoverishment by identifying the active processes that lead to these outcomes, rather than by treating them as deriving from the lack of an intangible rights ideal. Nonetheless, the adoption of a rights-based approach should inspire a serious repositioning of development agencies in relation to their fields of action (with renewed focus on the civil and political realm) and institutional partnerships (with potential alliances with lawyers, unions, and social movements). It cannot be a case of business as usual, and if development interventions are to be effective, agencies' work will inevitably become more political, of which more below.

The second key idea also relates to strategic positioning, but this time with reference to the very different local contexts within which development agencies seek to promote rights-based approaches. The abstract promotion of rights, often from a position of moral grandstanding, is more likely to aggravate than solve intractable social and economic problems, and shaming and blaming can only take things so far. This is not to make a relativist point regarding the allegedly Eurocentric character of human rights: for what it's worth, and although this is not an issue that our contributors touch on in depth, we clearly hold that rights are something universally held by all people everywhere. Rather it is to recognize that rights emerge in a myriad of different ways and forms in different times and places, and not always as a result of what might be recognizable as an outright "rights-based" approach. External efforts to promote rights need to be carefully calibrated to the efforts of progressive actors in particular circumstances and at particular moments, and must accept the fact that local actors may have diverse strategies to reach similar goals.

The third idea reflects the fact that the "politicization" of development work is central to the adoption and promotion of rights-based approaches. We welcome this. The reframing of development as a fundamentally political process is essential if development is to tackle the underlying causes of poverty and marginalization. We would depart from the position other recent observers have taken on this issue, whereby "P"olitics is defined as "partisan, promoting particular (self-serving) actors and nonconsensual interests and values"—such that "It is from such agendas and alliances that peace and development work ought to be free," and such that "P" is to be defied (Ball 2005, 283). It is not clear that the goals of equality, justice, and nondiscrimination associated with the inevitably "p"olitical rights-based approaches can be achieved outside of the world of "P"olitics. Political elites and political parties must be engaged in this struggle; development actors cannot afford to apply a peg to their noses and sidestep this world while still presuming to attain their ends. Only if political actors can be persuaded to join in the struggle for rights will efforts progress.

Finally, there remains the dilemma that rights can be linked to neoliberal regimes as well as to more progressive projects of social transformation. For those who favor the latter, including ourselves, we have suggested that the way forward involves an explicitly philosophical challenge. At its simplest, we need to ask the question: for what wider purpose are rights being promoted? To some this is a heresy, and suggests that rights are merely a means rather than a worthwhile end in and of themselves. We would respond that rights are intrinsically important in themselves in order for lives of dignity to be led, *and* that they are inevitably part of a wider social and political project, the nature of which may vary. Rights have been fought for by a variety of actors, and with very different objectives in mind—ranging from efforts to secure property rights to further bolster the neoliberal order to the elaboration of workers' rights as a challenge to this order in the name of socialism or social democracy. Such struggles also go further and deeper, beyond the ideological positions that wax and wane over relatively short spans of time, and involve older questions concerning what type of society—or vision of what Aristotle termed "the good life"—is being sought, and possibly fought for, and via what type of political process? Such ideals have often been framed in terms of happiness, freedom, or other such higher-level goals. And many, including Amartya Sen, have argued that rights are essential to the flourishing of human freedom for which all development efforts should ultimately be aiming.

Here we would differ from Sen by suggesting that rights can be most progressively linked to a broader project of social justice rather than of freedom. Once this move is made, we have an ethical benchmark against which to measure rights-based claims as they arise, whereas clearly the freedom of some will inevitably curtail the freedom of others (judge the influence of a businessman who exercises his free right to contribute huge sums to a particular party against the free vote of the ordinary elector). Justice offers a more progressive and substantive target than freedom, speaks more directly to the material problems of development, offers a means of building alliances between different social groups, and resonates with the clarion call of many movements that promote rights. Situating rights in relation to a broader social justice project also means we should be open to multiple routes of working toward justice, some of which may not be best achieved through the direct pursuit of a rights-based strategy (see Archer, Chapter 2; Patel and Mitlin, Chapter 7). It is against this benchmark of advancing social justice that rights-based approaches will ultimately be measured and judged, and it is to this project that they should be explicitly attached.

References

Ball, O. 2005. Conclusion. In *Reinventing development? Translating rights-based approaches from theory to practice*, edited by P. Gready and J. Ensor, 278–300. London: Zed Books.

Bebbington, A. J. and S. Hickey. 2006. NGOs and civil society. In *The Elgar companion to development studies*, edited by D. A. Clark, 417–423. Cheltenham: Edward Elgar.

Booth, D., ed. 1994. *Rethinking social development: Theory, research and practice.* Harlow: Longman.

Burchell, G. 1991. Peculiar interests: Civil society and governing "The system of natural liberty." In *The Foucault effect: Studies in governmentality*, edited by G. Burchell, C. Gordon and P. Miller, 119–150. Chicago: University of Chicago Press.

Cleaver, F. 2004. The social embeddedness of agency and decision-making. In *Participation: From tyranny to transformation? Exploring new approaches to participation in development*, edited by S. Hickey and G. Mohan, 271–277. London: Zed Books.

Dagnino, E. 2007. Challenges to participation, citizenship and democracy: Perverse confluence and displacement of meanings. In *Can NGOs make a difference?: The challenge of development alternatives*, edited by A. Bebbington, S. Hickey and D. Mitlin, 55–70. London: Zed Books.

De Soto, H. 2000. *The mystery of capital: Why capitalism triumphs in the West and fails everywhere else.* New York: Basic Books.

Dean, M. 1999. *Governmentality: Power and rule in modern society.* London, New Delhi, Thousand Oaks: Sage Publications.

Englund, H. 2004. Recognizing identities, imagining alternatives. In *Rights and the politics of recognition in Africa*, edited by H. Englund and F. B. Nyamnjoh, 1–29. London: Zed books.

Fraser, N.1995. From redistribution to recognition? Dilemmas of justice in a "post-socialist" age. *New Left Review* no. 212:68–93.

Friedman, M. 1962. *Capitalism and freedom.* Chicago: University of Chicago Press.

Gaventa, J. and A-M. Goetz. 2001. Bringing citizen voice and client focus into service delivery. IDS Working Paper no. 138. Sussex: IDS.

Green, D. 2008. *From poverty to power: How active citizens and effective states can change the world.* Oxford: OXFAM International.

Green, M. and D. Hulme. 2005. From correlates and characteristics to causes: Thinking about poverty from a chronic poverty perspective. *World Development* 33, no. 6:867–879.

Harriss-White, B. 2005. Destitution and the poverty of its politics—With special reference to South Asia. *World Development* 33, no. 6:881–892.

Hickey, S. 2008. The return of politics in development studies (I): Getting lost within the poverty agenda? *Progress in Development Studies* (forthcoming).

Holland, J., M. A. Brocklesby and C. Abugre. 2004. Beyond the technical fix? Participation in donor approaches to rights-based development. In *Participation: From tyranny to transformation? Exploring new approaches to participation in development,* edited by S. Hickey and G. Mohan, 242–268. London: Zed Books.

IDS [Institute of Development Studies]. 2003. The rise of rights: Rights-based approaches to development, *IDS Policy Briefing* no. 7. Sussex: IDS.

Jackson, C. 2003. Gender analysis of land: Beyond land rights for women? *Journal of Agrarian Change* 3, no. 4:453–480.

Jonsson, U. 2005. A human rights-based approach to programming. In *Reinventing development? Translating rights-based approaches from theory to practice,* edited by P. Gready and J. Ensor, 47–62. London: Zed Books.

Kabeer, N. 2002. *The Power to Choose: Bangladeshi Garment Workers in London and Dhaka.* London, New York: Verso Books.

Kanbur, R. 2001. Economic policy, distribution and poverty: The nature of disagreements. *World Development* 29, no. 6:1083–1094.

Mamdani, M. 1996. *Citizen and subject.* Princeton: Princeton University Press.

Mander, H. 2005. Rights as struggle—Towards a more just and humane world. In *Reinventing development? Translating rights-based approaches from theory to practice,* edited by P. Gready and J. Ensor, 233–253. London: Zed Books.

Manzo, K. 2003. Africa in the rise of rights-based development. *Geoforum* no. 34:437–456.

Moser, C. 2005. Rights, power and poverty reduction. In *Power, rights and poverty: Concepts and connections,* edited by R. Alsop, 29–50. Washington, DC: Oxford University Press for the World Bank.

Munro, L. 2008. Risk, rights and needs: Compatible or contradictory bases for social protection. In *Social protection for the poor and poorest: risk, needs and rights,* edited by A. Barrientos and D. Hulme, 27–46. New York: Palgrave Macmillan.

Nyamnjoh, F. B. 2004. Reconciling "the rhetoric of rights" with competing notions of personhood and agency in Botswana. In *Rights and the politics of recognition in Africa,* edited by H. Englund and F. B. Nyamnjoh, 33–63. London: Zed Books.

O'Connor, A. 2006. Global poverty knowledge and the USA: What it has been, why it needs to change. Paper prepared for the workshop "Concepts for analysing poverty dynamics and chronic poverty." Chronic Poverty Research Centre, University of Manchester, October 23–25.

Pieterse, J. N. 1998. My paradigm or yours? Alternative development, post-development, reflexive development. *Development and Change* 29, no 2:343–373.

Rafi, M. and A. M. R. Chowdhury. 2000. Human rights and religious backlash: The experience of a Bangladeshi NGO. *Development in Practice* 10, no. 1:19–30.

World Bank. 2000. *World Development Report 2000–2001. Attacking poverty.* Washington, DC: Oxford University Press for the World Bank.

World Bank. 2004. *World Development Report 2004. Improving service delivery.* Washington, DC: Oxford University Press for the World Bank.

World Bank. 2006. *World Development Report 2006. Equity and development.* Washington, DC: Oxford University Press for the World Bank.

Young, I. M. 1997. Unruly categories: A critique of Nancy Fraser's dual systems theory. *New Left Review* no. 222:147–160.

Notes

1. We have already considered another ideological division within development thought here, namely that between economic and social tendencies (Kanbur 2001; Pieterse 1998). We concluded that mainstream actors within the economic tendency would struggle to integrate a rights-based perspective into their professional work as analysts and policy advisers.

2. This juxtaposition of "state versus market" approaches to development tends to overlook the fact that civil society has increasingly been seen as a critical institutional arena in international development. Interestingly, proponents of both neoliberal and alternative perspectives on development have cast civil society as the natural arena within which the rights of citizens are fulfilled (Bebbington and Hickey 2006).

Contributors

Robert Archer is Executive Director of the International Council on Human Rights Policy, Geneva, an independent institute that conducts research into dilemmas and problems facing organizations that apply human rights. He worked previously with Christian Aid (London), where he set up its Policy Department, and with the Catholic Institute for International Relations (London), where he established its Asia program. He has degrees in English literature, philosophy, and African Studies, and has written books on Madagascar and South Africa as well as shorter reports.

Adriano Campolina Soares is an agronomist with a master's degree in Agriculture, Society and Development. He is an activist on food sovereignty issues (such as land reform, farmers' rights, etc.) and has worked with local NGOs, peasant movements, political parties, and labor unions in Brazil. He joined ActionAid Brazil in 2000 and worked as food campaigner, policy director, and program director. Currently he is ActionAid's international director for the Americas Region and Right to Food Theme.

Jennifer Chapman is currently working freelance, after three years heading an action research program for ActionAid on planning, reflection, and learning in people-centered advocacy work which led to the resource pack *Critical Webs of Power and Change*. She has extensive research and practical experience with NGOs and donors, with a particular focus on learning around rights-based approaches, advocacy, policy work, power, gender, and partnerships.

Frances Cleaver is a Reader at the Centre for International Development, University of Bradford. Her professional work is centered around understanding the collective management of natural resources and the implications for wellbeing of differing arrangements for resource governance. She is particularly interested in the use of participatory action research and ethnographic methods for exploring these themes, primarily through work in Africa.

Jeidoh Duni works with the Mbororo Social and Cultural Development Association in the North West Province of Cameroon as a paralegal field supervisor. He coordinates the paralegal extension component that is principally concerned with the legal education of the Mbororo Fulani and the protection and promotion of their rights. He is also a trainer, with particular expertise in the REFLECT adult literacy approach.

Michael Drinkwater is a sociologist and senior program advisor with CARE International, with which he has worked since 1994. He has over 25 years of experience, working extensively in Africa, particularly in the Southern African region, and, since 2000, in South Asia. His published doctoral thesis on the State and Agrarian Change in Zimbabwe's Communal Areas was completed at the University of East Anglia, Norwich. Michael now works with CARE's Program Impact, Knowledge and Learning Team, where he is involved with a range of program quality and action research initiatives.

Robert Nso Fon is a legal practitioner and a human rights activist in Cameroon. He runs a law firm and his legal practice is focused on defending the rights of the poor and marginalized. He started working with the Mbororo Social and Cultural Development Association in 1998 and is responsible for coordinating their Access to Justice programs. He is the coauthor of the Psycho-Legal Extension Model, an alternative paradigm for challenging social exclusion.

John Gledhill is Max Gluckman Professor of Social Anthropology and Co-Director of the Centre for Latin American Cultural Studies at the University of Manchester, Co-Managing Editor of the journal *Critique of Anthropology*, and Chair of the Association of Social Anthropologists (2005–2009). His publications include the books *Casi nada: Agrarian Reform in the Homeland of Cardenismo* (1991), *Neoliberalism, Transnationalization and Rural Poverty* (1995), *Power and Its Disguises: Anthropological Perspectives on Politics* (2000), and *Cultura y Desafío en Ostula* (2004).

Sam Hickey lectures on international development at IDPM, School of Environment and Development, University of Manchester. His research focuses on the politics of development, particularly the links between politics and poverty reduction, issues of citizenship and participation, and the role of civil society and NGOs in development. Recent papers have appeared in *World Development* and *Development and Change*, and he is coeditor (with Giles Mohan) of the collection. Participation: *From Tyranny to Transformation: Exploring New Approaches to Participation* (Zed Books, 2004), and (with Anthony Bebbington and Diana Mitlin) *Can NGOs Make a Difference? The challenge of development alternatives* (Zed Books, 2007). He currently coordinates research into the politics of exclusion within the Chronic Poverty Research Centre.

Leonith Hinojosa-Valencia is researcher and fellow lecturer at the School of Environment and Development in the University of Manchester. She studies local and regional processes of economic change with some focus on Andean countries. Her work and publications hinge around the economic and institutional dimensions of rural and territorial development strategies and NGOs. She is currently researching the political economy of extractive industries and socio-environmental conflicts. Her experience in NGOs is in management, monitoring, and impact assessment.

Katsuhiko Masaki is Associate Professor in the Department of Global Citizenship Studies at Seisen University in Japan. He holds a Ph.D. from the Institute of Development Studies (IDS) at the University of Sussex, UK. His major publications include: "'Inclusive Citizenship' for the Chronically Poor" (Chronic Poverty Research Centre Working Paper 96, 2007), and *Power, participation, and policy* (Lexington Books, 2007).

Valerie Miller has collaborated with grassroots organizations, NGOs, women's movements, and international agencies around the world as an organizer, educator, evaluator, researcher, and human rights advocate over the last 30 years. She currently serves as senior advisor to Just Associates, an international network of activists and scholars working on gender, movement-building, and social change strategies, and conducts online courses on advocacy with Human Rights Education Associates. She has written numerous articles and books on literacy, human rights, advocacy, and power.

Diana Mitlin is an economist and social development specialist, and works at both the International Institute for Environment and Development and the Institute for Development Policy and Management (University of Manchester). Her major focus is on issues of urban poverty reduction, in particular in the areas of secure tenure, basic services, and housing. Her work has explored a number of themes related to the contribution of civil society in addressing poverty and inequality issues. For the last ten years, she has worked with Shack/Slum Dwellers International. Recent publications include *Empowering Squatter Citizen* (2004, with David Satterthwaite) and *Confronting the Crisis in Urban Poverty* (2006, with Lucy Stevens and Stuart Coupe), and (with Anthony Bebbington and Sam Hickey) *Can NGOs Make a Difference? The challenge of development alternatives* (Zed Books, 2007).

Lauchlan T. Munro is Director of Policy and Planning at the International Development Research Centre in Ottawa. Before joining IDRC he was

Chief of Strategic Planning for UNICEF, 2000–2003; he also served in UNICEF field offices in Sudan, DR Congo, Zimbabwe, and Uganda. His research interests cover human rights, social protection, and public sector management, especially the aid business.

Sheela Patel is founder and director of the Society for the Promotion of Area Resource Centres, and is engaged with the National Slum Dwellers Federation and Mahila Milan. She has advised international agencies, and was part of the Millennium Project Taskforce on Slum Dwellers, the Advisory Board of the Asian Coalition for Housing Rights, and the Cities Alliance. She has published widely on the work of federations and on the tools and methods that are appropriate for working with grassroots organizations. In 2001, she was awarded the UN-Habitat Scroll of Honour.

Nuhu Salihu is a development practitioner and linguist. He has worked for the UK charity Village AiD as Africa Programme Coordinator for the last 7 years. He cofounded the Mbororo Social and Cultural Development Association and was one of its leading members from 1989 until his departure in 2005. Nuhu was the first second-generation Mbororo pastoralist to graduate from university. His main interests are in social justice, interethnic relations, cross-culture communication, and alternatives to mainstream development aid.

John Samuel is a human rights activist, campaigner, policy researcher, and institution builder with more than 20 years of experience with social movements and advocacy organizations in India and internationally. He is the International Director (Asia and Just Governance) of ActionAid. He is the founder and coeditor of Infochange News and Features (www.infochangeindia.org), one of the most frequented daily development channels in Asia, and a coeditor of the Citizens Report on Governance and Development (www.socialwatchindia.net).

Index

Also from Kumarian Press . . .

Rights and Development:

Human Rights and Development
Peter Uvin

Development and Rights
Edited by Deborah Eade

Non-State Actors in the Human Rights Universe
Edited by George Andreopoulos, Zehra Kabasakal Arat, and Peter Juviler

New and Forthcoming:

How the Aid Industry Works:
An Introduction to International Development
Arjan de Haan

Freedom From Want:
The Remarkable Success Story of BRAC, The Global Grassroots
Organization That's Winning the Fight Against Poverty
Ian Smillie

Coping with Facts: A Skeptic's Guide to the Problem of Development
Adam Fforde

green press

INITIATIVE

Kumarian Press is committed to preserving ancient forests and natural resources. We elected to print this title on 30% post consumer recycled paper, processed chlorine free. As a result, for this printing, we have saved:

3 Trees (40' tall and 6-8" diameter)
1,239 Gallons of Wastewater
2 million BTU's of Total Energy
159 Pounds of Solid Waste
299 Pounds of Greenhouse Gases

Kumarian Press made this paper choice because our printer, Thomson-Shore, Inc., is a member of Green Press Initiative, a nonprofit program dedicated to supporting authors, publishers, and suppliers in their efforts to reduce their use of fiber obtained from endangered forests.

For more information, visit www.greenpressinitiative.org

Environmental impact estimates were made using the Environmental Defense Paper Calculator. For more information visit: www.papercalculator.org.

 Kumarian Press, located in Sterling, Virginia, is a forward-looking, scholarly press that promotes active international engagement and an awareness of global connectedness.